Buddhist Thought and Ritual

Buddhist Thought and Ritual

David J. Kalupahana

MOTILAL BANARSIDASS PUBLISHERS
PRIVATE LIMITED • DELHI

Reprint Edition: Delhi, 2001

First Edition: USA, 1991
(Paragon House Publishers)

ISBN: 81-208-1773-7

Also available at:

MOTILAL BANARSIDASS

41 U.A. Bungalow Road, Jawahar Nagar, Delhi 110 007
8 Mahalaxmi Chamber, Warden Road, Mumbai 400 026
120 Royapettah High Road, Mylapore, Chennai 600 004
236, 9th Main III Block, Jayanagar, Bangalore 560 011
Sanas Plaza, 1302 Baji Rao Road, Pune 411 002
8 Camac Street, Kolkata 700 017
Ashok Rajpath, Patna 800 004
Chowk, Varanasi 221 001

Printed in India

BY JAINENDRA PRAKASH JAIN AT SHRI JAINENDRA PRESS,
A-45 NARAINA, PHASE-I, NEW DELHI 110 028 AND
PUBLISHED BY NARENDRA PRAKASH JAIN FOR
MOTILAL BANARSIDASS PUBLISHERS PRIVATE LIMITED,
BUNGALOW ROAD, DELHI 110 007

Dedication

To the late venerable (Dr.) Hammalawa Saddhatissa,
a monk who combined tradition and modernity in
Buddhist scholarship

Table of Contents

List of Abbreviations

A	*Anguttara-nikāya*, ed. R. Morris and E. Hardy, 5 vols., London: Pali Texts Society (PTS), 1885–1900.
D	*Dīgha-nikāya*, ed. T.W. Rhys Davids and J.E. Carpenter, 3 vols., London: PTS, 1890–1911.
DA	*Sumaṅgalavilāsinī*, *Dīgha-nikāya-aṭṭhakathā*, ed. T.W. Rhys Davids, J.E. Carpenter and W. Stede, 3 vols., London: PTS, 1886–1932.
Dh	*Dhammapada*, ed. S. Sumangala, London: PTS, 1914.
DhA	*Dhammapada-aṭṭhakathā*, ed. C.R. Norman, 4 vols., London: PTS, 1906–1914.
Khp	*Khuddakapāṭha*, ed. Helmer Smith, London: PTS, 1915.
M	*Majjhima-nikāya*, ed. V. Trenckner and R. Chalmers, 3 vols., London: PTS, 1887–1901.
Miln	*Milinda-pañha*, ed. V. Trenckner, London: PTS, 1928.
Psm	*Paṭisambhidā-magga*, ed. A.C. Taylor, 2 vols., London: PTS, 1905–1907.
Pug	*Puggala-paññatti*, ed. R. Morris, London: PTS, 1883.
S	*Saṃyutta-nikāya*, ed. L. Feer, 6 vols., London: PTS, 1884–1904.
Sn	*Sutta-nipāta*, ed. D. Anderson and H. Smith, London: PTS, 1913.
T	*Taishō Shinshu Daizōkyō*, ed. J. Takakusu and K. Watanabe, Tokyo: Daizo Shuppan Company, 1924 –1934.
Thag	*Theragāthā*, in *Thera-therī-gāthā*, ed. H. Oldenberg and R. Pischel, London: PTS, 1883.
Ud	*Udāna*, ed. P. Steinthal, London: PTS, 1948.
Vin	*Vinaya Piṭaka*, ed. H. Oldenberg, 5 vols., London: PTS, 1879–1883.
Vism	*Visuddhimagga*, ed. C.A.F. Rhys Davids, 2 vols., London: PTS, 1920–1921.

INTRODUCTION

THE ESSAYS PUBLISHED HERE have been selected from a larger collection presented at three Buddhist Intrareligious Conferences held in Chiang-mai, Thailand and in Colombo, Sri Lanka. These conferences were sponsored by the Council for the World Religions. The two conferences held in Chiang-mai dealt with general philosophical and cultural themes relating to the various Buddhist traditions, while the last one held in Colombo was on a more specific topic, namely, "Religious Harmony Through Rituals." The first eight papers are from the conferences held in Chiang-mai, and the last five from the Colombo conference. The first part of the present volume, therefore, deals with facets of Buddhist thought, both early and late, while the second part examines some of the more significant rituals in the Buddhist tradition.

The essay on "The Buddhist Doctrine of Anatta" by Y. Karunadasa, the well-known author of *Buddhist Analysis of Matter* (1967), is presented as the lead paper for obvious reasons. *Anatta* (no-self, non-substantiality,) as the author argues, is the most radical of the Buddha's doctrines, for it "sets Buddhism off from the two main currents of Indian thought and sets itself on a new path." It is a doctrine that has baffled many classical as well as modern writers on Buddhism. When it was presented by the Buddha as a way of clearing the philosophical background containing two fossilized theories, eternalism and nihilism, and as a foundation of the middle path represented by the principle of "dependent arising" (*paṭicca-samuppāda*, Sk. *pratītyasamutpāda*) most interpreters perceived it as a nihilistic doctrine. Karunadasa's paper provides a detailed treatment of this important doctrine indicating its epistemological, ethical, and social significance, as well as its relevance to the Buddha's conception of freedom.

My own paper that follows is on "*Pratītyasamutpāda* and the Renunciation of Mystery." It deals with the positive conception of "dependent arising" as formulated by the Buddha, and as understood by some of the outstanding philosophers of the Buddhist tradition. The mystery that the Buddha intended to renounce is none other than the "self" or "substance," either in the subject or in the object, that is, the mysterious entity (*atta*) the negation of which is the theme of Karunadasa's essay. For this reason, the analysis presented here complements that of Karunadasa. My analysis, however, is not confined to the first formulation of the doctrine by the Buddha. I have attempted to show that the Buddha's statement of the doctrine is faithfully followed by the later disciples like Moggalīputta-tissa, Nāgārjuna and Vasubandhu.

R.D. Gunaratne, a philosopher of science by training, examines the three concepts: space (*ākāśa*), emptiness (*śūnyatā*), and freedom (*nirvāṇa*) in Buddhism, and makes a bold attempt to interpret them in terms of the insights gained from the discoveries of modern science. Leaning toward the more absolutistic conception of space presented by the scientists, Gunaratne argues for similar absolutistic conceptions of space, emptiness, and freedom in the Buddhist context, yet without denying the relativism implied in the theory of dependent arising. This, however, is achieved on the basis of certain dichotomies such as the two truths: conventional or relative (*saṃvṛti*) and ultimate (*paramārtha*), which indeed are susceptible to a variety of interpretations.

P.D. Premasiri, with his paper on "The Social Relevance of the Buddhist Nibbāna Ideal," joins camp with the authors of the first two papers against Gunaratne and argues not only in favor of the social relevance of the conception of freedom (*nibbāna*), but also against any interpretation of it as an "absolute" or an "ultimate reality." The major part of this essay is devoted to an analysis of a cliche, prominent among the early interpreters of Buddhism, that *nibbāna*, the goal of Buddhism, is a transcendental reality beyond any conceptualization, and therefore the person who has attained this goal has nothing to do with the empirical world, hence with the social life of human beings. Utilizing the epistemological and psychological material in the early discourses of the Buddha, Premasiri defines *nibbāna* as the psychological and moral transformation of a human being as a result of his adopting a right view or perspective regarding life in general, and human life in particular. He leaves no room for the introduction of any form of absolutism or transcendentalism.

Sanath Nanayakkara's piece on "The Bodhisattva Ideal: Some Observations," is a challenging one. Contrary to the widely accepted view that the *bodhisattva* ideal is a Mahāyāna innovation, Nanayakkara argues persuasively that, in fact, it originated with Theravāda, and that the earlier versions found in both Theravāda and Mahāyāna represented a middle path between the two extreme forms of behavior: self-indulgence and self-mortification. It was a harmonious blend of self-interest and of the interests or welfare of others. That moderate ideal of *bodhisattva*, however, degenerated into an extremist view of absolute altruism in the hands of some of the later schools of Buddhism, both the Theravādin and Mahāyānist. A closer examination of the subject matter of Nanayakkara's paper will reveal that the controversy regarding the *bodhisattva* ideal is a reflection of the perennial philosophical problem relating to the conceptions of the "particular" and the "universal" and their application in moral discourse. The Buddha's middle path was intended to avoid sharp dichotomies in theory as well as in practice.

Interestingly, a problem similar to the one discussed by Nanayakkara in relation to the conception of *bodhisattva* reappears in the contribution by Shih Heng-ching, one of the leading Buddhist scholars from the National Taiwan University. This time it is presented in the form of "self-power" versus "other-power." It refers to the conflict between two Chinese Buddhist traditions—Ch'an, emphasizing "self-power," and Pure Land, underscoring "other-power." Her detailed treatment of the two traditions, as well as of the attempt by the later Chinese masters to syncretize Ch'an and Pure Land practices, clarifies for us the continued struggle by the later Buddhists to avoid extremes and to remain faithful to the middle path of the Buddha.

Yet another theme of integration of extremes is discussed in Masao Ichishima's work on "Integration of Sūtra and Tantra." Appeasement of thought (*ceto samatha*) or the freedom of thought (*ceto vimutti*) and freedom through insight (*paññavimutti*) were complementary aspects of the freedom attained by the Buddha and his immediate disciples. Subsequent explanations tended to distinguish these two aspects as two entirely different means: appeasement (*śamatha*) and insight or discernment (*vipaśyanā*), thereby generating absolute dichotomies that contributed to conflicts among various Buddhist schools. Ichishima's paper deals with an attempt to integrate one such dichotomy, that is, the dichotomy between exoteric (*sūtra*) and esoteric (*tantra*) forms of Buddhism by focusing upon the integration of the two aspects of freedom, namely, appeasement (*śamatha*) and discernment (*vipaśyanā*).

The paper by Cheng-mei Ku, another prominent Buddhist scholar from Taiwan, on the "Mahīśāsaka View of Women," may appear to be out of place among the themes discussed above. Considering the issue addressed in her paper and its current relevance, however, the editor deemed it appropriate for inclusion here, especially as a concluding statement on the problems relating to Buddhist thought. It clears up several misunderstandings regarding the way in which women were perceived in the Buddha's teachings and proceeds to identify the particular schools that downgraded their status. The importance of her paper lies in its attempt to trace the several doctrines which, when put together, were ultimately responsible for the emergence of a low profile regarding women.

The second set of papers deals with some of the prominent rituals in the Buddhist countries, especially Sri Lanka and China. The first two papers are on the *paritta* ("protection"), a ceremony little known outside the Sri Lankan Buddhist tradition. They represent the impressions of two authors, a Buddhist monk who would be involved in the performance of the ceremony, and a laywoman who would be a participant. Venerable H. Saddhatissa, a well-known Theravāda scholar-monk from England, provides an analysis of the text recited at the *paritta* ceremony, and on that basis explains the significance of *sūtra* recitation as a ritual for "protection" (*paritta*) of human life from evil forces. He argues that the *sūtra* recitation has a psychological impact on the listeners and thus provides for health and happiness. As such, it is not very different from the *mantra* recitation of the Tibetan or East Asian Buddhists.

The second paper, "The *Paritta* Ceremony of Sri Lanka: Its Antiquity and Symbolism," is by Lily de Silva, the editor of the monumental three-volume text of the *Dīghanikāya-aṭṭahakathā-ṭīkā*. It presents a history of the *paritta* ceremony and, more importantly, a detailed analysis of its symbolism. The paper is an excellent summary of the research she has conducted on the subject for several years. It is difficult to make sense of any ritual unless we are able to understand the symbolism involved. De Silva makes a valuable contribution by indicating the symbolic significance of each and every object utilized in the ceremony and relating them in such a way that renders the whole ceremony meaningful in a Buddhist context. (A paper on the Tibetan *mantra*-recitation would have been an interesting companion for the two papers on the *paritta* ceremony, providing for a comparative study of the meaning and relevance of *sūtra*-recitation in the different Buddhist traditions. Unfortunately, the Tibetan representative was unable to participate at the conference devoted to rituals.)

The next essay, by Premasiri, is on the "Significance of the Ritual Concerning Offerings to Ancestors in Theravāda Buddhism." The author traces the history of this very ancient practice in the Vedas and Brahmanical literature of the period before the rise of Buddhism, but endeavors to distinguish the Buddhist version from the Brahmanical by highlighting the moral and psychological character of the former. (Even though the essay is specifically on the ritual as practiced in a Theravāda country like Sri Lanka, considering the enormous popularity of the ritual in China and Japan, at least a brief reference to the nature of the ritual as practiced in those countries would have given a more complete portrayal of the subject matter.)

The ritual of self-sacrifice or self-immolation is one that can hardly be justified in a Buddhist context, especially in light of the very first discourse of the Buddha, "The Establishment of the Principle of Righteousness" (*Dhammacakkappavattana*), where he condemned both self-indulgence and self-mortification. Even though self-sacrifice came to be looked upon as a noble ideal both in Theravāda and in Mahāyāna at a later period, actual suicide as a religious ritual is extremely rare in the South Asian Buddhist tradition. Cheng-mei Ku's second essay included in this volume, "A Ritual of the Mahāyāna – Self-Sacrifice," explains how the conception of offering or charity (*dāna*), when combined with the Mahāyāna evaluation of the physical human personality (*rūpa*) as a created body (*nirmāṇa-kāya*), can contribute to the ritual of self-sacrifice. Hence its popularity in the East Asian Buddhist countries.

The final essay on "Chinese Buddhist Confessional Rituals: Their Origin and Spiritual Significance" is by Hsiang-chou Yo of the Chinese Culture University of Taipei. It is a detailed treatment of the significance of "confession" in the Chinese Buddhist monastic life. His manner of relating the Mahāyāna conception of "emptiness" (*śūnyatā*) to the confessional ritual will be of absorbing interest to those who have difficulty in harmonizing speculative metaphysics and down-to-earth rituals. (Unfortunately, Yo does not have much to say about the important place accorded to confession in the Buddha's own discourses. Even though he mentions that the great Chinese master, Tao An, who was the first to promulgate the confessional rituals in Chinese Buddhism, inherited this tradition from South Asian Buddhism, he makes no reference to the enormous popularity of the ritual in the monastic life of the South Asian Buddhists.)

The essays included in this volume provide for the reader the diverse and various facets of Buddhist thought and rituals. Not only does the work facilitate an understanding of the nature of Buddhist theory and practice but furthermore reveals the continuity in such theory and practice as Buddhism spread throughout the length and breadth of the vast continent of Asia.

PART 1

1

THE BUDDHIST DOCTRINE OF ANATTA

Y. Karunadasa

THE INTELLECTUAL MILIEU in which Buddhism originated in northern India in the 6th century B.C. is fairly well known. In fact the prevailing mood of the times is very well reflected in the Buddhist discourses themselves. A wide variety of mutually conflicting theories on the nature and destiny of man and his place in the cosmos dominated the scene. Despite their wide variety they can be subsumed under three main categories. The first includes all forms of religion current at the time, the second all forms of materialism which arose in direct opposition to religion, and the third all forms of skepticism which arose as a reaction against both.

Of the various forms of religion, some represented a linear development of the Vedic thought; others arose in direct opposition to it. Generally speaking, while the former movement was confined to the Brahmans, the latter was confined to the Samanas. In the former the trend is more towards theism and monism, but in the latter the trend is more towards non-theism and pluralism. Both groups in common advanced an array of metaphysical views which were at variance with each other. Questions pertaining to the nature and destiny of man, whether the cosmos is finite or otherwise in terms of time and space, the relationship between the soul and the physical body, the post-mortal condition of the liberated saint and what constituted spiritual purity and impurity became the subject of polemical discussions and this, in turn, gave rise to a bewildering mass of metaphysical views, each sure of its supreme excellence. Scriptural authority, divine revelation, the omniscience of the teacher, knowledge gained through yogic experience and arguments based on ***a priori*** reasoning were the main epistemological grounds on which these views were sought to be justified.

Although they represented a wide spectrum of views which were at variance with each other, they all subscribed to a common belief: the belief in a metaphysical self, a self which is immutable and distinct from the body (*aññaṃ jīvaṃ aññaṃ, sarīraṃ*).[1] Their thinking thus proceeded on a duality, on the duality between the metaphysical self and the physical body. It is the self that is in bondage. Hence salvation means salvation of the self, to be realized either by being absorbed with the macrocosmic soul or by gaining separate immortality for each self. The other point on which there was general agreement was that since the self is something immutable, unlike the physical body, it survives death as a separate entity. Now it was this belief in an immutable spiritual substance variously called an *atta*, *jīva*, *purisa*, a metaphysical belief more or less common to religions contemporaneous with the birth of Buddhism, that came to be referred to in Buddhist literature as *sassatavāda* (eternalism).[2] Accordingly, all religious views which subscribe to an eternal, self-subsisting spiritual entity—no matter under what term it is introduced—are but different species of *sassatavāda* and, as such, are subsumable under this generic term.

For *sassatavāda* the physical frame in which the elusive self is encased is not an instrument but a veritable obstacle for the self's deliverance, for what prevents its upward journey is the gravitational pull of the body (sense-pleasures). Hence deliverance of the self—in other words, its perpetuation in a state of eternal bliss—requires the mortification of the flesh (*attakilamathānuyoga*)[3] to restrain its influence over the self. It was this belief that led to a plethora of ascetic practices as a means to self-liberation.

The materialist tradition which arose in direct opposition to spiritualist religions had many votaries and more than one school of thought. Taking their stand on the epistemological ground that sense-perception was the only valid means of knowledge, they questioned the validity of theological and metaphysical assumptions which do not come within the ambit of sense experience.[4] From this it should not be concluded, as it has been sometimes, that the materialist view of existence was free from a belief in a self. For although it denied the religious version of *ātmavāda* according to which the self is different from the body, it also had its own version of *ātmavāda*, according to which the self is identical with the body (*taṃ jīvaṃ taṃ sarīraṃ*).[5] The line of argument which led it to this conclusion seems to be as follows: there is no observable self apart from the body, and since only the observable exists, the self must be identical with the body. Hence in its view the self is material and is a product of the four material elements (*ayaṃ attā rūpī cātummahābhūtiko*).[6] Thus for materialism the question at issue is not whether the self exists or not, but with what it should be identified. Since it identified the self with the body, it necessarily follows that at death, with the break-up of the body, the self itself gets annihilated without any prospect of post-mortal survival. Because of this inevitable conclusion to which the materialist view of existence led, all forms of materialism came to be referred to in Buddhist literature as *ucchedavāda* (annihilationism).[7] For what is called *ucchedavāda*, therefore, there is no duality within man, for it believes in the identity of the body and the self. In its view, man is a pure product of the earth; after death there is no more. Hence all pleasures must be enjoyed here and now, in this life itself. The aim of life is not the suppression of the senses in search of an elusive eternal bliss but the indulgence in sense pleasures (*kāmasukhallikānuyoga*).[8] Thus what are called *attakilamathānuyoga* and *kāmasukhallikānuyoga* represent the spiritualist and the materialist views of existence, what Buddhism refers to as *sassatavāda* and *ucchedavāda*.

It is fairly certain that it was this polarization of intellectual thought into two main traditions, with a number of contending sects and sub-sects within each tradition, that led to the birth of skepticism. That it also led, not as a linear development but in dialectical opposition to it, to the birth of Buddhism, too, is clearly suggested by the Buddha's very first sermon, the sermon on the Setting in Motion of the Wheel of Righteousness (*Dhamma-cakka-ppavattana sutta*).[10] For herein it is against the contemporary intellectual background that the Buddha sets out his newly discovered (*pubbe ananussutesu dhammesu*)[11] path to deliverance. This newly discovered path to deliverance is called the *majjhimā paṭipadā* (*via media*) because it is said to avoid the two extremes of self-mortification and sense-indulgence. It is an avoidance of the two extremes *in toto* (*ubho ante anupagamma*)[12] and not a compromise between the two, for it transcends their mutual opposition. The avoidance of the two extremes does also mean the avoidance *in toto* of what serves as their *raison d'être*, i.e. *sassatavāda* and *ucchedavāda*, the metaphysical and the physical views of the self.

In fact, it was also through personal experience that the Buddha was convinced of the futility of sense-indulgence and self-mortification as a means to self-perfection. If his life as Prince Siddhārtha exemplifies one extreme, his life as an ascetic practicing austerities exemplifies the other. And his attainment of enlightenment by giving up both extremes shows the efficacy of the Middle Path – the path that leads to self-perfection and deliverance.

In Buddhism's view, both the metaphysical and the physical versions of the self have a psychological origin: the former springs from man's excessive desire for the perpetuation of individuality in eternity (*bhava-taṇhā*), and the latter, from his equally excessive desire for sense-gratification (kāma-taṇhā) before his final annihilation at death. Since this latter view is accompanied by man's fear of moral retribution, it abhors any prospect of post-mortal existence (*vibhava-taṇhā*).[13] Thus, according to Buddhism the conflict between *sassatavāda* and *ucchedavāda* represents not only the perennial conflict between the spiritual and materialist views of existence but also the human mind's oscillation between two deep-seated desires.

It must, however, be noted that although the Buddha rejects both the spiritual version of the metaphysical self and the materialist version of the physical self, he is more sympathetic towards the former and more critical of the latter. Hence it is that, although sense-gratification which represents the physical view of the self is described as lowly (*hīna*), vulgar (*gamma*), and worldly (*pothujjanika*), the same description is not extended to self-mortification which represents the metaphysical view of the self.[14] The implication seems to be that although the metaphysical version of the self does not lead to the realization of the ideal of liberation (*anatthasaṃhita*), it, nevertheless, does not lead to the collapse of the moral life. It is not subversive of the higher ideals of human culture. For it recognizes moral retribution (*kamma-vāda*). On the other hand, the materialist version of the self leads to the erosion of the moral fabric of human society. It encourages a view of existence which takes sense-gratification as the ultimate purpose in life. It takes for granted that man's present existence is purely due to fortuitous circumstances and, as such, he is not responsible in any way for what he does during his temporary sojourn here in this world.

What we have introduced as Buddhism's unique doctrine of *anatta* amounts to a critique and rejection of both *sassatavāda* and *ucchedavāda*. Stated in brief, it amounts to the fact that none of the constituents of the empiric individuality can be considered as one's self: The physical form is transient (*anicca*); whatever is transient is unsatisfactory (*yad aniccaṃ taṃ dukkhaṃ*); whatever is unsatisfactory is non-self (*yaṃ dukkhaṃ tad anattā*).[15] Whatever is non-self, that is not mine (*n'etaṃ mama*), that I am not (*n'eso'ham asmi*), that is not myself (*n'eso me attā*).[16]

The same situation is true of the other constituents of the empiric individuality, namely sensations (*vedanā*), perceptions (*saññā*), mental formations (*saṃkhāra*) and consciousness (*viññāṇa*). The application of the characteristic of non-self even to *viññāṇa* (consciousness) which includes all forms of innermost mental experience, is very significant. For this shows that any state of consciousness, even the consciousness that I am I, is also subject to the three characteristics of sentient existence.[17] "Hence the learned and noble disciple does not consider corporeality, sensations, perceptions, mental formations, or consciousness as the ego, nor the ego as the owner of these factors, nor these factors as included within the ego, nor the ego as included within these factors."[18]

The non-identification of any of the constituents of the empiric individuality with self has given rise to the question whether there is a self over and above the constituents.[19] As far as Buddhism is concerned, the question has no relevance. For Buddhism explains the totality of conditioned existence and deliverance therefrom in such a way that it simply rules out the very necessity of raising the question. In the first place, none of the Buddhist doctrines presupposes such a self and, in the second, none of the Buddhist doctrines becomes more meaningful by such an assumption. What is more, if there is such a self, it is certainly not attested to by what in Buddhism is called *abhiññā* or higher knowledge realized through the higher stages of mental culture. Even the states of jhanic experience, where consciousness has attained a sublime level of refinement, do not provide evidence for the existence of such an entity. In fact Buddhism recognizes the likelihood of interpreting the content of jhanic experience in a manner not warranted by the facts. This seems to be the reason why the meditator is advised to review the content of jhanic experience in the light of the three marks of conditioned existence, namely impermanence (*anicca*), unsatisfactoriness (*dukkha*), and absence of a substance persisting through the phenomena (*anatta*).[20] Such a practice has the salutary effect of precluding the possibility of erroneously interpreting the content of jhanic experience as some kind of absorption with, or as manifestation within, the meditator of a transcendental reality.

It is in man's suffering—suffering understood in its broadest sense—and its complete elimination that Buddhism is mainly interested: "Both formerly and now, Anurādha, I declare only suffering and its cessation".[21] "As the vast ocean, O disciples, is impregnated with one taste, the taste of salt, even so this doctrine and discipline is impregnated with one taste, the taste of deliverance."[22] But the realization of this deliverance does not depend on the solution of the metaphysical question—whether it is solvable or not is another question—whether the soul and the body are identical or different: "The religious life, O Mālunkyaputta, does not depend on the dogma that the soul and the body are identical, nor does it depend on the dogma that the soul and the body are different. Whether the dogma obtains that the soul and the body are identical or that the soul and the body are different, there still remain birth, old age, death, sorrow, lamentation, grief and despair, for the extinction of which in this present life itself, I am prescribing."[23] If the purpose of religious life is to attain a state of perfect freedom in which all worldly imperfections have vanished forever, a freedom from all limitations, a state of being unconditioned by anything empirical or trans-empirical, the realization of such freedom and the path that leads thereto, does not require the assumption of an elusive, unverifiable, transcendental entity that serves as a background to, and by implication, as *raison d'être* of the world of experience: "Verily I declare to you, my friend, that within this very body, mortal as it is and only a fathom high, but conscious and endowed with mind, is the world and the waxing thereof and the waning thereof and the way that leads to the passing away thereof."[24]

What is most radical about the Buddhist doctrine of *anatta* is that through it Buddhism sets itself off from the two main currents of Indian thought and sets itself on a new path. In fact it forms the very basis of the Buddha's scheme of salvation and, therefore, all its attendant concepts flow from it. It serves as a rationale not only for Buddhism's practical doctrine and discipline which has the realization of nirvana as its goal but also for its social ethics and social philosophy.

If the belief in an ego-entity is a wrong view, how it comes to be and why it prevails at all is another question to which Buddhism has given much attention. This forms the main subject of discussion particularly in those aspects of Buddhist thought which come under Buddhist psychology and epistemology. It is an issue that has been approached from many points of view and over which many arguments are adduced. In brief, they seek to inquire into the psychological mainsprings of this belief and also the epistemological grounds over which it is sought to be justified. The Buddhist view is that this belief in an ego-entity is the result of an incorrect interpretation of the data of psychological experience and that the tenacity with which men cling to the ego-notion prevents them from seeing the truth of egolessness. It is also maintained that the epistemological grounds on which this belief is sought to be justified such as scriptural authority (*anussava*) and *a priori* reasoning (*takka-vimaṃsa*) are not valid.[25] It is not proposed here to go into all the relevant details, for this is a subject that has been discussed in a number of modern works, particularly in K.N. Jayatilleke's monumental work on the *Early Buddhist Theory of Knowledge*.

However, one important aspect that deserves mention here is that according to Buddhism even our linguistic habits can sometimes lead to the erroneous belief in a self-entity. For there is a tendency on our part to interpret the nature of reality according to the structure of language. In Buddhism's view this can lead to many a wrong conclusion, because the human mind has an inveterate tendency to imagine ontological entities corresponding to linguistic expressions. Thus, for example, when we say, "It rains" or "It thunders," we dichotomize a single process by the use of the word "It." In the same way, when we say, "I think," we tend to believe that there is an I-entity in addition to the process of thinking. How such a way of thinking can lead to the wrong belief in an elusive self is very well illustrated by the Buddha's answer to the question: "But who, Venerable One, is it that feels?" Buddha says in reply: "This question is not proper. I do not teach that there is one who feels. If, however, the question is put thus: 'Conditioned through what does feeling arise?,' then the right answer will be: 'Through sense-impression is feeling conditioned.' " Again when the Buddha is asked: "But what are old age and death and to whom do they belong?",[26] the Buddha says in reply: "I do not teach that there is one thing called old age and death and that there is someone to whom they belong." That although language is necessary to convey the nature of reality, the structure of the language does not necessarily picture the nature of reality is also brought into focus by the well-known statement of the Buddha: "These, O Citta, are names, expressions, turns of speech, designations in common use in the world. And of these a *Tathāgata* makes use indeed, but is not led astray by them."[27]

Now, this Buddhist view of existence, expressed through the doctrine of *anatta*, invests the concept of man with a new dimension. In accordance with this view there is no spiritual substance in man which relates him to some kind of transcendental reality. His is not a microcosmic soul emanating from, and awaiting to be absorbed with, the macrocosmic soul. Nor is he, as materialism (*ucchedavāda*) asserts, a product of fortuitous circumstances awaiting to be annihilated at death. For although Buddhism does not subscribe to the metaphysical view of the self, unlike materialism, it does not deny continuity (*punabbhava*) and moral responsibility (*kammavāda*). Thus the Buddhist view of human personality cannot be explained either in terms of a soul that outlasts death or in terms of a soul that gets annihilated at death. Avoiding the two extremes of idealism and materialism, it explains human personality as a process of psycho-physical phenomena interconnected by causal relations, as a process of alimentation (*āhāraṭṭhitika*) feeding itself on four kinds of nutrients, namely, material food (*kabaliṅkāra-āhāra*), sensory impression (*phassa*), mental volition (*mano-sañcetanā*), and consciousness (*viññāṇa*).[28] However, this way of explaining human personality does not deprive it of the possibility of perfection, for within the human personality there is the necessary potential and the wherewithal to reach the highest levels of perfection, as we find this ideal translated into actual experience in the lives of the Buddhist saints.

If the doctrine of *anatta* gives a new dimension to the concept of man, the four Noble Truths provide a statement, in consonance therewith, of man's present predicament (pathological), the causes thereof (diagnostical), deliverance therefrom (ideal) and the path that leads to its realization (prescriptive). Man's present predicament, as Buddhism understands it, is not due to his fall from an original state of perfection, for Buddhism speaks of no such original state of perfection. Nor is it due to his estrangement from his true self because no such self is assumed. Nor is it due to his habit of identifying his true self with what is not the self, because the very idea of the self is an unnecessary assumption. On the contrary, in Buddhism's view man's present predicament, which is characterized by suffering (*dukkha*), is directly traceable to the belief in an illusory self, because it leads to the equally illusory duality between the self and the non-self plus all that it presupposes and entails. Hence Buddhism's interest in self is not to develop it or to make it more healthy, but to eliminate it completely. What is emphasized here is not deliverance of the self, but deliverance from the self-notion.

If the self is not assumed, how can man's perfectibility and deliverance become possible is a question that has often been raised. The Buddhist answer is that it is the very assumption of a self, both in its spiritual and materialist versions, which makes perfectibility and deliverance impossible: "Verily, if one holds the view that the self is identical with the body, in that case there can be no holy life. Again, if one holds the view that self is one thing and the body another, in that case, too, there can be no holy life. Avoiding both extremes the Perfect One teaches the doctrine that lies in the middle."[29]

The middle doctrine alluded to here is Buddhism's explanation of empirical existence through its empirical doctrine of dependent co-origination (*paṭicca-samuppāda*). Just as the Noble Eightfold Path is called the Middle Way (*majjhimā-paṭipadā*) because it avoids the two extremes of self-mortification and sense-indulgence, even so the doctrine of dependent co-origination is called the Middle Doctrine (*majjhena dhammaṃ deseti*)[30] because it avoids, in the self-same manner (*ubho ante anupagamma*) the philosophical views which serve as their *raison d'être*. The significance of the Middle Doctrine is due to the fact that it avoids not only the eternalist view that everything exists absolutely (*sabbaṃ atthi*), but also the opposite nihilist view that absolutely nothing exists (*sabbaṃ natthi*). It also avoids not only the monistic view which reduces the diversity of phenomenal existence to a common ground, to some sort of self-existing substance (*sabbaṃ ekattaṃ*), but also the opposite pluralistic view which analyses existence to a concatenation of discrete entities (*sabbaṃ puthuttaṃ*).[31] Avoiding all these extremes, the doctrine of dependent co-origination explains that phenomena arise in dependence on other phenomena, without assuming, however, a persistent substance behind the phenomena.

NOTES

1. *M* 1.246; *S* 4.375 H.
2. *D* 1.13; 3.108; *S* 2.20; 3.99; 4.400; *Pug* 38; *Psm* 1.155.
3. *D* 3.113; *S* 4.330; 5.421; *M* 3.230.
4. See K.N. Jayatilleke, *Early Buddhist Theory of Knowledge*, London, 1963, 69 ff.
5. *M* 1.246; *S* 4.375 H.
6. *M* 2.56.
7. *D* 1.34; *S* 2.18; 4.401; *A* 4.174; *Pug*. 38.
8. *S* 4.330; 5.421; *D* 3.113.
9. See K.N. Jayatilleke, *op. cit.*, 109 ff.
10. *Vin* 1.14H; *S* 5.420 H.
11. *Ibid.*, *loc. cit.*
12. *Ibid.*, *loc. cit.*
13. *D* 3.216; *Vin* 1.10.
14. See note 10, above.
15. *Vin* 1.15; *S* 4.283; *M* 2.35.
16. *Ibid.*, *loc. cit.*
17. O.H. de A. Wijesekara, *The Three Signata*, Kandy, 1960, 10.
18. *S* 3.122.
19. See e.g. George Grimm, *The Doctrine of the Buddha*, Berlin, 1958; Edmond Holmes, *The Creed of Buddha*, London, 1957 (reprinted); Ananda Coomaraswamy, *Buddha and the Gospel of Buddhism*, Bombay, 1956 (reprinted).
20. *M* 1.350; *A* 2.43.
21. *S* 4.384. *Pubbe caham Anurādha etarahi ca dukkhañ ceva paññapemi dukkhassa ca nirodhaṃ.*
22. *Vin* 2.235: *Seyyathāpi bhikkhave mahāsamuddo ekaraso loṇaraso evam eva kho bhikkhave ayaṃ dhammavinayo ekaraso vimuttiraso.*
23. *M* 1.430: *Taṃ jīvaṃ taṃ sarīran ti Mālunkyaputta diṭṭhiyā sati aññaṃ jīvaṃ aññaṃ sarīran ti vā diṭṭhiyā sati attheva jāti atthi jarā atthi maraṇaṃ santi soka-parideva-dukkha-domanassupāyāsā yesāhaṃ diṭṭhe va dhamme nighātaṃ paññapemi.*
24. *S* 1.62. *Api khvāhaṃ āvuso imasmiññeva vyāmamatte kalebare saññimhi samanake lokaṃ ca paññapemi lokasamudayaṃ ca lokanirodhaṃ ca lokanirodhagaminiṃ ca paṭipadaṃ.*
25. See K.N. Jayatilleke, *op. cit.*, 169 ff.
26. *S* 3.12.
27. *D* 1.202.
28. *M* 1.48; *S* 2.11; *D* 3.228.
29. *S* 2.61.
30. *Ibid.*, 5.421.
31. *Ibid.*, 2.17, 77.

2

PRATĪTYASAMUTPĀDA AND THE RENUNCIATION OF MYSTERY

David J. Kalupahana

WRITING ABOUT "ESCAPE FROM PERIL" in his popular and significant work, *The Quest for Certainty*, John Dewey writes: "Man who lives in a world of hazards is compelled to seek for security. He has sought to attain it in two ways. One of them began with an attempt to propitiate the powers which environ him and determine his destiny. It expressed itself in supplication, sacrifice, ceremonial rite and magical cult. In time these crude methods were largely displaced. The sacrifice of a contrite heart was esteemed more pleasing than that of bulls and oxen; the inner attitude of reverence and devotion more desirable than external ceremonies. If man could conquer destiny he could willingly ally himself with it; putting his will, even in sore affliction, on the side of the powers which dispense fortune, he could escape defeat and might triumph in the midst of destruction."[1]

Interpreting the Buddhist philosophical tradition, Brahmanical scholars like S. Radhakrishnan seem to give the impression that the revolution brought about by the Buddha in the Indian religious tradition is no more than the abandoning of the "crude methods" (referred to above by Dewey) in favor of the "sacrifice of a contrite heart." In other words, the Buddha did not bring about a radical change in the philosophical thinking in India, but was merely satisfied with reforming the corruptions that had crept into the Brahmanical religion.[2]

In the following pages, we propose to show that not only was the Buddha criticizing and condemning the meaningless beliefs and practices of the Brahmanical religion, but also was shaking up the very foundation of pre-Buddhist Indian philosophical thought, both Brahmanical and non-Brahmanical.

Just as much as the ordinary man in pre-Buddhist India sought refuge in the mysterious powers that surrounded him, so did the philosophers fall back upon something extremely mysterious, the knowledge of which could exalt him to the level of a divinity. The *Upaniṣads* clearly represent this attempt on the part of a contemplative (*yogin*) to impart knowledge of a "mysterious self" (*ātman*) to a disciple in "secret session." The whole idea of an eternal and permanent self lying within the human personality and which is identical with the reality embodied in everything (*sarvam*) was intended as an intellectual way of overcoming anxiety and attaining some form of security. The Materialist thinkers who rejected the Upaniṣadic emphasis on the psychic nature of this self offered sacrifices at the altar of their divinity, namely, the material or physical nature (*svabhāva*), denying the ability on the part of man to change the course of nature. In the case of the *Upaniṣads*, the mysterious substance was both within and without, and in the case of the Materialists it is not within but without. Both "self" (*ātman*) and "nature" or "substance" (*svabhāva*) are permanent and eternal. Dewey has the following to say about such verities:

> Practical activity deals with individualized and unique situations which are never exactly duplicable and about which, accordingly, no complete assurance is possible. All activity, moreover, involves change. The intellect, however, according to the *traditional doctrine*, may grasp universal Being, and Being which is universal is fixed and immutable. Wherever there is practical activity we human beings are involved as partakers in the issue. All fear, disesteem and lack of confidence which gather about the thought of ourselves, cluster also about the thought of the actions in which we are partners. Man's distrust of himself has caused him to desire to get beyond and above himself; in pure knowledge he has thought he could attain this self-transcendence.[3]

It is true that the Buddha claimed knowledge and certainty. Such knowledge-claims are often expressed in statements like: "Knowledge and insight arose in me: 'Imperturbable is my freedom of thought, this is my last life, now there would be no rebirth.' "[4] This statement, in addition to explaining the destiny of the freed one, also describes his present state of consciousness or thought. It throws light on his psychological constitution and is therefore relevant to an understanding of the nature of knowledge and insight he has gained. He is one who has gained stability of thought. It is not a stability achieved as a result of renouncing the unstable and ever-changing sense experiences, as the Upaniṣadic thinkers would require. For the Buddha, stability of thought is engendered not by a renunciation of sense experience and conception but by the relinquishing of a metaphysical search or a metaphysically oriented investigation associated with sense experience. This metaphysical search prompted by anxiety and leading to further anxiety is explained in the following passage:

> In this case, monk, it occurs to somebody: "What was certainly mine is certainly not mine (now); what might certainly be mine, there is certainly no chance of my getting." He grieves, mourns, laments, beats his breast, and falls into disillusionment. Even so, monks, does there come to be ***anxiety*** (***paritassanā***) about something objective that does not exist.
>
> In this case, monk, the view occurs to someone: "This world is this self; after dying I will become permanent, lasting, eternal, not liable to change, I will stand fast like unto the eternal." He hears the doctrine as it is being taught by the Tathagāta or by a disciple of the Tathāgata for rooting out all resolve for bias, tendency and addiction to the determination and conditioning of views, for the appeasement of all dispositions, for the relinquishing of all attachment, for the waning of craving, absence of lust, cessation and freedom. It occurs to him thus: "I will surely be annihilated, I will surely be destroyed, I will surely not be." He grieves, mourns, laments, beats his breast, and falls into disillusionment. Thus, monks, there comes to be ***anxiety*** about something subjective that does not exist.[5]

There can be little doubt that the "something objective that does not exist" (***bahiddhā asati***) and the "something subjective that does not exist" (***ajjhattaṃ asati***) are not simply the experience of objectivity and subjectivity but the search for a metaphysical object, an eternal substance (***nimitta***) with its accompanying qualities (***anuvyañjana***) and a metaphysical subject, an eternal self (***ātman***) that could be identified with an ultimate reality. The non-existence of such an object or of a subject became evident to the Buddha when he fleshed out sense experience and conception by practicing the higher contemplations (***jhāna***), as if he were peeling off the trunk of a plantain tree without discovering an inner essence.

The overcoming of anxiety by renouncing the search for mysterious entities, subjective as well as objective, provided the Buddha with the stability of thought and enabled him to examine whatever is available through sensory experience and conception. The examination of the subjective aspect of experience gave him insight into the psychophysical personality without revealing any hidden mystery.

> With his thought thus serene, made pure, translucent, cultured, devoid of evil, supple, ready to act, firm, and imperturbable, he applies and bends his thought to knowledge and vision. He comes to know: "This body of mine has material form, it is made up of the four great elements, it springs from mother and father, it is continually renewed by so much boiled rice and juicy foods, its very nature is impermanence, it is subject to erasion, abrasion, dissolution and disintegration, and there is in this consciousness of mine, too, bound up, on that it does depend.[6]

It is this knowledge of the psychophysical personality with no substantial agent that is embodied in the doctrine of aggregates (*khandha*): material form (*rūpa*), feeling (*vedanā*), perception (*saññā*), dispositions (*saṅkhāra*) and consciousness (*viññāṇa*)[7] or in the theory of six elements (*dhātu*): earth (*paṭhavi*), water (*āpo*), heat (*tejo*), air (*vāyo*), space (*ākāsa*) and consciousness (*viññāṇa*).[8]

The manner in which the human person, this psychophysical personality, proceeds with the act of conception is the next subject of investigation.

> With his thought thus serene...and imperturbable, he applies and bends his thought to the creation of a mind-made body (*manomayaṃ kāyaṃ*). From this body he creates another body, having material form, made of mind, possessed of all limbs and parts, not deprived of any organ.

This statement, taken in itself, could justify an extreme form of idealism. However, placed in the context of the knowledge described earlier, it simply explains the manner in which an ordinary human being conceptualizes. Thus, instead of consciousness (*viññāṇa*), referred to in the previous passage as well as in the doctrines of aggregates and elements and which is intended to account for experience, this latter passage introduces a faculty, namely, the mind (*mano*), as the instrument of conceptualization. The manner in which the mind functions in relation to consciousness is explained elsewhere when the Buddha, describing the six sensory faculties, maintained that, while the first five faculties survey their respective fields, the mind (*mano*) has the extended capacity to survey the sensory fields of other faculties.[9] This may be represented as follows:

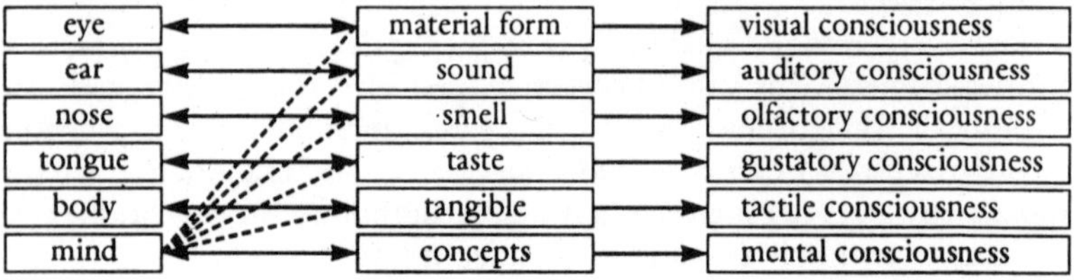

The functions of consciousness (*viññāṇa*) and mind (*mano*) are not at all identical, even though these terms are mistaken to be synonyms. Consciousness represents experience. In the explanation of the human personality, both in terms of aggregates and in relation to elements, the psychic part is always referred to as consciousness, not as mind. The difference between consciousness and mind is exemplified by their verbal forms, *vijānāti* and *maññati*; the former accounting for knowledge and the latter explicating the process of reflection. It is this reflective function of mind that enables it to enjoy the fields of other faculties, thus giving it a pre-eminent position in the matter of conceptualization.

This conceptualization can function in two different ways. First, it can serve as a *substitute* for experience. Thc six forms of consciousness (*viññāṇa*) are discriminated on the basis of the six faculties and their corresponding objects and then conceived (*saṅkhaṃ gacchati*) in terms of the reflective capacity of the mind (*mano*). Thus, when an object is perceived, and this involves the coming together of the sense organ, the object of sense and consciousness, one recognizes it and names it as such and such. Such recognizing and naming are possible only because of the functioning of the mind which can deal with the so-called *substitute*, that is, concepts (*dhammā*). Second, it is possible to ignore the fact that a concept is a mere substitute or intellectual shorthand for an experience and extend the process of conceptualization far beyond its limits. Philosophers thus fall into the Platonic snare when they look upon a concept not merely as a substitute for a percept but as something in itself revealing a permanent and eternal entity or structure. The result is the belief in an eternal subjective self (*ātman*) or an immutable substance (*svabhāva*) or both.

Of these two functions of mind, the former could be characterized as being "dependently arisen" (*paṭiccasamuppanna*) and the latter as being fabricated (*saṅkhata*). For the Buddha, the world of the ordinary unenlightened human beings is full of such fabricated mysterious entities. Their consciousness or experience is overwhelmed by such mysteries. They take refuge in such entities. It is this obsession, this mooring or anchoring (*ālaya*) on the part of human beings, that prevents them from perceiving dependent arising (*paṭiccasamuppāda*) and attaining freedom (*nibbāna*).[10]

Buddhism thus recognizes the enormous influence that the conceptualizing human mind can exert upon human knowledge and behavior.[11] The metaphysical search for "something" (*kiñci*), mysterious and hidden, is the product of *mano*, (*maññati*), *citta*, or (*cinteti*), and not of *viññāṇa* or (*vijānāti*).[12] The mind, through its power of conceptualization, can soar into heights of divinity and absolutism, as it did in the case of some of the Upaniṣadic thinkers, or sink into its lowest depths, as it did with some of the materialists. For this reason, mind becomes the faculty that needs to be brought under control or restraint. The Buddha often spoke of the need to restrain the mind (*mano*) and the thought process (*citta*) associated with it, and never spoke of the restraint of consciousness (*viññāṇa*).

The middle path that avoids the extremes of conceptualization, as embodied in theories of eternalism (*sassatavāda*) and annihilationism (*ucchedavāda*), is "dependent arising" (*paṭiccasamuppāda*).[13] It is a conceptualization that remains faithful to experience, namely, the perception of phenomena that are "dependently arisen" (*paṭiccasamuppanna*). The one who has abandoned the search for "something" (*kiñci*) is called *akiñcana*. In the Buddha's discourses, *akiñcana* is an epithet applied to a freed one (*nibbuta*), not because such a person has no sense experience and does not resort to conceptualizations, but because he has renounced the metaphysical search on occasions of sense experience and conception. Perceiving things, both subjective and objective, as being dependently arisen (*paṭiccasamuppanna*) and conceiving the idea of "dependent arising" (*paṭiccasamuppāda*) as a principle of explanation, he remains aloof from dogmatic assertions about an unseen "beauty queen" (*janapada-kalyāni*).[14]

This seems to be the context in which the Buddha admonished Bāhiya Dārucīriya saying:

> Then, Bāhiya, thus must you train yourself: "In the seen there will just be the seen; in the heard, just the heard; in the reflected, just the reflected; in the cognized, just the cognized." That is how, Bāhiya, you must train yourself. Now, Bāhiya, when in the seen there will be to you just the seen;...just the heard;...just the reflected;...just the cognized, then, Bāhiya, you will not identify yourself with it. When you do not identify yourself with it, you will not locate yourself therein. When you do not locate yourself therein, it follows that you will have no 'here' or 'beyond' or 'midway-between,' and this would be the end of suffering.[15]

Relinquishing the metaphysical search for something on occasions of sense experience, that is, being *akiñcana*, also implies freedom from grasping (*anādāna*).[16] Abandoning the search for metaphysical entities and mysterious causes, the Buddha was willing to recognize things as they have come to be (*yathābhūta*), that is, to take

1. the seen as the mere seen (*diṭṭha-matta, dṛṣṭa-mātra*),
2. the heard as the mere heard (*suta-matta, śruta-mātra*).
3. the reflected as the mere reflected (*muta-matta, smṛta-mātra*),
4. the cognized as the mere cognized (*viññāta-matta, vijñāta-mātra*), and this same attitude is to be adopted in relation to conception or convention (*vohāra-matta, vyavahāra-mātra*).[17]

For the Buddha, truth or reality is to be measured in terms of practical consequences. This highlights the "dependently arisen" (*paṭicca-samuppanna*), the experienced event, and reduces the mystery that may be associated with the principle of "dependent arising" (*paṭicca-samuppāda*). Furthermore, the emphasis upon practical consequences rather than particular consequences eliminates any teleological implications. Predictability comes to be grounded upon probability rather than absolute certainty. It is only recently that Western philosophers have realized that the more comprehensive our account of the *effect*, the better is our chance of understanding necessary connections, while with the most comprehensive account of the *cause* we need to be satisfied with sufficiency.[18] Almost 2500 years ago, the Buddha seems to have realized this when he admonished his disciples that in aspiring for freedom (*nibbāna*) one cannot and should not attempt to determine when one's thought (*citta*) would be free from influxes (*āsava*), just as a farmer cannot and should not hope to determine beforehand how and when his crop is going to mature and produce the harvest.[19] The language of conditionality in which the principle of dependent arising is expressed, that is, "when that exists, this comes to be; on the arising of that, this arises," renders the principle sufficiently flexible to accommodate the "unusual" (*abbhūta*).

The application of this principle of dependence in the sphere of morality produced far-reaching results, especially in eliminating conflict and strife (*kalaha*, *viggaha*) and inculcating harmony (*sāmaggi*). Just as much as Buddhism disregarded ultimate truths, it avoided the sponsorship of strict and absolute moral laws. Speaking about the actual and the ideal, another pragmatist from America, William James, has said:

> But this world of ours is made on an entirely different pattern, and the causistic question is here most tragically practical. The actually possible in this world is vastly narrower than all that is demanded; and there is always a *pinch* between the ideal and the actual which can only be got through by leaving part of the ideal behind.[20]

A similar pragmatic attitude is reflected in the Buddha's admonition to monks when he said: "Monks, even the good should be relinquished, let alone the evil" (*Dhammā pi...pahātabbā pageva adhammā*).[21] This flexibility enabled the Buddha not only to modify the rules of discipline he prescribed for his disciples taking into consideration varying times and circumstances, but also to move around in the world, even among the most dogmatic thinkers, without coming into conflict. He was prepared to claim: "Monks, I do not conflict with the world. However, the world conflicts with me" (*Nāhaṃ bhikkhavṃ lokena vivadāmi, loko ca mayā vivadati*).[22]

The reluctance to accept strict moral rules did not mean either the acceptance of moral solitude as the best way of life or abandoning moral principles altogether. Evaluating behavior in terms of fruitfulness, a middle path that recognizes happiness of oneself as well as others was accepted as a fair and just moral standard. Selfishness, self-indulgence, or self-aggrandizement was looked upon as "low (*hīna*), vulgar (*gamma*), individualist (*puthujjanika*), ignoble (*anariya*), and unfruitful (*anatthasaṃhita*)." A life of self-mortification, self-immolation, or extreme altruism was viewed as "painful (*dukkha*), ignoble (*anariya*), and unfruitful (*anatthasaṃhita*).[23] Taking the common denominator, it seems that these two ways of life are both ignoble and unfruitful. The moral life that avoids these two extremes should therefore be at least noble (*ariya*) and fruitful (*atthasaṃhita*). For this reason, a life that contributes toward one's own happiness as well as the happiness of others is recommended as the highest ideal a man can follow.

However, in order to follow the moral life referred to above the ordinary human person requires a stronger and more powerful incentive than the subtle philosophical rationalization. Abandoning the conception of a Supreme Being who is generally supposed to offer rewards to the good and punish the evil, the Buddha had also eliminated such incentives. For this reason, he had to emphasize the doctrines of moral retribution (*kamma*) combined with the possibility of survival (*punabbhava*) in order to re-introduce the incentive for a moral life. The very same argument used by Blaise Pascal to inculcate morality based upon the belief in a Supreme Being, an argument that is popularly known as "Pascal's Wager" was utilized by the Buddha and in his case it was the idea of survival that could serve as an incentive for the moral life.[24]

A few centuries after the Buddha's death the search for a mysterious something emerged in the Buddhist tradition, especially with the speculations of the Sarvāstivādins and the Sautrāntikas. The Sarvāstivāda notion of a "substance" (*svabhāva*) existing during the past, present, and the future heralded that search. The Sautrāntikas, rejecting the Sarvāstivāda view, propounded a similarly mysterious something, namely, a subtle personality (*puggala*). The introduction of these metaphysical views and their survival in some form or another within the Buddhist tradition provided opportunities for several Buddhist thinkers to gain prominence as undisputed leaders in a crusade against substantialized metaphysics. We take up three prominent figures, Moggalīputta-tissa, Nāgārjuna, and Vasubandhu, for treatment even though there were numerous others who could be seen as doing the same thing. Even though the methods adopted by these three thinkers may vary slightly, their mission was the same, namely, to re-establish the non-substantialist teachings of the Buddha.

During the 250 years following the death of the Buddha, the substantialist ivy was spreading far and wide that the non-substantialist teachings of the Buddha could have been a relic of the past if not for the erudition and logical acumen of a philosopher like Moggalīputta-tissa. He provided the foundation for the first "great purge" in the Buddhist tradition carried out by the Emperor Asoka. His *Kathāvatthu* represents the first attempt to utilize sophisticated arguments to draw out the implications of the metaphysical theories of personality (*puggala*) and of substance (*sabbaṃ sabbadā atthi*). The result was the re-establishment of the non-substantiality of both a person (*pudgala-nairātmya*) and elements (*dharma-nairātmya*). Unfortunately, this valuable piece of Buddhist scholarship has remained unrecognized not merely because of the difficulties in dealing with its contents but also on account of the Theravāda-Mahāyāna sectarianism that has overwhelmed modern critical scholarship.

The self-same sectarian differences, however, have been responsible for over-stating the contribution of another equally significant philosopher, namely, Nāgārjuna. Unlike Moggalīputta-tissa, whose name is not familiar to most Buddhist scholars, Nāgārjuna has become a household name, sometimes even overshadowing the historical Buddha. His primary philosophical treatise, the *Mūlamadhyamakakārikā*, has remained a puzzle, especially for those who were looking for ways and means to magnify the sectarianism referred to earlier. In a recent publication I have provided sufficient evidence to show that Nāgārjuna's goal was not to improve upon the teachings of the historical Buddha or to provide a philosophical foundation for any form of sectarianism, but rather to return to the original teachings of the Buddha by weeding out the substantialist metaphysics that continued to thrive even after the *Kathavātthu*.[25] Nāgārjuna's method was primarily "analytical." However, that analytical method was applied primarily to the refutation of substance (*svabhāva*), subjective as well as objective. Having devoted 25 out of 27 chapters of his work to an analysis of substantialist metaphysics and re-establishing the non-substantialist standpoint of the Buddha, Nāgārjuna concludes his 25th chapter as follows:

> The Buddha did not teach the appeasement of all objects, the appeasement of obsessions and the peaceful as some thing (*kiṃcit*) to some one (*kaśyacit*) at some place (*kvacit*).

Placing this statement in the context in which the Buddha emphasized the need to relinquish the search for a mysterious something (*kiñci*) and adopt a more empirical explanation of existence as "dependent arising," one can appreciate not only Nāgārjuna's epistemology and ontology but also his ethical reflections. Unfortunately, his views about knowledge, reality, and morals are interpreted in the light of a rather mysterious conception of "emptiness" (*śūnyatā*). Ignoring Nāgārjuna's warning against perceiving emptiness as an ultimate reality,[26] instead of a "dependent concept" (*upādāya prajñapti*),[27] most interpreters of Nāgārjuna have re-introduced that element of mystery which he attempted to eliminate precisely by anchoring "emptiness" (the abstract conception) on "the empty" (*śūnya* = the concrete), the ideal (*paramārtha*) on the practical (*artha* = *saṃvṛti* = *vyavahāra*). Indeed, Nāgārjuna was enthusiastic in placing "dependent arising" (*pratītyasamutpāda*) in the context of the "dependently arisen" (*pratītyasamutpanna*), as the Buddha himself did, when he denied that there could be any *dharma* that is not dependently arisen.[28]

Nāgārjuna's devastating criticism of substance (*svabhāva*) left the metaphysician with no room to introduce any form of substantialism except in the area of personal experience, and soon the seeds for a metaphysical theory of idealism were being sown, especially in the *Laṅkāvatāra-sūtra* which openly criticized the "middle path" proposed by Nāgārjuna without understanding it.[29] "Consciousness-only" (*vijñāna-mātra*) or "thought-only" (*citta-mātra*) becomes the "ultimate reality" and the "originally pure" (*prakṛti-prabhāsvara*) or the "location of the womb (of enlightenment)" (*garbha-saṃsthāna*).[30]

It was left to Vasubandhu to rescue the Buddha-word from such metaphysical reflections. He was therefore compelled to examine critically the psychological material in early Buddhism and see whether there was any room for idealism within it. His teacher, Maitreya, had already attempted this in a rather unsystematic way. Vasubandhu's *Vijñaptimātratāsiddhi* deals with the same problems in a more critical and systematic way.[31] The first part of the treatise, the *Viṃśatikā*, is devoted to an examination of the routinely accepted view of commonsense that an object exists independent of experience, an uncritical assumption that leads to the belief in something hidden in phenomena. William James, whose views compare well with those of the Buddha and, therefore, of Vasubandhu, provides the following explanation of the common sense assumption:

> The reason why we believe that objects of our thoughts have a duplicate existence outside, is that there are *many* human thoughts, each with the same objects, as we cannot help supposing. The judgment that *my* thought has the same object as *his* thought is what makes the psychologist call my thought cognitive of an outer reality.[32]

A challenge to this epistemologist's claim is posed by James in a footnote. "If but one person sees an apparition we consider it his private hallucination. If more than one, we begin to think it may be a real external presence."[33] A critical philosopher will be compelled to raise questions, in spite of their incompatibility, not because he is interested in demolishing the validity of all human knowledge, but because he is keen on getting rid of the dogmatism with which certain views are upheld even by very sophisticated philosophers. A superficial reading of Vasubandhu's *Viṃśatikā* may give the impression that he is critical of the reality of external objects because he wanted to propound a theory of "idealism." On the contrary, Vasubandhu was interested primarily in getting rid of the dogmatic tendency to look for something mysterious in the object rather than denying objectivity in human knowledge. Having critically examined the realist metaphysics, Vasubandhu speaks of "mere concept" (*vijñaptimātra*). This should not be confused with "mere consciousness" (*vijñāna-mātra*) or "mere thought" (*citta-mātra*) of the *Laṇkāvatāra*. To state that an event is "mere consciousness" would be to tip the scale in favor of idealism. However, to say that it is a "mere concept" leaves room for equal play on the part of both consciousness and object in the explanation of experience. In emphasizing the idea of "mere concept" Vasubandhu was underscoring the conceptual element in all forms of knowledge-claims, whether that be experience or reason.

This leads him to the examination of the process of cognition (*vijñāna*) and the manner in which the mind (*manas*) influences that process of cognition. This is the "transformation of consciousness" (*vijñāna-pariṇāma*) he undertakes to explain in the second part of his treatise, the *Triṃśikā*. The three transformations are listed as follows:

1. the resultant (*vipāka*) =*ālaya-vijñāna*
2. reflection (*manana*) = *mano nāma vijñāna*, and
3. conception of object (*viṣaya-vijñapti*) =*ṣaḍvidhaṣya viṣayasya upalabdhi*.

In the first place, *ālaya-vijñāna* is not the primordial consciousness. It is a resultant. This eliminates a substantialist interpretation of consciousness and is in conformity with the Buddha's own explanation of consciousness as being dependently arisen. The *ālaya* does not imply a metaphysical "storehouse" or an "unconscious process," but carries the same implication as *ālaya* in the Buddha's discourse where it means "anchoring" or "obsession." With such attachment or obsession functioning in consciousness, the *ālaya-vijñānu* is not a passive recipient of sensory impressions, a sort of *tabula rasa*. The following definition is provided by Vasubandhu:

It is unidentified in terms of concepts of objects and location, and is always possessed of [activities such as] contact, attention, feeling, perception, and volition. In that context, neutral feeling is uninterrupted and not defined. So are contact, etc. And it proceeds like the current of a stream.[34]

The phrase "unidentified" (*asaṃviditaka*) applies to the two concepts (*vijñapti*) of object and location only, not to all activities such as contact, attention, feeling, perception, and volition. This would not leave room for a metaphysical "unconscious process," let alone a "collective unconscious." In other words, the *ālaya-vijñāna* refers to the continued and uninterrupted flow of experience together with its flights and perchings conditioned by interest, yet unconditioned by excessive lust or hatred to break up this neutral feeling. William James' "stream of consciousness" is the modern counterpart of *ālaya-vijñāna*.[35]

According to the explanation given above, *ālaya-vijñāna* functions in terms of contact, feeling, perception, and volition. These can operate as long as an element of interest exists. However, this element of interest can give rise to the four-fold activity: "self-view" (*ātma-dṛṣṭi*), "self-confusion" (*ātma-moha*), "self-esteem" (*ātma-māna*) and "self-love" (*ātma-sneha*). With this possibility, the *ālaya* also becomes the seed of everything (*sarva-bījaṃ*). The four-fold activity is called *manana* and this is the function of *manas*, the faculty that deals with concepts (*dharma*) in producing *mano-vijñāna*.

The difference between *ālaya-vijñāna* and *manas* as envisaged by Vasubandhu is reflected in a definition of mind provided by William James:

Each mind, to begin with, must have a minimum of selfishness in the form of instincts of bodily self-seeking in order to exist. This minimum must be there as a basis for all further conscious acts, whether of self-negation or of a selfishness more subtle still. All minds must have come by way of the survival of the fittest, if by no direct path, to take an interest in the bodies to which they are yoked, altogether *apart from any interest* in the pure Ego which they also possess.[34]

Consciousness which cannot function without interest is *vijñāna*. This interest also can turn out to be a search for a "mysterious something," thereby producing obsession or anchoring (*ālaya*). The appeasement of that obsession eliminates the search for something mysterious leaving consciousness to function in terms of simple interest. Thus, with the restraining of *manas*, the *ālaya*-part of consciousness (*vijñāna*) dissipates, leaving consciousness or the function of being conscious intact. Vasubandhu calls this *arhatva*.

However, if *manas* is allowed to have its sway over all forms of conscious activity, if it were to be made the primordial, as in the case of

Descartes' *cogito* or Kant's transcendental unity of apperception, and leave consciousness as a mere subsidiary phenomenon, the conceptual component of experience can be exaggerated to the neglect of experience or consciousness. A transcendental unity of apperception also could lead to the conception of the unity of the object, a mysterious substance in which all qualities inhere but which is not given in experience. The unwarranted activities of *manas* are thus responsible for the generation of the belief in a substantial object that is supposed to remain even when not experienced.

Vasubandhu's *Triṃśika* is intended to show that conscious life (*vijñāna*) can transform itself from a state of bondage (*saṃsāra*) to one of freedom (*nirvāṇa*) if and when the reflective function of mind (*manas*) can be restrained to remain within its appropriate limits, that is, without going beyond experience. In brief, it is a subtle way of indicating how "interest" could be prevented from turning out to be a "search for a mysterious something (*kiṃcit*)."

Here, then, are three famous disciples of the Buddha, one who has been branded as a Theravādin and the other two as Mahāyānists, faithfully following the "ancient path" (*purāṇaṃ maggaṃ*), assiduously clearing up the weeds of substantialist metaphysics, and enthusiastically exerting themselves to reach the one goal (*ekayāna*), namely, freedom from suffering. Following their example it would be appropriate for anyone who is interested in the Buddha's message to consider Theravāda or Mahāyāna as a "mere convention" (*vohāra-matta*), or a "dependent concept" (*upādāya prajñapti*) or a "mere concept" (*vijñapti-mātra*) and strive for one's own happiness as well as the happiness of others without making a dogmatic claim about any one of these traditions as: "This alone is true; all else is falsehood" (*idam eva saccaṃ moghaṃ aññaṃ*).[35]

NOTES

1. John Dewey, *Quest for Certainty* Gifford Lectures, 1929, New York: G. P. Putnam's Sons, 1960, 3.
2. See *2500 Years of Buddhism*, ed. P. V. Bapat, New Delhi: Government of India, 1956, xiii.
3. *The Quest for Certainty*, 6–7, emphasis added.
4. *M* (PTS) 1.167, 173; 3.162.
5. *Ibid.*, 1.136–137.
6. *D 1.76.*
7. *M* 1.140, 190, 228, 435, 551; 3.16.
8. *Ibid.*, 3.239.
9. *Ibid.*, 1.295.
10. *Ibid.*, 1.167.
11. *Dh* 1–2.
12. See *M* 1.1 ff.
13. *S* 2.17.
14. *D* 1.193.
15. *Ud* 8.
16. *M* 2.196; *Dh* 396, 421.
17. *S* 1.14–15.
18. Donald Davidson, "Causal Relations," in *The Logic of Grammar*, ed. Donald Davidson and Gilbert Hartman, Encino, California: Dickenson, 1975, 250–251.
19. *A 1.240.*
20. "Moral Philosopher and the Moral Life," in *Essays in Pragmatism*, ed. A. Castell, New York: Hafner, 1948, 78.
21. *M* 1.135.
22. *S* 3.138.
23. *Ibid.*, 5.421.
24. *M* 1.403.
25. *Nāgārjuna*, *The Philosophy of the Middle Way*, Albany: The State University of New York, 1986.
26. *Mulamadhyamakakārikā* XII.8.
27. *Ibid.*, XXIV.18.
28. *Ibid.*, XXIV.19.
29. *Laṇkāvatāra Sūtra* (ed. Nanjio), 310.
30. *Ibid.*, 358.
31. See my recent work on Vasubandhu, *The Principles of Buddhist Psychology*, Albany: The State University of New York Press, 1987.
32. William James, *The Principles of Psychology*, New York: Henry Holt, 1908, I.271–272.
33. *Ibid.*

34. *Vijñaptimātratāsiddhi*, *Triṃśikā*, 3–4.
35. *The Principles of Psychology*, I.224–290.
36. *Ibid.*, I.323–324.
37. *D* 1.187; *M* 3.212.

3

SPACE, EMPTINESS AND FREEDOM

(ĀKĀŚA, ŚŪNYATĀ, AND NIBBĀNA)

R.D. Gunaratne

THIS IS, BASICALLY, AN ESSAY in Buddhist cosmology. Cosmology, as the term is understood today, has two uses: one belonging to philosophy and the other to science, although these two are not necessarily without intermingling.

The two senses are well indicated by Milton K. Munitz in his article on cosmology in the *Encyclopedia of Philosophy*. Munitz refers to A.E. Taylor's and A.N. Whitehead's conceptions to indicate the philosophical use. Taylor assigns to philosophical cosmology the task of considering "the meaning and validity of the most universal conceptions of which we seek to understand the nature of individual objects which make up the experienced physical world, " 'extension', 'succession', 'space', 'time', 'motion', 'change',...and the more complex categories of 'matter'...'causality'...and so forth." Whitehead uses the term even more broadly, "as being synonymous with speculative philosophy in its most comprehensive sense." Thus in Whitehead's *Process and Reality*, whose subtitle is "An Essay in Cosmology," an attempt is made to construct a categorical scheme of general ideas "in terms of which every element of our experience can be interpreted."

On the contrary, "the term 'cosmology' designates a science in which...the observational astronomer and the theoretical physicist are devoted to giving an account of the large scale properties of the astronomical or physical universe as a whole."[1]

In this paper I shall be concerned primarily but not exclusively with the philosophical use of the term. But the reader will find in this essay that the philosophical and the scientific uses often impinge on each other.

The essay is woven around one cosmological concept—that of space or *ākāśa*. The purpose of this study is to examine the Buddhist conception of space and the rather interesting role it seems to have played in both Theravāda and Mahāyāna Buddhism.

Space (*ākāsa* Skt. *ākāśa*) was one of the five great elements (*mahābhūtas*) [the other four being earth (*pṛthvi*), water (*āp*), fire (*tejas*), and air (*vayu*)] in most Indian systems of thought like the Vedānta, Sāṃkhya, Nyāya-Vaiśeṣika, Caraka (medical tradition), although the Nyāya-Vaiśeṣika considered it non-corporeal.[2]

Space seems to have had a certain priority among the great elements. In Sanskrit philosophical literature, space stands for the subtle and the real plenum which pervades the universe.[3] And it seems to take priority among the great elements in the creation of the universe.[4] To quote Radhakrishnan, "The Upanisads look upon the earliest material world as one of extension in space of which the characteristic feature is vibration." And "vibration (sound or *ākāśa*), in order to create forms, needs *vāyu*, *tejas*, *āp* and *pṛthvi*." Again, "the development of the world is a steady grossing of the subtle *ākāśa* or space. All physical objects...are built by these five elements."[5]

Naturally, some of these ideas find reflection in Buddhist thought. However, Buddhism, along with Jainism,[6] did not consider space to be a great element. It, like the materialist Lokāyata,[7] recognized as great elements only the other four. Early Buddhism, as Y. Karunadasa argues convincingly, distinguishes two concepts of space. One is termed the "element of space" (*ākāśa-dhātu*), the other simply space (*ākāśa*).[8] The element of space is a derived form (*upādā-rūpa*) intimately associated with matter. It refers to the cavities and interstices both in the human body (*ajjhattika*) and in the external (*bāhira*) world. It is also referred to as "delimiting form" (*pariccheda-rūpa*), that is, it delimits matter and is in turn delimited by matter. In this sense, it is dependent on material objects and ultimately on the four great elements (*mahābhūtas*).

The other concept, referred to by the term *ākāśa* alone, is a non-*saṅkhata dhamma*, that is, it is a non-conditioned reality. It is not born of causes, it does not perish, and therefore is eternal, infinite, real but not material.[9] *Milindapañha* enumerates its characteristics in the following terms: (i) It is everywhere, impossible to grasp. (ii) It is the resort of (all) things. (iii) It inspires terror. (iv) It is infinite, boundless, and immeasurable. (v) It does not hang on to anything or rest on anything and is not stopped by anything.[10] It is thus a conception of absolute space, which was current along with the other concept of the "element of space" (*ākāśa-dhātu*).

Buddhism distinguished between space (*ākāśa*) and extension (*paṭhavi*).[11] It also distinguished between the universe, considered as consisting of all the *loka* or worlds, and *ākāśa*, or absolute space, and allowed the possibility that space extended beyond the universe. For, while *ākāśa* is categorically asserted to be infinite, Buddha, in the well-known "unanswered questions" (*avyākata*), did not answer the question whether the universe is finite or infinite.[12] This is significant in view of the fact that the Buddha's conception of the universe was that it consisted of "innumerable" worlds (*lokas*) other than our own, and that all these worlds were in space—i.e., they were *ākāśa-loka*. On this conception K.N. Jayatilleke, for example, refers to the *Visuddhimagga* passage where it is said, "As far as these suns and moons revolve, shining and shedding their light in space, thus far extends the thousand fold universe (*sahassadhā-loka*)".[13] Still, the universe could be finite, while space is infinite.

In later Buddhism, including Theravāda, the conception of space (*ākāśa*) is gradually reduced to a *paññatti*, a mental construction, and hence devoid of any reality.[14] In the more idealistic Buddhist traditions, space was again denied any reality.[15] The appreciation of these different conceptions—absolute, relative and "unreal"—as well as of the difficulty involved in clarifying a unique conception of space, is facilitated by the realization that these views of space are seen even in current science. Thus, while Newtonian science considered space as absolute, Einstein's Theory of Relativity, which merged the notions of space and time, was at first thought to give only a relative (matter or energy dependent) concept of space-time.[16] But that this is the only concept compatible with or necessitated by relativity is now in dispute. It is argued by some that relativity of space-time is only epistemological, whereas absolute space is ontologically precedent.[17] In two further conceptions, space-time appears to be a "disposable" concept (i.e. like a *paññatti*). For it is maintained by some that if field theory is absorbed by particle theory, physics will be rid of the space-time concepts[18]; others consider empty space as only an immense background of energy.[19] This last view perhaps merges also with the idea that space is energy dependent.

We thus see three conceptions of space in the early Buddhist tradition: two of them—i.e. of absolute space (*ākāśa*) and "relative space" (*ākāśa dhātu*)—running parallel, and the other—i.e. space as mental construction – absorbing them in the later traditions of Buddhism, both Theravāda and Mahāyāna. The question that interests us here is (i) What was the concept of space at the beginning of Mahāyāna? (ii) Does it show any relationship to the philosophical standpoint of the Mahāyāna tradition?

In the discussion that follows, Nāgārjuna's Mādhyamika will be considered to have laid the foundation for Mahāyāna. Nāgārjuna, particularly his *Mūlamadhyamaka-kārikā*, expounds his philosophy of emptiness (*śūnyatā*). In two of his discourses, the Buddha discusses the empty (*suñña*) nature of life and being.[20] But it was Nāgārjuna who in his philosophy emphasized the emptiness of "everything" (*sarva-dharma-śūnyatā*).

Before we proceed, we should take note of two questions relating to meaning or reference of the term *śūnyatā*. It has been understood in a number of ways. *Śūnyatā* literally means "emptiness." In Buddhism it also refers to the relativity of the *dharmas* or existences, in the sense that these do not have any own-being (*svabhāva*). The two meanings perhaps coalesce but they could also be considered as two different aspects of a single idea. The third is the meaning of the term *śūnyatā* used as a characteristic of "everything." In Buddhism, *dharma* are categorized into *saṅkhata* and *asaṅkhata* – the conditioned and unconditioned. All natures, except *nibbāna* are conditioned. In other words, the life-process (*saṃsāra*) is conditioned, while "freedom" (*nibbāna*) is not. So, when we consider everything as "empty" (*śūnya*), does it mean that both *saṅkhata dhamma* (i.e. *saṃsāra*) and *asaṅkhata dhamma* (i.e. *nibbāna*) are "empty"? Or should we restrict the meaning of everything here only to *saṃsāra*? We would find that this turns out to be an intriguing question.

Generally, in the early Buddhist tradition, *saṃsāra* and *nibbāna* are considered different or as polar opposites. The conception of this difference has an ontological tinge be it great or small. I emphasize the word tradition here because, as we shall see, one can question how close the tradition was to Buddha's views themselves.

This situation of (*saṃsāra*) being relative and *nibbāna* being sort of an absolute has its parallel in the relationship between the relative *ākāsa-dhātu* and the absolute *ākāśa*. Indeed we now indicate that *ākāśa* was more or less identifiable with *asaṅkhata* – which only *nibbāna* is. There certainly was close association between *ākāśa* and *nibbāna*.

That *ākāśa* is a concept which almost tallied with *nibbāna*. The *summum bonum* of Buddhism can be seen when we note that there was hardly a characteristic which *nibbāna* had and *ākāśa* did not have. For *nibbāna* was real, boundless, eternal, immeasurable, and neither mental nor material and so on, and *ākāśa* had the same qualities. This naturally led to a difficulty. *Nibbāna* is the only unconditioned *dhamma* and *state* in Buddhism. It is *asaṅkhata*. Was *ākāśa* also *asaṅkhata* thereby placing it on a par with *nibbāna*? The Vaibhāṣikas insisted that *ākāśa* is an *asaṃskṛta dharma*. The Theravādins, who were not bold enough to uphold such a position while admitting that the *ākāśa* is not a *saṅkhata dhamma*, reserved the term *asaṅkhata* to characterize *nibbāna* alone. Thus *Milindapañha* tacitly avoids calling *ākāśa* an *asaṅkhata*, and the *Kathāvatthu* is explicit that it should not be called an *asaṅkhata* (for if *ākāśa* is *asaṅkhata* there ought to be two *nibbānas*).[20]

This is not all. *Ākāśa* was one of the major themes of contemplation (*kasina*) in Buddhist meditation, which is supposed to lead one to *nibbāna*. Thus, in the *Mahā-Rāhulovāda sutta*, the Buddha advises his son Rāhula to practice mental concentration which is compared with open space.[21] Moreover, the first of the higher mental states (*jhāna*) is *ākāsānañcāyatana*, where one contemplates the bounded space, becomes aware of it, enters into and dwells within the sphere of boundless space. The specification unbounded (*ananta*) here refers not only to space (*ākāśa*) but also to the state of mind which pervades space without bounds.[22] *Ākāsānañcāyatana* is also the first *arūpa-loka* (non-material state) mentioned in Buddhism, and it is often mentioned in the eight stages of deliverance (*aṭṭha vimokkha*).[23] Indeed a monk who attains and abides in the sphere of infinite space is said to have "won access to the imperturbable" (*ānejjappatto*); and this was taken to mean that this state was unconditioned (*asaṅkhata*).[24] However, we saw the Theravādin refusing to apply this term to anything other than *nibbāna*.

One thus sees that mundane *ākāśa* is the concept which came nearest to the supra mundane *nibbāna*, and thus it could help one to get some understanding or inkling of *nibbāna*. And through meditation, it certainly leads one towards the supreme ideal.

Given the literal meaning of "emptiness" to *śūnyatā*, one immediately feels that *ākāśa* ("empty space") and *śūnyatā* of Nāgārjuna perhaps have some association. And *śūnyatā* being the *paramārtha* truth it probably is the (nature of) *nibbāna*. On the contrary, *śūnyatā* is also the (underlying) nature of *saṃsāra*. All this goes well with Nāgārjuna's not making a radical distinction between *saṃsāra* and *nibbāna*. But we saw that *śūnyatā* is understood as lack of *svabhāva* or own-being. That is to say that all things are only relative or conditioned. Nāgārjuna's view here, as we shall see, is not without problems.

This leads us to the two interpretations of Nāgārjuna's conception of *nirvāṇa*. Murti, in his well known *Central Philosophy of Buddhism*, seems to favor an absolutistic and ineffable conception of *nirvāṇa*.[25] Kalupahana, in his admirable *Nāgārjuna: The Philosophy of the Middle Way*

(1986), persuasively "de-mystifies" Nāgārjuna, and maintains that Nāgārjuna was not prepared to create an unbridgeable chasm between *saṃvṛti* and *paramārtha*. He goes on to say, that freedom (*nirvāṇa*) is not something to be sharply distinguished from the life-process (*saṃsāra*), even though they are not identical. Indeed we have Nāgārjuna's line:

"There is no distinction between *nirvāṇa* and *saṃsāra*."[26]

Apart from the intrinsic interest in the nature of *nibbāna*, the point which interests us in Nāgārjuna's *Kārikā* is that, in the *dhātu-parīkṣā*, Nāgārjuna takes the *ākāśa-dhātu* as the central concept to analyze and shows that there is no essence in each *dhātu* as such. As Kalupahana points out, a person was considered to be formed of the six elements (*dhātu*)[27] namely, water (*āpa*), heat (*teja*), air (*vāyu*), earth (*paṭhavi*), space (*ākāśa*), and consciousness (*viññāṇa*); and Nāgārjuna says none of these constituents can be taken to have an essence of its own. Nāgārjuna's position of *dhātu* as *śūnya*, which was the explicit position of the Buddha, lends support to Kalupahana's position that Nāgārjuna was only a very faithful exponent of the Buddha's teachings.[28]

A question that interests us is that Nāgārjuna has considered here only the concept of *ākāśa-dhātu* which was a relative conception. But *ākāśa* was an absolutist conception, and it is intriguing that Nāgārjuna did not examine that concept at all. In view of the very significant place it was accorded in early Buddhist schools, Nāgārjuna would certainly have been aware of this distinction. Buddha himself could have lent support to this distinction as the *Maha-Rāhulovāda sutta* refers to concentration which is like open space, and again in the first *jhāna* where a person is first advised to meditate on bounded space and then on unbounded space.

Moreover, Nāgārjuna devoted a full chapter to *kāla parīkṣā* (examination of time) but did not take up *ākāśa parīkṣā* (examination of space). He only examined *ākāśa-dhātu* under the *dhātu parīkṣā*.

While Kalupahana's analysis that Nāgārjuna's bases in the argument were epistemological (and empiricist, operationalist, or pragmatic) is probably correct, I find it difficult to see why Nāgārjuna ignored the concept of *ākāśa* which has been, in a sense, associated with *nibbāna* itself. Does an ontological question raise its head (due to this negligence) here?

This leads us to the question as to what is the relationship between *nirvāṇa*, *paramartha*, and *śūnyatā* in Nāgārjuna. On the one hand, they are identical for the *paramārtha* (truth) is *śūnyatā* and the *paramārtha* is *nirvāṇa*. On the other hand, *śūnyatā* is the nature of (all and) particularly the *saṃvṛti* truths. (A crude parallel in modern terms would be like our saying that the commonsense objects like chairs, tables, mangoes, etc. are conventional *saṃvṛti* truths, while the real (*paramārtha*) truth is that they are made of electrons and other sub-atomic particles).

Now here is at least an apparent paradox. *Śūnyatā* is speaking about the *saṃvṛti*. But *paramārtha* truth is also *śūnya*. This appears incorrect, if not impossible. For what is dependent or conditioned, and therefore lacking in *svabhāva*, are the *saṅkhata dhamma*. *Paramārtha* or *nibbāna* is an *asaṅkhata dhamma*. While it may be allowable to say that *saṅkhata dhamma* are in the *paramārtha*, can *asaṅkhata* also be *śūnya* in the sense of being relative or dependent? If one takes up that position one is either ignoring the sense of *śūnya* or giving up the *saṅkhata-asaṅkhata* distinction.

We may press our earlier analogy to clarify the ideas here. If chairs, tables etc. are made of electrons and sub-atomic particles, either the sub-atomic particles are ontologically basic, in which case they are *paramārtha*, or, if they are not, and these sub-atomic particles themselves could be split up, as is now evident,[29] then they would not be *paramārtha*. If so, it happens that the *paramārtha* is the *principle* (a *dhammatā*) that there is nothing fundamental, and that principle is the *unchangeable*. It is here, I think, that *intuitively* the two meanings of "emptiness" and "relativity" coalesce. It is here also that *saṅkhata* and *asaṅkhata* or *saṃsāra* and *nibbāna* also link up. *Nibbāna* is the realization, nay the experience, of this "emptiness" of each thing and everything.

Kalupahana considers that Buddha's non-substantialist position, which he associates with a non-absolutistic conception of *nibbāna*, was maintained by Moggaliputta-tissa and Nāgārjuna, whereas some of the early Buddhist schools and the Vedantic interpretation of Nāgārjuna or Mādhyamika had absolutistic conceptions of *nibbāna*. While I think there is much to be said for Kalupahana's view, it is not the intention of this paper to go into this controversy. But we saw that Nāgārjuna himself has been given both the absolutistic and the "relativistic" interpretations. I think that one factor which allowed the absolutistic interpretation to be given to Nāgārjuna was his not examining the early Buddhist conception of (absolute) *ākāśa*. It is not sufficient to say that, as a true follower of the Buddha, Nāgārjuna took up only the conception of *ākāśa-dhātu* which seems to be the only conception that the Buddha had, according to Kalupahana. Nāgārjuna was demolishing the early Buddhist misconceptions and *ākāśa* was one of the most troublesome of these, as Kalupahana himself notes. Although Kalupahana seems to think that by examining *ākāśa-dhātu*, Nāgārjuna examines *ākāśa* itself, this is by no means clear. He examines *ākāśa* only as a *dhātu*, which will mean that he examines the early Buddhist conception of *ākāśa-dhātu* and not of *ākāśa*. The concept of *ākāśa* was exactly what Nāgārjuna should have considered. By failing to do so Nāgārjuna seems to have wittingly or unwittingly slipped one important point where he could have been explicitly non-absolutistic.

All the same, I think Nāgārjuna's position that *saṃsāra* and *nirvāṇa* are linked, has blossomed in Mahāyāna Buddhism, with branches like Zen emphasizing the role of nature and daily life in attaining *satori* or freedom.[30]

Again, the "view of Emptiness in Mahāyāna is not a result of analysis, as in Theravāda, where individual things are minutely analyzed, but a synthetic view seen by intuition...."[31]

This intuition comes through meditation or great mental concentration. I conjecture that the concept of *ākāśa*, and meditation based on it, could have been, and would be, the ideal instrument to reach this idea of emptiness. *Ākāśa* is empty, almost by definition. In meditation one first contemplates on bounded space (*ākāśa-dhātu*) and then on unbounded space (*ākāśa*). Perhaps one could thus see the objects melting into the *ākāśa*, into "nothingness." Then perhaps, you yourself melt into "nothingness" with the objects, and "identify" yourself with *ākāśa*, emptiness—the *śūnyatā*. And here *nibbāna* and *saṃsāra* merge. Isn't the conception of Ākāśagarbha, the Mahāyāna Bodhisattva, of great significance?

Writing on Zen Buddhism, D.T. Suzuki once said:

> "Man came from Nature in order to see Nature in himself...."

This is objective thinking, to say that Man sees himself through Nature, or that Nature sees itself through Man....This probing into subjectivity is probing into the very bases of Nature as it is in itself.[32]

To this, we could perhaps add the rejoinder,

"If you really experience *ākāśa*, the *ākāśa* with pervading emptiness, then you see what you are, and what Nature is."

That probably is somewhere near the realization of the *śūnyatā*, the *satori*, the *nibbāna*. And, in the broad sense of cosmology which a philosopher like Whitehead gives to the term,[33] aren't some of these also cosmological concepts along with *ākāśa*?

NOTES

1. *Encyclopedia of Philosophy*, ed. Paul Edwards, London and New York: Macmillan and Free Press, Vol. 2, 237–8.
2. See, e.g. *Sinhala Encyclopedia*, Colombo: Dept. of Cultural Affairs, Government of Ceylon, Vol. 2 (hereafter, *SE*) 370–384.
3. cf. *Encyclopedia of Buddhism* (ed. G.P. Malalasekera) Government of Ceylon, Vol. I. (hereafter, EB) 340.
4. Mittal, K.K., *Role of Materialism in Indian Thought*, New Delhi: Munshiram Manoharlal Publishers, 1974. Mittal also quotes from Deussen's translation of an upanishadic passage which includes the following, "from this atman, in truth has the ether (space) arisen, from the ether the wind, from the wind the fire...." (90).
5. *Loc. cit.*
6. Karunadasa, Y., *Buddhist Analysis of Matter*, Colombo: Department of Cultural Affairs, 1967 (hereafter, Karunadasa) 16.
7. Karunadasa, 91–98.
8. *Loc. cit.*
9. *Miln*, 320–321 gives the following description. *"Yato mahārāja ākāso na jāyati, na mīyati na cavati na uppajjati evam eva kho mahārāja nibbānaṃ na jāyati...."*
10. *The Question of King Milinda* (Translated T.W. Rhys Davids) Pt. II. Dover Publications Inc. New York, 1963, 316–17.
11. See *EB* 341.
12. *D* 1.22–23.
13. Jayatilleke, K.N., Buddhist Conception of the Universe, in *Facets of Buddhist Thought*, Kandy: Buddhist Publications Society, 84 ff.
14. Karunadasa, 98.
15. Stcherbatsky, T.H., *Buddhist Logic*. Vol. I., New York: Dover Publications, Inc. 84ff.
16. E.g. see Jammer, Max, *Concepts of Space*, Cambridge, Mass,: Harvard University Press. 2.
17. See Grunbaum, Adolf. The Philosophical Retention of Absolute Space in Einstein's General Theory of Relativity, reproduced in *Problems of Space and Time* (ed. Smart J.J.C.) New York: Macmillan, 1964, 315–16.
18. See Smart, J.J.C., *Problems of Space and Time* (ed. Smart) Introduction, 16–17.
19. Bohm, David, *Wholeness and the Implicate Order*, Art paperbacks, London, 1980. 191ff.
20. Karunadasa, 93ff.
21. *M* 1.424.
22. *EB*. 347.
23. *Loc. cit.*
24. *Loc. cit.*

25. Murti, T.R.V. *Central Philosophy of Buddhism*, London: George Allen and Unwin Ltd., 1956.
26. Kalupahana, David. J. *Nāgārjuna. The Philosophy of the Middle Way*, State University of New York Press 1986. (hereafter, Kalupahana) 355 ff.
27. Nāgārjuna, *Mūlamadhyamakakārikā*, XXV, 19.
28. Kalupahana, 447.
29. See, e.g. Capra, Fritjof, *The Tao of Physics*, Fontana Paperbacks 1983 edition, 209ff.
30. See Suzuki, D.T., Role of Nature in Zen Buddhism, in *Zen Buddhism*, in selected writing of D.T. Suzuki, (ed. William Barret), Doubleday Anchor Books, New York 1956, (Hereafter Suzuki, D.T.)
31. Suzuki, D.L. *Mahāyāna Buddhism*, London: George Allen and Unwin, 1981, 85.
32. Suzuki, D.T. 236.
33. See Munitz, Milton, K., article on Cosmology in *Encyclopedia of Philosophy*, ed. Paul Edwards, Vol. 2. 238.

4

THE SOCIAL RELEVANCE OF THE BUDDHIST NIBBĀNA IDEAL

P.D. Premasiri

NIBBĀNA IS THE *SUMMUM BONUM* OF BUDDHISM. The attainment of the goal of *nibbāna* is the sole aim, remote or immediate, of both Buddhist layman and monk. It is said that the holy life is lived under the Buddha to attain this goal.[1] Given the facts about the nature of the universe and ourselves, this goal was considered in early Buddhism as the highest, the supreme which each and every individual ought to attain sooner or later. Although there is unanimity regarding the view that *nibbāna* is the ultimate goal, there is wider divergence of opinion, regarding the way in which Buddhist *nibbāna* should be conceived. For some interpreters *nibbāna* represents a transcendental reality beyond any form of conceptualization or logical thinking. It is a metaphysical reality, something absolute, eternal and uncompounded, a nominal behind the phenomenal. For others it is merely an extinction of life, an escape from the cycle of suffering which in the ultimate analysis is equivalent to eternal death. Such opinions which are diametrically opposed to one another can be seen, from the point of view of the Pali canonical scriptures, to be a result of not paying heed to the warnings given by the Buddha himself on the conflict in reason generated by our speculative interest in attempting to seek categorical answers to questions which cannot be so answered. The object of the present paper is to point out that later interpreters have distorted the concept in mystifying it and unduly emphasizing its other-worldly aspect. This will in turn unravel the fact that the Buddhist goal of *nibbāna* has much to do with this world.

This, however, contradicts the prevalent opinion in a wider circle of scholars that Buddhism is an "otherworldly," a "life denying," and a "salvation religion" having nothing to do with this world. We shall show with supporting evidence from one of the principal scriptural traditions which has a recognizable claim to antiquity and orthodoxy, viz. the Pali Nikayas, that Buddhism does not see any opposition between an improvement of the conditions of this world and man's striving for salvation. It is a considerable distortion of Buddhism to interpret it as a religious ideal which ignores the progress of mankind in this world, to escape into an euphoric bliss in a mystical and metaphysical realm of transcendental being.

Heinz Bechert says in his foreword to *The World of Buddhism*, "The Buddha's teaching is for all mankind, but its original aim was not to shape life in the world but to teach liberation, release *from* the world."[2] Max Weber made similar remarks some decades earlier. He described Buddhism as a "salvation religion" and according to him, "Its salvation is an absolutely personal performance of the single individual."[3]

> Salvation is an absolutely personal performance of the self-reliant individual.... The specific social character of all genuine mysticism is here carried to its maximum.[4]

Spiro speaks of a distinction between "Nibbānic Buddhism" and "Kammatic Buddhism" and believes that "Nibbānic Buddhism" is properly characterized as a religion of radical salvation.[5] Spiro says:

> Ideationally, its conception of salvation is indeed a radical one, entailing the transcendence of the entire physicotemporal world. Sociologically, its character for a soteriological community is equally radical: in order to transcend the physicotemporal world, it is necessary to abandon the sociopolitical world. But physical retreat from the world is not sufficient; it is merely a necessary condition for yet another psychologically radical act: having abandoned the world, one must sever all ties to it and withdraw all cathexes from it. Salvation can only be achieved by a total and radical rejection of the world in all its aspects. Nibbānic Buddhism demands no more; it demands no less.[6]

Such a disparate attitude towards the affairs of the world and the goal of *nibbāna* or salvation does not appear to accord with the doctrinal standpoint of the Buddha. For degeneration in the affairs of the world is, according to Buddhism, closely linked with the lack of a sound moral ideal, and the ideal of *nibbāna* introduces precisely the kind of ideal that is necessary for the promotion of a better and harmonious world order. Nibbānic beings are considered to be an essential ingredient in an ideal society. For by nature they perform a vital role in giving moral direction to society, without which no stable society can be founded. Contrary to the opinion of those who tried to introduce artificial dichotomies into Buddhism in terms of such categories as "Nibbānic Buddhism" and "Kammatic Buddhism," the Buddhist view of an ideal social order effectively integrates its salvation ideal with the ideal of the creation and maintenance of a righteous social order.

One main reason for considering *nibbāna* as a world-denying ideal is the interpretation of it as a mystical and metaphysical concept. When Buddhism is seen in comparison with the background, on which it arose, one of its distinguishing features is its avoidance of metaphysics and the demystification of the spiritual life. This is clearly seen in the Buddha's refusal to commit himself to the positions taken up by his contemporaries on the major metaphysical issues (*avyākata* theses), his non-conformity to the then most dominant view that divine creation is the explanation for the first beginnings of the cosmos and his criticism of the mystical notions of Vedic ritual and sacrifice. However, later forms of Buddhism seem to have been influenced by the absolutistic views stemming from the Upaniṣadic metaphysical tradition. The Theravāda tradition itself, which otherwise remained faithful to the empirical and analytical approach of early Buddhism, seems to have been influenced by the view that *nibbāna* is a transcendental absolute. Buddaghosa, the principal Theravāda commentator of the fifth century A.D., for instance, is found asserting that *nibbāna* is an existent entity (*bhava*).[7]

Radhakrishnan attributed to the Buddha the conception of an absolute metaphysical being. He says:

> Nirvana is an eternal condition of being, for it is not a *saṃskāra*, or what is made or put together, which is impermanent. It continues while its expressions change. This is what lies behind the khandhas which are subject to birth and decay. The illusion of becoming is founded on the reality of Nirvana. Buddha does not attempt to define it, since it is the root principle of all and so is indefinable.[8]

The weight of the evidence in the Pali Nikāyas warrants the conclusion that a distinctive feature of the Buddha's doctrine was the denial of an immutable soul inhering within or outside the empirically observable factors of personality. The enlightenment experience of the Buddha was never formulated in the Pali Nikāya literature as consisting of an insight into an underlying reality of the self. However, Radhakrishnan, in his enthusiasm to interpret the early Buddhist conception of *nibbāna* in absolutistic terms, even tried to attribute the theory of a timeless self to the Buddha. He says:

> ...Nirvana is timeless existence, and so Buddha must admit the reality of a timeless self. There is a being at the back of all life which is unconditioned, above all empirical categories, something which does not give rise to any effect and is not the effect of anything else.[9]

There is no evidence whatsoever to suggest that the Buddha did talk explicitly or implicitly of such a self. On the contrary Buddhism characterized the doctrines of those who propounded the theory that such a self exists as a false view which falls into the theoretical extreme of eternalism (*sassatavāda*).

Most scholars including Radhakrishnan who have favored an absolutistic interpretation of *nibbāna* have made use of an *Udāna* passage which refers to *nibbāna* as *ajāta*, *abhūta*, *akata*, and *asaṅkhata*. Influenced by the metaphysical monism and absolutism of the Vedāntic teachings these scholars render the terms into English as "unborn," "unmade," "uncaused," and "unconditioned" respectively. If this rendering is justified it is easy to read a metaphysical meaning into the *Udāna* statement. But the entire issue hinges on the correctness of the rendering.

It does not appear to be a justifiable procedure to take the *Udāna* passage in isolation, severed from the general context of the Buddhist theory of reality and give it an arbitrary interpretation which suits the fancies of the interpreter. It is important to consider the actual meanings that can be given to the terms used in the *Udāna* passage in conformity with the other approaches to the theory of reality generally represented in the Pali Nikāya literature.

Nibbāna, unlike *brahman* or *ātman* in the *Upaniṣads*, is not a concept which serves to explain the absolute beginnings of the universe and its varied content. It is not the ultimate principle from which the plurality of existence emanates or into which the apparent plurality can be reduced or assimilated. The function of the concept is therefore clearly non-metaphysical. The notion that Buddhist *nibbāna* is the unconditioned ground of the illusory world of plurality derives no support from the early Buddhist sources. *Nibbāna* does not perform any explanatory role in Buddhism in the field of cosmological or cosmogonical speculation.

An interpretation of the *Udāna* passage which does not misrepresent the fundamental tenets of early Buddhism should take into account the place that *nibbāna*, as the goal of spiritual endeavor of a Buddhist, occupies in the context of the Buddhist theory of reality and its scheme of salvation. Buddhism takes as the starting point of its doctrine not any metaphysical postulate as an explanation for existence but the experiential and existential evident fact of the unsatisfactoriness of life (*dukkha*) as it is lived in man's unenlightened condition. *Nibbāna* stands for the freedom that is attainable by man here and now from this unsatisfactory condition by eliminating its causes, which are primarily of a psychological nature, by diligently pursuing a path of self-discipline, mental culture, and development of wisdom. Buddhism chooses to use a term which in the ordinary language of the time was used to express the idea of extinguishing or blowing out a fire. Man in his unenlightened condition was conceived in Buddhism as being afflicted by the fires of passion. The term *nibbāna* in this sense had a figurative meaning as well, in that it signified the blowing out of the fires of passion.

Early Buddhism attempted no metaphysical characterization of *nibbāna*, but laid great emphasis on its empirical characteristics which could be ascertained in the living experience of a person who has attained it in this life itself. In the living experience of a person it is said to be a perfectly blissful attainment. Its blissfulness is said to be a result of a certain transformation of mental attitudes and dispositions. It is a mistake to believe that the Buddha refrained from describing the nature of *nibbāna*. The Buddha was reluctant to answer any question about the after-death state of one who realizes *nibbāna*, precisely because such an answer leads to metaphysical views about the nature of a person. From this it does not follow that the Buddha considered *nibbāna* as an indescribable state of being. The Buddha's descriptions of *nibbāna* took a purely psychological form. It is described as the elimination of lust (*rāgakkhaya*), elimination of hatred (*dosakkhaya*), and elimination of delusion (*mohakkhaya*).[10] *Nibbāna* was also conceived as a state of moral purification, knowledge and bliss. The Buddha was interested in characterizing *nibbāna* only to the extent that it was a state attained by a person in this life itself. He did not attempt, nor did he think it profitable, to speculate on the nature of the after-death state of a person who has attained *nibbāna*. However, he categorically stated that for a person who has eradicated the defiling tendencies of the mind there is no more process of repeated birth and death in the *saṃsāric* cycle.

In terms of the doctrine of the dependent co-origination (*paṭiccasamuppāda*) the Buddha explained the human predicament as a viciously circular process consisting of *jāti* (birth), *bhava* (becoming), *kamma* (volitional action) and *saṅkhāra* (psychologically conditioned impulses). The Buddha discovered in his own experience that there is a possibility of overcoming the fetters of *jāti*, *bhava*, etc. by following a certain path of spiritual culture. It was the transformation that occurs at the fruition of this path that the Buddha called *nibbāna*. Here, the factors associated with the cyclic process of *dukkha*, such as *jāti*, *bhava*, *kamma*, and *saṅkhāra* cease to operate. The *Udāna* passage which is often mistakenly quoted to give a metaphysical interpretation to Buddhism says nothing more than the fact that man is capable of putting an end to the operations of *jāti*, *bhava*, *kamma*, and *saṅkhāra*. It is easy to see that the terms used in the *Udāna* passage are the negative past participles derived from the verbal roots *jan*, *bhū*, and *kṛ* in the following manner:

a	+	*jan*	=	*ajāta*
a	+	*bhū*	=	*abhūta*
a	+	*kṛ*	=	*akata*
a	+	*saṃ* + *kṛ*	=	*asaṅkhata*

For the reasons given above it is plausible to conclude that the significance of the *Udāna* passage can be interpreted in ways which do not entail an absolutistic conception of *nibbāna*.

There is also the possibility that the kind of knowledge that the Buddha described as *abhiññā* (higher knowledge), *pariññā* (comprehensive knowledge), and *paññā* (wisdom) associated with the realization of *nibbāna* be misconstrued to mean a form of mystical intuition. It is evident from the Buddhist concept of knowledge represented in the Pali Nikāyas that the Buddha was not concerned with any mystical intuition which awakens man to the ultimate reality of a realm of really real objects in such a way that such an awakened soul could relegate the entire world of sense experience to the sphere of illusion. The Buddha did not consider the world of sense experience as illusion. He cautioned philosophers against the metaphysical traps into which they could fall by trying to interpret the world of sense experience. Emancipating knowledge (*vimutti-ñāṇadassana*), according to the Buddha, consists in seeing the transient and unsubstantial nature of the empirical world itself. *Nibbāna* refers to the peace that follows such seeing from the proper perspective. Such knowledge is characteristically described in Buddhism as self-transforming knowledge. It is called *āsavakkhayañāṇa*, "knowledge leading to the eradication of the cankers." Unlike in the Platonic scheme of knowledge, there is no suggestion in Buddhism of an intellectual intuition into a realm of Ideal Forms.

The Buddhist position is that in the ultimate analysis the goal of all rational beings is happiness or felicity. In order to determine what the true happiness of man is, it is necessary to understand the nature of man and the human predicament. *Dukkha*, resulting from factors which are not within the power of the human will to avoid, such as birth, old age, decay, and death, which are all instances of the transient nature of things, can, according to Buddhism, be totally ended only by ending the process of *saṃsāra*. Ending the process of *saṃsāra* occurs with the total elimination of greed (*lobha*), hatred (*dosa*), and confusion (*moha*), which is the same as the attainment of *nibbāna*. On the one hand, this attainment therefore ensures a person the liberation from the *saṃsāric* process associated with misery. On the other hand it brings about a moral and psychological transformation of the individual amounting to a total elimination of unwholesome mental traits (*sabbākusaladhammapahāṇa*) and the cultivation of wholesome mental traits (*kusaladhamma-samannāgata*). This latter aspect of *nibbāna* has significant implications on the social life of this world.

Human suffering, with the exception of that part of it which is brought about by natural material causes, is to a large extent a result of human action itself. Interpersonal relationships, particularly in terms of the workings of human social institutions, are largely determined by the sort of individuals of which society is constituted. Harmony and conflict, war and peace, justice and injustice depend largely on the general moral standards prevailing in human societies. The bulk of human suffering is, according to Buddhism, produced by human depravity. Violent and aggressive acts of war and terrorism, deprivation of basic human rights by dominant groups exercising political authority, drug addiction, alcoholism, and sexual crimes are but a few glaring examples of social evils of the contemporary world. Buddhism sees these evils as rooted in greed (*lobba*), hatred (*dosa*), and confusion (*moha*) which are exactly antithetical to the traits of character to be developed by those pursuing the goal of *nibbāna*. For, according to Buddhism, a person who is greedy, hateful, and deluded, overcome by greed, hatred, and delusion (*lobhena*, *dosena*, *mohena abhibhūto*) generally has the tendency to commit deeds which cause suffering to himself and others as well as to encourage others also to behave as he does.[12] Buddhism believes that the cultivation of wholesome traits of character and the elimination of unwholesome ones by each individual is essential for the promotion of a harmonious social order. In so far as *nibbāna* involves the elimination of greed, hatred and delusion and the path leading to it is a progressive fulfillment of this ideal of perfection, the pursuit of the goal of *nibbāna* has important social implications. If it is agreed that human depravity, consisting of unchecked greed and hatred fed by ignorance, is the universal cause of social conflict and moral evil, then one cannot deny the universal social relevance of the Buddhist concept of the supreme goal of *nibbāna*.

The relevance of the Buddhist goal of *nibbāna* to the improvement of the conditions of social living can be understood by paying attention to the Buddhist analysis of the nature and origin of social conflict. Conflicts occur at different levels of social interaction as *kalaha* (quarrels), *viggaha* (disputes), and *vivāda* (contentions). Rulers come into conflict with other rulers (*rājāno pi rājūhi vivadanti*) and members of one social group come into conflict with other members of the same social group as in the case of the ruling aristocracy quarrelling among themselves (*khattiyā hi pi khattiyehi vivadanti*). Such conflict ends up in violent acts against one another resulting in the exhibition of unwholesome conduct as well as injury, death, and destruction (*te tattha kalaha-viggahavivādam āppanā maraṇaṃ pi nigacchanti maraṇamattam pi dukkhaṃ*).[13] In such conflict there is the taking up of destructive arms (*daṇḍādāna, satthādāna*). The behavior exhibited in a situation of conflict is unequivocally described in Buddhism as evil and unskilled (*papakā akusalā dhammā*).

According to the *Sakkapañha-sutta* of the *Dīgha-nikāya*, conflict is a common occurrence among all classes of sentient beings. It occurs despite the desire of beings to live in unity, harmony, and concord.

> Devas, men, Asuras, Nāgas, Gandhabbas and whatever other different types of communities are there, it occurs to them that they ought to live without mutual hatred, violence, enmity and malice, yet for all they live with mutual hatred, violence enmity and malice.[14]

The Buddha's answer to the question "How do conflicts arise?" (*kuto pahūtā kalahā vivādā*) is what is most relevant to our discussion. While considering this question in a plurality of perspectives, the Buddha emphasizes the moral and psychological origins of social conflict. It is significant that when the Buddha was questioned once as to what his doctrine or thesis was, he answered that it was one which enabled a person to live without coming into conflict with anyone in this world consisting of devas, māras, brahmas, religious communities, rulers, and men.[15] This is really a reference to the ultimate goal of Buddhism, the goal of *nibbāna* which is reached by eradicating all the unwholesome traits of the mind.

Buddhism shows by means of psychological analysis that the factors generating conflict in society are born in the human mind in the very activity of sense-perception. Buddhism considers conflict as endemic in human society. It insists that conflict can be eliminated in society to the extent that man transforms himself spiritually. In the case of any particular individual there is the possibility of disentangling himself totally from conflict through a total transformation of his mental dispositions.

This can have a wide-ranging influence on society as a whole, especially when such transformation occurs in individuals who set the pace for the rest of society. A society which recognizes this is, from the Buddhist perspective, one which is on the path of conflict reduction.

The spiritual transformation leading to the cessation of conflict behavior with respect to a particular individual involves the elimination of the latent tendencies of the mind described as *rāgānusaya* (latent tendency of lust), *paṭighānusaya* (of hatred), *diṭṭhānusaya* (of dogmatic views), *vicikicchānusaya* (of doubt), *mānānusaya* (of conceit), *bhavarāgānusaya* (of lust for becoming), and *avijjānusaya* (of delusion). In order to put an end to conflict behavior, the Buddha recommends a self-transformation involving a cessation of what is described as "thoughts of conceptual obsession" (*papancasaññāsaṅkhā*).[16]

Conflict is found to occur more frequently in circumstances where heterogenous groups of people with various kinds of identities (such as class, ethnicity, religion etc.) interact. According to Buddhism identity becomes an obsession, and the initial stage of this obsession is traced to our tendency to identify ourselves with the components of our psycho-physical personality which is analyzable into five transient groups or aggregates (*pañcakkhandha*). This, according to Buddhism, is the outcome of *papañca*. The label "I" which is a useful linguistic device for purposes of human interaction, is transformed into an emotionally charged "ego clinging," intellectually justifying it through the assertion of the dogma of an enduring *ātman* (*attavāda-upādāna*). This is the most crucial starting point of conflict. *Papañca* is said to consist of three types, namely, *taṇhā* (craving), *diṭṭhi* (dogmatic views), and *mānā* (measuring). *Taṇhā*, *māna* and *diṭṭhi* are considered as three aspects of the self same ego-consciousness. *Papañca* is said to cease along with the cessation of the clinging to the notion of "I" and "mine." Bhikkhu Ñāṇananda aptly sums up the Buddha's standpoint represented in the *Madhupiṇḍika-sutta* thus:

> If one does not entertain craving, conceit and views (*taṇhā*, *mānā*, *diṭṭhi*) with regard to the conditioned phenomena involved in the process of cognition, by resorting to the fiction of an ego, one is free from the yoke of proliferating concepts and has thereby eradicated the proclivities to all evil mental states which breed conflict both in the individual and in society.[17]

According to Buddhism all tension-creating identities are merely extensions of the ego-clinging. *Nibbāna* is the point at which the tendency to ego-clinging is utterly annihilated (*asmimānasamugghāta*).

The *nibbāna* ideal of Buddhism, when viewed from a demystified perspective which is more faithful to the original teaching of the Buddha, may be seen as one which provides the spiritual foundation for a just, harmonious, and healthy society. The Buddhist ideal of *nibbāna* may be said to be lacking in social and worldly concern only if by social and worldly concern is meant an involvement in the unenlightened acts of wickedness, greed, and folly to which mankind is generally prone due to its depraved condition.

According to Buddhism, immoral action can be explained at a more fundamental level by reference to its deeper psychological roots. Being the most psychological of all religions, the spiritual path of Buddhism is characterized by a systematic theory of moral psychology. Morality (*sīla*), concentration (*samādhi*), and wisdom (*paññā*) constituting the scheme of three-fold training (*sikkhā*) in Buddhism, are meant to tackle systematically, with deep psychological insight, the problem of moral evil. Immorality in human action is only a manifestation, at the surface level, of man's evil dispositions. Buddhism speaks of the existence of impurities (*kilesas*) or defilements (*āsava*) at three different levels. First, they are in the dormant or dispositional condition (*anusaya*). Second, they are manifested at the level of thought and emotion (*pariyuṭṭhāna*). Third, they are manifested at the level of action by word and deed (*vītikkama*). The graduated path of spiritual training proceeds from the gross to the more subtle levels in which these tendencies exist, and systematically removes the psychological roots of moral evil. *Sīla* tackles immorality at the level of bodily and verbal deeds, *samādhi* at the level of thought and emotion, and *paññā* at the dispositional level, or at the original root of all evil.

Buddhism concentrates on character traits, for they are what prompt a man's actions. Actions, according to Buddhism, are merely the surface manifestations of the deeper psychological structures. To interpret Buddhism as a system lacking social concern is, therefore, to grossly misrepresent it. According to Buddhism, a morally good person, a person whose mind is free from *lobha*, *dosa*, and *moha* will feel social concern and will do what is right as a matter of course.

The Buddha and his immediate disciples were the first of those who attained the goal of *nibbāna*. Having attained this goal they spent the rest of their lifetime not in seclusion, withdrawn from society, but in the service of humanity. The Buddha himself has given clear expression to the social role of the perfected person when he addressed his first sixty disciples who attained the goal of *nibbāna* in the following words:

> Go ye forth and wander for the gain of the many, for the welfare of the many, out of compassion for the world, for the good, for the gain and for the welfare of gods and men. Let not two of you go the same way.[18]

According to the Buddha such noble persons who are free from sensuous intoxication and negligent behavior, established in patience and gentle demeanor, who restrain themselves from evil, cultivate peace within themselves and make themselves totally tranquil, play a vital role in society, giving it moral direction and guidance. Examples of the Buddha's disciples who courageously and zealously performed their social role are not lacking in the history of Buddhism.[19]

From the Buddhist point of view, the spiritual values associated with the *nibbāna* ideal are a necessary basis for wholesome social action. It is a mistake to think that social conflict could be resolved, and all social evils could be removed purely by installing suitable institutional structures. For institutions operate through the instrumentality of individuals. As long as individual behavior is governed by what the Buddha calls the roots of evil (*akusalmūla*), namely, greed (*lobha*), hatred (*dosa*), and confusion (*moha*), social institutions cannot function for the common well-being. It is for this reason that most of the Buddha's social and political doctrines were intended to inculcate a sense of spiritual values in the rulers and other persons in authority. Social commitment without a proper spiritual basis is dangerous. For craving for power, self-interest and other egoistic concerns can easily be disguised as social concern.

The *nibbāna* ideal of Buddhism has no conflict with a this-worldly interest so far as such interest does not violate the principles of righteousness. In fact the pursuit of the *nibbāna* ideal is considered in Buddhism as a way of reducing and even eliminating the tensions of this world. For the pursuit of this ideal involves a transformation of human character traits which in turn influences interpersonal relationships in society. This explains the Buddha's interest in preaching the doctrine (*dhamma*) to persons who held key positions of authority such as kings and ministers with a view to guiding such a person also on the path of moral perfection. Dichotomies such as the welfare of this world as opposed to the welfare of the other world, welfare of the self as opposed to the welfare of others, welfare of the individual as opposed to the welfare of the society, have, according to Buddhism, no real foundation in the ultimate sense.

NOTES

1. *M* 1. 148, *Anupādā parinibbanatthaṃ kho āvuso bhagavati brahmacariyaṃ vussatiti.*
2. Edited by Heinz Bechert and Richard Gombrich, London: Thames and Hudson Ltd., 1984, 7.
3. *The Religion of India: The Sociology of Hinduism and Buddhism*, Glencoe, Illinois, 1958, 206.
4. Ibid., 213.
5. Melford E. Spiro, *Buddhism and Society*, New York: Harper & Row, 1970, 65.
6. *Ibid.*
7. *Vism* 507.
8. *Indian Philosophy*, London: George Allen and Unwin Ltd., 1929, vol. I, 449.
9. *Ibid.*, 452.
10. *S* 4.251; 5.8.
11. See D.J. Kalupahana, *Buddhist Philosophy: A Historical Analysis*, Honolulu: The University Press of Hawaii, 1976. 75f.
12. *A* 1.189.
13. *M* 1.86.
14. *D* 2.276.
15. *M* 1.109.
16. *D* 2.277.
17. *Concept and Reality in Early Buddhist Thought*, Kandy: Buddhist Publication Society, 1971, 18.
18. *Vin* 1.21.
19. *M* 3.267 H.

5

THE BODHISATTVA IDEAL

SOME OBSERVATIONS

Sanath Nanayakkara

THERE IS A GENERALLY ACCEPTED VIEW, prevailing especially among the Western scholars on Buddhism—a view which almost amounts to a sacred belief—that the Bodhisattva ideal is a Mahāyānic creation. The origin of this view becomes clear when one traces the history of the introduction of Buddhism to the West. The primary sources of introduction of Buddhism to the West are Mahāyāna works. To the West, therefore, until the Pali tradition became well-known and established, Buddhism was co-terminus with Mahāyāna. In fact, even at present there is an influential school of thought which considers Mahāyāna to be the early or even original form of Buddhism. This appears to be due to the fact that even after Theravāda became known, the theistic and mystic ideas embodied in Mahāyāna were capable of capturing the interest of Westerners imbedded in similar traditions. So, there has been and there is in them an inborn inclination, a particular bias towards Mahāyāna.

Moreover, this bias is towards the popular teachings and cults of Mahāyāna and not towards its philosophical core which is not different from that of the Theravāda. It is this favorable attitude they adopt as regards Mahāyāna that has led them to consider many salient and important tenets, norms, and doctrines that originated in Theravāda as being creations of Mahāyāna Buddhism. Attributing the invention of the *bodhisattva* concept to Mahāyāna is also a consequence of this favored attitude.

The term *bodhisattva* is the Sanskrit equivalent of the Pali term *bodhisatta*. Har Dayal, in his *Bodhisattva Doctrine*,[1] enumerates a number of possible interpretations of the term suggested by numerous scholars. After enumerating them, Har Dayal himself makes the following observation: "But the safest way is always to go back to the Pali without attaching much importance to lexicographers and philosophers." Yet it becomes evident that the interpretation he suggests is not quite in keeping with the cautious approach he sets up as the best guiding principle. His interpretation is as follows:

> Now the bodhisatta in the Pali texts seems to mean "a bodhi-being." But *satta* here does not denote a mere ordinary creature. It is almost certainly related to the Vedic word *satvam*, which means "Krieger," "a strong or a valiant man, hero, warrior." In this way we can also understand the final *dpah* in the Tibetan equivalent. *Satta* in Pali *bodhisatta* should be interpreted as 'heroic being, spiritual warrior.' The word suggests the two ideas of existence and struggle and not merely the notion of simple existence.

Undoubtedly Har Dayal is reading too much into the term *bodhisatta* and impregnating the simple Pali term denoting an equally simple concept with Mahāyānic ideas of a later date. This is an unwarranted attempt at sanctification of an originally simple concept to help it to measure up to its later developed meaning.

A perusal of the canonical texts shows that the earliest use of the term *bodhisatta* is traceable to passages containing accounts of the Buddha's recalling the life he led prior to his attainment of enlightenment. Thus, in the *Ariyapariyesana-sutta*,[2] the Buddha in his reminiscence of the days prior to his realization of bodhi, that is, when he lived as a householder aware of the problem of life and thinking of a way out, refers to himself as *bodhisatta*. The text clearly defines this stage as a phase in the life of the Buddha prior to his attainment of enlightenment (*pubbeva sambodhā*). There is no special reference to his heroic qualities or to his spiritual valor. This discourse depicts the *bodhisatta* as a seeker after truth, just one among the many we come across in the religious scene of the time. True, he was not a mere ordinary creature, for ordinary creatures are not generally interested in such abstruse problems. But his special quality is not denoted by the term *satta* as suggested by Har Dayal. The "ordinary" being (*satta*) becomes "out of ordinary" due to his being interested in obtaining enlightenment (*bodhi*) regarding the problems of life. So the significant part of the compound is *bodhi* and not *satta* as suggested by Har Dayal.

According to canonical references, the earliest usage of the term thus denotes a being (*satta*) who is earnestly interested in obtaining enlightenment (*bodhi*) on the question of human suffering. Such a seeker of enlightenment came to be referred to as *bodhisatta*. When such a *bodhisatta* succeeds in obtaining enlightenment, he is referred to as one who has attained *bodhi*, one who has obtained enlightenment, i.e., a Buddha. Thus it is seen that the term *bodhisatta* in its earliest use denotes a specific "phase" in the life of the Buddha that coincides with the arising of an interest in obtaining enlightenment on, or solution to, the problem of life up to the moment of attaining enlightenment (*bodhi*).[3]

This meaning, however, did not remain static for long. One could easily observe its extension at a subsequent stage to cover even the period of life prior to setting his mind on the attainment of enlightenment (*bodhi*) regarding the problem of life. This extension of meaning is seen in the *Acchariyabbhutadhamma-sutta*.[4] Herein, the term *bodhisatta* is used to refer to him from the time of his penultimate birth in the Tusita world. This retrospective extension of the meaning of *bodhisatta* is carried to a still further stage and used to denote the previous births of the Gautama Buddha. This is evident from the *Mahāsudassana-sutta*[5] and the Mahāgovinda-sutta,[6] as well as the *Makhādeva-sutta*.[7] The *Jātaka* firmly established and popularized this usage.

When the idea of the plurality of the Buddhas came into vogue the term *bodhisatta* was employed to cover not only the last birth of all Buddhas, but their previous births as well. In passing it may be mentioned that commentarial literature uses the term *pacceka-bodhisatta* to refer to the pre-enlightened stage of *Pacceka-buddhas*.[8]

Thus, it is seen that the concept of *bodhisatta* had its origin in Theravāda Buddhism. Even as an ideal to be emulated it was first put forward by the Theravādins. However there is neither a *bodhisattva* "doctrine" nor a *bodhisattva* "cult" in the Theravāda. Har Dayal observes:

> The *bodhisattva* doctrine was the necessary outcome of two movements of thought in early Buddhism, viz. the growth of *bhakti* (devotion, faith, love) and the idealization and the spiritualization of the Buddha. *Bhakti* was first directed towards Gautama Buddha. But he was soon idealized, as has already been indicated. He then became an unsuitable and unattractive object for the pious Buddhist's *bhakti*. The deep rooted feeling found an outlet in the invention and adoration of the *bodhisattvas*.

Whether the *bodhisattva* doctrine is the necessary outcome of both movements of thought mentioned by Har Dayal is an arguable point. Though there is a host of *bodhisattvas* referred to in the Mahāyāna texts, only one out of this large number, namely Avalokiteśvara, really became an object of adoration and worship with a highly developed cult around him. Bodhisattva Avalokiteśvara is certainly an object of devotion (*bhakti*). But Avalokiteśvara is not a necessary outcome of the growth of *bhakti*. It is more probable to consider that the *bhakti*-cult was drawn in to enhance and enrich the Avalokiteśvara *bodhisattva* cult which came into existence in consequence of both compelling circumstances.

From the very beginning, the Theravāda ideal was considered hard to attain. Not only the popular masses, but even those who took up religious life as a full-time vocation found it extremely difficult to endure the rigor of this spiritual journey. So, the general human tendency to find "short cuts," to make others do the difficult jobs for them, necessitated the invention of a being capable of ferrying the faithful to safety. Gautama Buddha emphatically stated that he was not there to perform the role of a savior. On his own admission and declaration he was a mere guide, a pathfinder, a teacher at the most. The admonition given to monk Vakkali clearly proves how he thwarted attempts made by the faithful to create a savior out of him.[9] Yet he was not completely successful in rooting out these attempts. During his lifetime, and on an extensive scale after his demise, the faithful set at work to magnify his supreme human qualities and transform him into a merciful superhuman or a divine being. The Buddha in this changed form had all the characteristics of a savior, and the *bhakti* concept gave all the backing required to sustain and develop faith in this new savior. However, this metamorphosis went a step further and finally changed the human Buddha into an abstruse metaphysical concept, a universal principle. The masses could neither grasp this change nor appreciate it. Such a metaphysical concept did not serve any purpose to them, and it is at this juncture the quality of *mahākaruṇā* (great compassion) of the Buddha came to be epitomized in the form of Avalikitesvara. This epitomization was greatly facilitated by the *bodhisatta* ideal already made popular by the Theravādins.

Thus, the idealization and the spiritualization of the Buddha was a major circumstance that led to the development of the *bodhisattva* cult.

Another view over-emphasized and enthusiastically championed by some scholars is that the Theravādins pursue exclusively the *śrāvaka* (disciple) ideal leading to *arahanthood*, whereas the Mahāyānists totally dedicate themselves to the attainment of the *bodhisattva* ideal leading to Buddhahood, and that the *bodhisattva* ideal is the result of the Mahāyānist protest against the self-centered approach of the Theravāda scheme of salvation.

To evaluate this view it is necessary to understand what the goal, the purpose of Buddhism is. Both Theravāda and Mahāyāna schools agree that the ultimate goal of Buddhism is to put an end to unsatisfactoriness, conflict, or simply *dukkha*. This is possible, according to both schools, by realizing the Truth or the Four Noble Truths. Similarly, the two schools agree regarding the path leading to this realization. How is this realization attained? Is it through one's own effort or through the help or grace of some external power or agency?

There is no gainsaying the fact that early Buddhism maintained and vigorously championed the view that one is one's own master;[10] one's purity or impurity depends on oneself[11]; one desirous of realizing the end of *dukkha* should be self-reliant, and one should rely on effort, perseverance, and courage. While the Buddha never presented himself other than as a guide (*maggassa akkhātāro*) or teacher (*satthā*), he categorically discouraged followers from cultivating blind devotion or faith in him. Instead, he encouraged the disciples to build reasoned confidence (*ākāravatī saddhā*) in the Buddha, Dharmma, and the Sangha.

The Buddha and his disciples dedicated themselves to teach and to direct the followers to liberation. It appears that the Mahāyānists, as well as their present apologists who label the Theravāda ideal as narrow and self-centered, have disregarded the Buddha's exhortation to the first sixty *arahants* to go on tour, with no two disciples taking the same route, disseminating the new-found doctrine for the well-being of all.[12]

If "altruism" means regard for others as the principle of actions; then the activities engaged in by the Buddha for 45 years after his enlightenment, as well as the tireless activities of his many disciples, clearly show that both the Buddha and the *arahants* were in ample possession of this quality. But if it means working for the welfare of others, neglecting one's own welfare, then neither the Buddha nor his disciples were altruistic in their outlook. Let no one neglect one's own good for the sake of another's, however great,[13] is the Buddhist attitude. Buddha always believed in crossing the ocean of *saṃsara* himself first and then helping others to cross; disciplining himself before disciplining others; enlightening himself before directing others towards enlightenment.[14] This undoubtedly is a marked difference between the Theravāda *bodhisattva* ideal and the Mahāyāna *bodhisattva* doctrine.

Sometimes it is said that this allegation of self-centeredness, selfishness, or lack of altruism is not levelled against the Buddha or his immediate disciples but against the monks of a later period. But such an allegation is unfounded, for there is no definite ground to prove that the Theravāda monks as a whole or even a majority of them exclusively behaved in a self-centered manner. If such an allegation is ever made, it should be commonly levelled against all monks irrespective of their particular religious inclination, for at this later stage monks were generally far away from the "ideal," more prone to secular activities, or fully engrossed in scholasticism. To a majority of them the "noble quest" (*ariyapariyesanā*) appears to have been of little significance; and to some it was only a subject of academic interest.

Those who accept and propagate the view that the *bodhisattva* concept is a Mahāyānic invention also subscribe to the corollary view that the Theravādins pursue exclusively the *śrāvaka* (disciple) ideal leading to *arahanthood*, while the Mahāyānists exclusively strive for the *bodhisattva* ideal leading to Buddhahood. From this they arrive at the conclusion that the purpose or the aim of Theravāda is to lead its followers to liberation through the attainment of *arahanthood*, while the objective of Mahāyāna is to lead its followers to liberation through Buddhahood. This is cited as the main point of divergence in the paths adopted by the two systems.

It has already been pointed out that both Theravāda and Mahāyāna schools agree on the goal (that is the attainment of enlightenment or *bodhi*) and the path (*magga*) leading to it. The most common and comprehensive designation used by the Theravādins to denote a person who has reached the goal is "*arahant*."

Gautama, who was the first to become enlightened (*buddha*), was also the first *arahant*. His disciples or *śrāvakas*, once they reached the goal, were designated as those who have attained enlightenment (*bodhi*). But as they realized enlightenment after Gautama, they are often referred to as *buddhānubuddha* (those who are enlightened after the Enlightened One).[15] The content of enlightenment of both the Buddha and *śrāvakas* is the same. Occasionally the term *sambodhi* (complete or full-enlightenment) is used in early texts to denote the enlightenment of both the Buddhas and *śrāvakas*.[16] The potentiality to attain the goal which is referred to as *buddhattva*, *buddhatā*, *buddhabhāva*, *buddhasvabhāva* is said to be innate in all, in varying degrees. Thus, it is apparent that Theravāda categorically accepted the position that the Buddhahood is open to all.

If such is the factual position, how did the Buddha-*śrāvaka* dichotomy, as two distinct ideals, arise? A close scrutiny of the facts reveals that this dichotomy was created by the Theravādins themselves. Even a casual perusal of the canonical texts reveals signs of the appearance of a gap between the Buddha and the *śrāvakas*. The gap widened rapidly due to the boundless devotion and veneration of the average Buddhist and to the unchecked scholasticism of the academics. Docetic theories that were put forward hastened this alienation of the teacher-pupil relationship. The content of the Buddha's enlightenment became so expansive as to include within its scope all conceivable forms of knowledge of which some are not even remotely connected with the original conception of enlightenment. Consequently the Buddhahood came to be considered a unique position attainable only by an aspirant who for innumerable eons has perfected the special qualities of perfection (*pāramitā*) with the declared intention of attaining Buddhahood. And, further, it was accepted that during the dispensation (*sāsana*) of a particular Buddha there cannot be another Buddha.[18]

This development is quite contrary to the original Theravāda position. In the original conception, the distinction between the Buddha and the *śrāvaka* was only a distinction between teacher and pupil. The content as well as the final outcome of their enlightenment was similar. All were enlightened (*buddha*). Original Buddhism did not encourage any postponement of the attainment of enlightenment. It stressed the necessity and possibility of attaining *bodhi* here and now (*diṭṭhe'va dhamme*) while yet living. But to attain *bodhi* "here and now," total dedication was essential. Householders, who formed the majority of Buddhists, could not follow such a full-time spiritual calling. Yet, they did not want to be completely left out from this spiritual journey. Besides, even the full-timers found this ideal difficult to attain. So the majority favored the idea of postponement of enlightenment. The belief in rebirth supplied the necessary psychological background for this. These circumstances paved the way for a more practical ideal, an ideal that could be fused with the household-life of the laity and the secular-bent or scholastic life of the clergy. The *bodhisattva* ideal fitted in perfectly to these demands. And the Theravādins popularized this ideal through the *Jātakas*. But there were inherent conflicts in this new position. *Bodhisattva* originally meant a "Buddha in the making." But at this stage of development the view held was that there can only be one Buddha during the dispensation of a particular Buddha. So Theravādins had to maintain the illogical position that though the *bodhisattva* ideal is open to all, only one such aspirant could become a Buddha during a particular dispensation. It was the Mahāyānists who resolved this apparent contradiction. They adopted the *bodhisattva* ideal made already popular by the Theravādin, and allowed it to reach its logical end, the attainment of *bodhi* thus making the Buddhahood open to all. In doing this the Mahāyānists were really retrieving the original Theravāda position.

But unfortunately Mahāyānists did not remain content with this. Being inborn innovators, rich in imagination, their urge was to ramify, vivify, multiply, and complicate. They made the originally simple *bodhisattva* concept extremely complex by a vigorous process of dehumanization and deification. The *bodhisattva* ideal adopted to suit both the clergy and laity once again showed signs of becoming the exclusive preserve of the clergy, for it became compulsory for a *bodhisattva* to give up family life and social relations and retire into the forest.[19] In this respect the Mahāyāna *bodhisattva* ideal surpassed the *śrāvaka* ideal which the Mahāyānists condemned as being withdrawn and aloof from society.

While retrieving the original Theravāda position, Mahāyānists, in their attempt to popularize Buddhism by catering to the demands of the masses, have effected changes which are also contrary to the original teachings. One such change is the excessive emphasis laid on compassion or *karuṇā*. In original Buddhism there is a fine blend of wisdom (*prajñā*) and compassion (*karuṇā*), the two characteristics that contribute to transform an ordinary human being into a noble enlightened being, who could be compassionate while remaining dispassionate. But in the Mahāyāna *bodhisattva* cult, *karuṇā* triumphed over *prajñā*, upsetting this balance. The Avalokiteśvara cult graphically depicts this change. It allowed the free employment of *bhakti*.

Because of this change, self-reliance (*atta-saraṇa*)[20] gave way to external-reliance (*añña-saraṇa*). Bodhisattva Avalokiteśvara became the epitome of altruism as one who has postponed his well-being for the sake of others; he is the destroyer of all suffering, fear, and sorrow. The mere recollection of his name came to be considered as being effective enough to induce him to save the supplicants. Though precepts were there, their practice was regarded as less important than Avalokiteśvara's grace. One could easily observe Mahāyānists vying among themselves to make the path to salvation easier and smoother. Originally it was action (*kiriya*)[21], now it was inaction; earlier it was self-effort, self-reliance, perseverance, courage; now it was mere self-surrender. The Mahāyāniṣts, who at one turn retrieved original Buddhism, at the next turn drowned it in popular rituals and cults. It is their over-enthusiasm to cater to the demands of the masses that made them over-accommodating, resulting in the dilution of Buddhism.

The rapid development of this Avalokiteśvara concept and along with it the development of the *bhakti* cult is well documented in India itself. The *Saddharmapuṇḍarīka-sūtra*, the *Sukhāvatīvyūha*, and the *Amitāyurdhyāna-sūtra* clearly demonstrate his rise to supremacy above all the other *bodhisattvas*. Though the *Saddharmapuṇḍarīka-sūtra* is not wholly devoted to describe Avalokiteśvara, it devotes one full chapter to eulogize his greatness. Herein he, referred to by the epithet Samantamukha, is presented as a full-fledged savior of all beings. He surpasses even the Buddhas in greatness. It is said that mere thinking of him is more meritorious than honoring a thousand Buddhas. He is represented as being capable of taking any form at will. He saves beings not only from getting drowned in the fathomless ocean of *saṃsara*, but also from all imaginable calamities.

An important development that is evident is his capability of bestowing children on women who adore him. This "child-giving" quality had far-reaching repercussions and had been instrumental in popularizing the Avalokiteśvara cult in China, under the appellation of ***kuan-yin***. The *Larger Syukhāvatīvyūha* presents him as the Lord of the Western Paradise, the Sukhāvatī. The *Amitāyurdhyāna-sūtra* still magnifies his greatness. His body assumes fantastic proportions, making it an abode of numerous Buddhas and *bodhisattvas*. His hands are said to embrace all beings. The influence of brahmanic mythology is quite evident from the description found in this text.

The *Karaṇḍavyūha* represents a further step in this development, in which his supremacy over all the Buddhas is clearly established. There is a clear attempt to place him above all the gods in the Hindu pantheon.

The Avalokiteśvara cult was not confined to India. It went as a necessary companion of Mahāyāna to all countries where Mahāyāna spread. In China, Avalokiteśvara underwent a change of sex. The "child-giving" quality referred to in the *Saddharmapuṇḍarīka-sūtra* was presented with full vigor in China by effecting this metamorphosis. And it is this form of Avalokiteśvara that caught the fancy of the populace. As Kwan-non or Kan-non he is worshipped throughout Japan. Here, too, confusion regarding his sex remains. He is commonly regarded as being female, while the academics prefer to consider that the sex of a *bodhisattva* is indeterminable.

The influence of his cult is seen in Tibet and Sri Lanka as well. As Spyan-ras-gzigs (chenrezigs) he is the most popular *bodhisattva* in Tibet. Even the Dalai Lama is supposed to be an incarnation of this *bodhisattva*. As Nātha (abbreviated from Lokeśvaranātha) he is worshipped in Sri Lanka, and literary evidence reveals that Nātha worship was at its peak in the 15th century. The Nātha shrine located to the west of the Temple of the Tooth in Kandy bears testimony to the popularity of his cult.[22]

As evident from the popularity of *bodhisattva* worship there is no doubt that it helped the numerical growth of the Buddhists. But, the question is: At what cost? Have any of these later developments conduced to the qualitative growth of Buddhism? Buddhism which has become unique due to its emphasis upon character building, views on freedom of thought and free investigation, self-reliance, supremacy of the human and oneness of mankind and a host of other similar revolutionary teachings has not profited qualitatively by these popular innovations. If the *bodhisattva* concept did not develop along these mythological lines, and instead developed and gained popularity as a practicable ideal, a model on which both clergy and laity could mould their lives, it would almost certainly have conduced to producing better

Buddhists. In fact the development of the *bodhisattva* ideal on these lines did commence among the Mahāyānists themselves as clearly evident from the *Vimalakīrtinirdeśa*. Vimalakirti, the hero of *Vimalakīrtinirdeśa*, is a *bodhisattva*, a Buddha-in-the-making. Yet he is a householder, carrying on all his household duties in a way beneficial to both oneself and others. He leads a householder's life while at the same time observing pure monastic discipline. Though possessing a wife and children, he holds himself aloof from worldly pleasures and practices pure virtues. Though he profits by all professions he is unsmeared by them. He behaves like an ordinary man, but is not misled as ordinary men are.

The *Vimalakīrtinirdeśa* describes the *bodhisattva* prince as follows:

> Only for the sake of the necessary means of saving creatures; abundantly rich, even careful of the poor, pure in self-discipline, obedient to all precepts, removing all anger by the practice of patience, removing all sloth by the practice of diligence, removing all distractions of mind by intent meditation, removing all ignorance by fullness of wisdom; though he was but a simple layman, yet observing the pure monastic discipline; though living at home, yet never desirous of anything; though possessing a wife and children, always exercising pure virtues, though surrounded by his family, holding aloof from worldly pleasures; though using the jewelled ornaments of the world, yet adorned with spiritual splendor; though eating and drinking, yet enjoying the flavor of the rapture of meditation; though frequenting the gambling house, yet leading the gamblers into the right path; though coming in contact with heresy, yet never letting his true faith be impaired; though having a profound knowledge of worldly learning, yet ever finding pleasure in the things of the spirit as taught by the Buddha; though profiting by all professions, yet far above being absorbed by them; benefitting all beings, going wheresoever he pleases;, ever teaching the young and ignorant, when entering the hall of learning; manifesting to all the error of passion when in the hours of debauchery; persuading all to seek the higher things when at the shop of the wine-dealer; preaching the law when among wealthy people; teaching the ksatriyas patience; removing arrogance when among brahmans; teaching justice to the great ministers; teaching loyalty and filial piety to the princes; teaching honesty to the ladies of the court; persuading the masses to cherish virtue.[23]

However, this ideal did not succeed in attracting the attention of the majority of the Mahāyānists. While Mahāyānists preferred to surrender themselves and entrust their salvation to Avalokiteśvaras, it appears that the Theravādins, especially of Sri Lanka, who for the most part remained faithful to the core of early Buddhism, preferred the ideal which resembles closely the one outlined in the *Vimalakīrtinirdeśa*. Among the Sri Lanka Buddhists there is a practice of referring to a pious, religious person, whether lay or clergy, as a *bodhisattva*. This practice is not new; there is textual evidence to show its prevalence even in early times. Many of the pious Buddhist kings are referred to as *bodhisattvas*. King Sirisaṅghabodhi (251–253 AD) is a well-known example of such a "*bodhisattva*" king. It was popularly held that only a *bodhisattva* had the right to kingship. Even present-day pious people, leading harmless and religious lives, dedicated to the service of others are described as possessors of *bodhisattva* qualities (*bodhisattva guṇopeta*).

This undoubtedly is due to the influence of the *Jātaka* book which popularized the *bodhisattva* ideal among the Buddhists. It will certainly prove to be an interesting study if one were to examine the possibility of the *Jātaka* book influencing the *Vimalakīrtinirdeśa*.

What is apparent from the above discussion is that the Mahāyāna *bodhisattva* concept, which had its origin among the Theravādins, bifurcated at a certain stage of its development, one leaning toward deification and mythology and the other remaining close to the original concept. The former is demonstrated by the Avalokiteśvara cult and the latter by the *bodhisattva* character epitomized by prince Vimalakirti in the *Vimalakīrtinirdeśa*. The former line of development is evidently contrary to the original teachings of Buddhism. But such innovations are unavoidable in any popular religion. It is also apparent that such innovations affect only the externals of a religion. This is so with regard to Buddhism. Popular doctrines that were channelled through the *bodhisattva* cult have not affected the core of Buddhism, of both Theravāda and Mahāyāna. As already pointed out this "core" is of one essence. Therefore, if the present day Buddhists, both Theravāda and Mahāyāna, earnestly desire to bridge the gap which exists between the peripheral features of the two schools and revive the original spirit of Buddhism, they should approach the subject without bias, and redirect the energy they expend on highlighting minor differences between the two schools, on discovering the causes that led to differences and on identifying similarities that lie concealed behind these differences. This certainly is bound to be a rewarding effort.

NOTES

1. Har Dayal, *The Bodhisattva Doctrine*, London, 1932.
2. *M* 1.163.
3. This rousing of interest is referred in Buddhist Sanskrit literature as *bodhicittotpāda*.
4. *M* 3.118 H.
5. *D* 2.169 H.
6. Ibid., 2.220ff
7. *M* 2.74f.
8. See Kloppenborg, Ria, *The Paccekabuddha, a Buddhist Ascetic*, Leiden, 1974, Revised edition, Wheel Publication, Nos. 305, 306, 307.
9. *S* 3.119.
10. *Dh* 160.
11. Ibid., 165.
12. *Vin* 1.21.
13. *Dh* 166.
14. *M* 1.235.
15. *Thag* 679, 1246.
16. *M* 1.17, 163; *S* 1.181; *Sn* 693, 696; also *M* 3.8.
18. *A* 1.29.
19. Har Dayal (op. cit.) p. 22.
20. *D* 3.100.
21. *M* 1.406–407; A 1.287.
22. *Encyclopaedia of Buddhism*, II fasc 3 s.v. Avalokiteśvara.
23. *Encyclopaedia of Buddhism*, III fasc 2 s.v. Bodhisattva.

6

THE SYNCRETISM OF CHINESE CH'AN AND PURE LAND BUDDHISM

Heng-ching Shih

CHINESE BUDDHISM can be conveniently divided into two periods: pre-T'ang and post-T'ang Buddhism. Pre-T'ang Buddhism represents very interesting developments in Chinese Buddhist history—its introduction into a highly developed civilization, its struggle to be accepted, its adjustment into that culture, its final "conquest" of China, and its formation of diverse schools characterized by profoundly philosophical systems of doctrines.

Post-T'ang Buddhism is regarded as the period of gradual decline of a once glorious religion, because no new important sūtras were translated; no outstanding Buddhists emerged; no new school of Buddhist thought was formulated; and the moral discipline of the Sangha degenerated. However, it was also a period with special features. It was marked by the growing popularity of lay Buddhism and by its emphasis on (1) religious practice rather than doctrinal speculation, and on (2) syncretism rather than sectarian rivalries, not only within Buddhism but also with indigenous Chinese systems of thought and religion.

This paper will not center on either pre-T'ang or post-T'ang Buddhism per se, but will focus on a very significant link between them—the movement of Ch'an–Pure Land syncretism. It is important because it is rooted in pre-T'ang Buddhism, matures at the end of T'ang, and becomes the predominant feature throughout post-T'ang Buddhism. Above all, it represents a unique form of Buddhism which reflects the Chinese characteristic of harmonization, and is a sinicized implementation of Mahāyāna doctrines and an outcome of some particular historical events.

Historically, the culmination of Ch'an–Pure Land syncretism after T'ang was mainly due to the devastating T'ang Hui-ch'ang Persecution (845). When Chinese Buddhism reached its apogee during the T'ang dynasty, eight major schools flourished. However, the persecution wiped out the vitality of the academically oriented schools, such as the T'ien-t'ai and Hua'yen schools, which were dependent on well established institutions of monasteries and libraries. The practice-oriented Ch'an and Pure Land became the only remaining "living" schools that survived the persecution. They survived for a number of reasons. They did not have to rely as heavily on scriptures as the philosophical schools did. They were economically self-sufficient without depending on imperial patronage. And they were "portable," that is, they could be practiced almost anywhere and under most circumstances.

After suffering from the blow of the persecution, post-T'ang Buddhism, mainly Ch'an and Pure Land schools, faced new challenges for their survival. With the loss of its intellectual, "aristocratic" tradition of learning within the confines of monasteries, Buddhism found a good opportunity to address itself to the people at large. Since specialized Buddhist scholarship in the philosophical schools of Buddhism was difficult to recover, and was not the main concern of the surviving Ch'an and Pure Land Buddhism anyway, post-T'ang Buddhism turned toward a new direction. This was characterized by simplicity, pragmatism, flexibility, and accessibility from which the Ch'an–Pure Land syncretism was born. It was simple, direct, and forceful in that Ch'an–Pure Land syncretism did not involve itself in philosophical speculation, but advocated personal, religious experience. It was pragmatic in that through the dual practices of both Ch'an and ***nien-fo*** (Buddha-recitation) along with other disciplines, final liberation was assured. Also it was flexible in that sectarianism broke down within the syncretism of the two distinctive schools. Finally, it was accessible because Ch'an–Pure Land syncretism provided an egalitarian salvation to the religious populace regardless of their spiritual capabilities.

Doctrinally, no other characteristic of Chinese Buddhism is more unique and controversial than that of Ch'an–Pure Land syncretism, for it is a rapprochement and synthesis of two radically distinct traditions.

Ch'an emphasizes "seeing into one's own nature" (*chien-hsing*) through one's own effort, while Pure Land stresses salvation through faith in the "other power." One practices meditation, the other *nien-fo*. Both doctrines and practices seem irreconcilable. Yet the simultaneous practice of these two different patterns of devotional and meditative disciplines has been observed side by side after T'ang.

The instrumental figure for the promotion and popularization of this movement is Yung-ming Yen-shou (904–975), who was an enlightened Ch'an monk and a Pure Land practitioner.[1] He was one of the greatest syncretists China ever produced. Before him, there already existed syncretic thought, especially concerning the reconciliation of Ch'an and doctrinal Buddhism (*chiao*).[2] However, it was Yung-ming who synthesized all systems of Buddhist thought in theory, and more importantly, united all approaches of Buddhist disciplines, especially Ch'an meditation and *nien-fo* (Buddha-recitation), in practice. We will specifically investigate and evaluate his Ch'an–Pure Land syncretism.

Yung-ming's Ch'an–Pure Land Syncretism

There are three factors which led to Yung-ming's advocacy of the joint practice of Ch'an and Pure Land. The first factor was the strong antagonism, prevailing at the time of Yung-ming, between Ch'an and Pure Land schools. Ch'an practitioners denigrated Pure Land believers as simple-minded seekers of the external instead of the true self, whereas the Pure Land followers criticized Ch'an monks as arrogant and undisciplined. Yung-ming saw the harm caused by the extremely unconventional (anti-scriptural and anti-ritual) attitude cherished by some Ch'an followers, which often led them to indulge in the "wild Ch'an" in which they utilized various fanatic and eccentric gimmicks to demonstrate their understanding of Ch'an. Some even went so far as to ignore all disciplines and disregard totally the accepted codes of morality on the pretext of practicing non-attachment. To Yung-ming, the application of the "wild Ch'an" was dangerous if the person applying it had no genuine insight but only superficial understanding. Thus Yung-ming incorporated *nien-fo* practice, as well as other disciplines,[3] into Ch'an so as to counteract the one-sided practice of Ch'an.

The second factor that led to Yung-ming's Ch'an–Pure Land syncretism was the sociopolitical conditions during his time.[4] It was a very turbulent era in which the suffering populace cried out for salvation. The Ch'an meditation was too difficult and demanding for the masses, but when Ch'an was accompanied by *nien-fo*, it became an accessible, effective, and egalitarian approach, for it suited people with high or low spiritual endowment.

The third factor was his non-sectarian attitude towards all systems of Buddhist thought in general, and the Ch'an and Pure Land Buddhism in particular. This syncretic thought was consistent with the traditional Chinese philosophy of harmony.[5]

Although in the syncretic mind of Yung-ming, there is no theoretical and practical contradiction in the joint exercise of Ch'an meditation and *nien-fo*, yet traditionally, Ch'an and *nien-fo* are radically different. Therefore, let us first examine how these two distinctive types of Buddhist experience differ from each other, and how Yung-ming syncretized them.

"Other-power" Versus "Self-power"

One of the most apparent differences between Ch'an and Pure Land lies in the "self-power"-oriented salvation of Ch'an versus "other-power"-oriented salvation of the Pure Land. The following quotations from Shan-tao and Hui-neng, which are representatives of the devotional Pure Land and the intuitively experientialist Ch'an, demonstrate well their perceptions on the approach to salvation. Shan-tao, the systematizer of the Pure Land teaching, said:

> Buddha Amitābha, through his forty-eight vows, takes in sentient beings who by harboring no doubt and worry and relying on the saving power of the Buddha's vows, are certainly to attain birth [in the Pure Land].[6]

On the other hand, in response to a question regarding the attainment of birth in the Pure Land, Hui-neng said:

> The deluded person concentrates on Buddha and wishes to be born in the other land; the awakened person makes pure his own mind.... If only the mind has no impurity, the Western Land is not far. If the mind gives rise to impurity, even though you invoke the Buddha and seek to be born [in the West], it will be difficult to reach.... If you awaken to the sudden Dharma of birthlessness, you will see the Western Land in an instant. If you do not awaken to the Sudden Teaching of Mahāyāna, even if you concentrate on the Buddha and seek to be born, the road will be long. How can you hope to reach it?[7]

From the above quotations, we see a sharp distinction between these two kinds of Buddhist soteriology: the "path of Pure Land," based on the other-power from the grace of the Buddha, and the "path of the sages" based on good work and religious exercises such as meditation, scholarship, ascetic disciplines and generally any attempt to realize enlightenment by one's own efforts.

Traditionally, the notion of "other power" denotes the absolute surrendering of oneself to the saving power of the Buddha. But what does "other-power" really mean and to what extent can one rely on it? Is there absolute "other-power"? In other words, is the working of "other-power" possible without some sort of response from "self-power"? Let us first examine how "other-power" has been interpreted in the context of Chinese Buddhism. In the *Ten Questions Concerning the Pure Land* (*Ching-t'u-shih-yi lun*), Chih-I was quoted as defining "other-power" as follows:

> Other-power means that if one believes that the power of the compassionate vow of Buddha Amitābha takes to himself all sentient beings who are mindful of him, then one is enabled to generate the mind of Bodhi, practice *nien-fo samadhi*, detest the body which is within the three words, and practice giving, morality, and merit. And if within each of these various practices, [the merit is] transferred [to others], and if one vows to be born in the Pure Land of Amitābha by relying on the power of the Buddha's vows, one's nature and the Buddha's response will be in mutual accord, and one will be born [in the Pure Land][8]

In this definition of "other-power," obviously it is the faith in the saving power of the Buddha which generates the Bodhi-mind as well as other practices. But it is through "other-power" accompanied by "self-power" that "one's nature and the Buddha's response are in mutual accord," and this harmony actualizes birth in the Pure Land. Hence, the "other-power" is not the exclusive factor leading to the Pure Land. If this interpretation sounds unorthodox, let us examine some interpretations from the orthodox Pure Land masters. T'an-luan defined the two powers—self and other—in the following:

> I regard "other-power" as the helping condition. How could it be otherwise? Now, I shall set forth again a metaphor of self-power and other-power.
>
> [Self-power] is like a person who, because he is afraid of the three evil *gates*, keeps the precepts; because he keeps them, he is able to practice *samādhi*; because of *samādhi*, he is able to exercise supernatural power; because of the supernatural power, he is able to traverse the four corners of the world.
>
> Again, the, [other-power is] like an inferior person, who cannot even mount on a donkey [with his own strength]; yet if he accompanies the flight of the *cakravartin* (Universal King), he can then traverse the four corners of the world without hindrance.[9]

T'an-luan illustrated the "other-power" method of salvation through the analogy of a weak man going everywhere in the world by relying on the power of the *cakravartin*, yet he called "other power" a "helping condition" in the sense that "other-power" was not the exclusive condition. Just as the power of the *cakravartin* is of no avail if the person has no desire for travel, so the saving power of the Buddha cannot function if men do not send out the "corresponding power," which can be in the forms of austere discipline, desire for birth in the Pure Land, or *nien-fo* practice. Otherwise, motivated by infinite compassion, the Buddha would have liberated all beings long ago through his saving power alone. Hence, in the context of Chinese Pure Land Buddhism, usually three factors or conditions are necessary for assurance of birth: faith, vow, and practice, although the practice here does not necessarily refer to the traditional Buddhist disciplines of *sīla*, *samādhi* and *prajñā*. Nevertheless, "other-power" in Chinese Pure Land Buddhism never means total abandoning of one's own spiritual effort. As long as some sort of self-effort is required to correspond with the "other-power," it seems that the gap between these two seemingly contradictory approaches can be bridged.

This conception of "some sort of self-effort" changed as Pure Land thought developed from the "five mindfulness" of Vasubandhu's *Sukhāvatīvyūhopadeśa*, to the vocative *nien-fo* of Shan-tao, and even to the "faith and faith alone" of Shinran. Yet regardless of the forms and the emphasis of the self-effort, the self-effort from the devotee is indispensable. For example, even the Primal Vow of the Buddha Amitābha is regarded as the basic teaching of devotees. The Primal Vow says, "If the beings in the ten directions, when I have attained Buddhahood, should believe in me with all sincerity of heart, desiring to be born in my country, and should, say ten times, think of me and if they should not be born there, may I not obtain enlightenment."

According to this vow, the belief in the Buddha with sincerity of heart, the desire to be born in the Pure Land and ten times of thinking (*nien*) of the Buddha are the conditions for the working of the Primal Vow. To put it in another way, the saving power can transmit only to those who utter the name of Amitābha with sincerity of heart and desire for birth in the Pure Land. The "self-power" appears in the forms of arousing faith and *nien-fo* on the part of Pure Land seekers. And since that is the case, should we not say *nien-fo* exercise based on strong faith is a form of "self-power"?

It is in this notion of self-powered *nien-fo* that Yung-ming finds the simultaneous cultivation of self-power-oriented Pure Land practices and other-power oriented Ch'an meditation possible.

Nien-fo Versus Meditation

The other main difference between the Pure Land and Ch'an which is closely related to the notion of "self-power," "other-power" polarity, is the devotional *nien-fo* practice of the Pure Land and the rigorous meditation of Ch'an. Psychologically, there are four approaches to *nien-fo*.[10]

The first is to think of the Buddha as fully enlightened and thus to take him as a model to follow for one's moral training. The second is to call upon the name, since the calling of the name itself contains innumerable merits. This form of ***nien-fo*** is based on the belief in the mystery of the name as well as of the sound produced by pronouncing it. The third form of ***nien-fo*** is to call upon the Buddha's name as the saving power and the last resort for liberating beings from worldly sufferings. The psychological impact of this type of ***nien-fo*** is so powerful that the Pure Land devotees believe that only one calling of the Buddha with much intensity at the time of death will warrant a response from the saving power of the Buddha and thus assure one's birth in the Pure Land.

Since this third form of ***nien-fo*** is the genuine devotional type of Pure Land Buddhism, the Pure Land teaching appears to be dualistic. It is dualistic as long as Amitābha is taken as existing on the other shore of the transmigration and sinful beings on this side. In other words, the dichotomy arises when Amitābha stands for the object of adoration and mortals for the adoring subjects, and when there is a separation of that Pure Land of the Buddha from this defiled land of beings. The practice of ***nien-fo*** based on this dualism is thus often criticized, especially by Ch'an followers, as seeking an external form which contradicts the Mahāyāna doctrines of no-form and no-birth.

It is in the fourth type of ***nien-fo*** that Yung-ming found some common ground between the devotional ***nien-fo*** and the speculative Ch'an meditation. This form may be termed ***wei-hsin nien-fo*** (mind-only ***nien-fo***) or ***i-hsin nien-fo*** (one-mind ***nien-fo***). Yung-ming defines it as follows:

> The Mind-only ***nien-fo*** means contemplating that the Mind pervades all dharmas. After realizing that the phenomenal is created by the Mind and that Mind itself is the Buddha, then whatever one thinks of is nothing but the Buddha. The ***Pratyutpanna Sūtra*** says, "For example, a man is delighted to see seven kinds of jewel and his relatives in his dream, but after waking up, he is unable to find their whereabouts." The Mind-only ***nien-fo*** is also like this, because it is made from the Mind. It is existing and at the same time empty; therefore, [the Buddha] neither comes nor goes away. Because [the form of ***nien-fo*** is] unreal like an illusion; one should get rid of the notion of the Mind and the Buddha. But on the other hand, because the illusory form of ***nien-fo*** exists, one should not get rid of the thought of the Mind and the Buddha. When emptiness and existence are mutually unobstructive, there is neither coming nor going [of the Buddha], yet this does not prevent one from universally seeing [the Buddha]. Seeing is no-seeing. This complies with the principle of the Middle Way.[11]

Based on the doctrine of mind-only, the mind-only ***nien-fo*** then turns from being dualistic and devotional to being monistic and speculative. It is a kind of ***nien-fo*** carried out with "one-mind undisturbed" (***i hsin pu*** *luan*). When one dwells on the name of the Buddha in continuous and uninterrupted succession, one creates a state of consciousness similar to that derived from deep meditation. This is why the Fo-tsang Ching defines *nien-fo* the following way: "*Nien-fo* means leaving behind all thoughts. When no thoughts arise, the mind gives rise to no discrimination, names, hindrances, desire, grasping or discernment."[12] However, this samādhic state of consciousness is different from merely hypnotic trance, for in the *nien-fo* consciousness, a true self shines out, and the cognizing subject is united with the cognized object. This "one-mind" is thus the link between Ch'an meditation and *nien-fo*, for this "one-mind *nien-fo*" is nothing but "seeing into one's own nature" of the Ch'an school. Although the devotional Pure Land followers might disagree with this Ch'anistic interpretation of *nien-fo*, this does not mean that *nien-fo* and Ch'an meditation cannot be reconciled.

The Non-Duality of the Two Truths

Another key philosophical principle used by Yung-ming to rationalize the unification of *nien-fo* and Ch'an meditation is the doctrine of the non-duality of any dichotomy based on the doctrine of one-mind. Yung-ming sees the One-mind in its two aspects: the Mind's essence (*t'i*) and its function (*yuan*). Although there are two minds in terms of essence and function, there is only one mind. Applying the same principle of the non-duality of essence-function, Yung-ming expounds the non-duality of the Two Truths, or broadly speaking, the non-duality of all polarities.

Ultimate Truth (*paramārtha-satya*) refers to the unconditioned, ineffable wisdom, *prajñā*, which is the realization of Emptiness of all realities. Conventional Truth (*saṃvṛti-satya*), the domain of compassion and expediency, pertains to the phenomenal world of everyday life. The deluded and dualistic mind makes a distinction between the non-differentiable Absolute from the differentiable empirical world. However, Mahāyāna Buddhism does not stop at the differentiation of these two truths. The gist of the theory of Two Truths lies in the Middle Way: the undifferentiation of the two-fold truth through the realization of emptiness. This is to say, when one realizes that all existing things are empty of self-nature, because of dependent co-arising, then a Mahāyāna conception of religious life can be positively applied.

The reason that Yung-ming emphatically advocated the teaching of non-duality was to refute those who clung to the Ultimate Truth and were not able to move back into the sphere of the Conventional Truth. They rejected the validity of the Conventional Truth under the pretext that "all forms are empty." According to their thinking, all religious practices are characterized by form and should therefore be rejected. Yung-ming argued that only when an individual could move from "form" to "emptiness" and back from "emptiness" to "form" did he have true understanding of the Two Truths and complete fulfillment of religious experience. This was so because a religious practice without a base on the Ultimate of Truth of *śūnyatā* accrued worldly virtues only, whereas a religious realization lacking constructive application of that realization in the empirical world was nothing but a dry, cold, and irrelevant experience.

To further demonstrate the non-duality and complementarity between Ch'an and Pure Land, Yung-ming listed ten pairs of non-dual and complementary polarities as doctrinal proofs. They are:

1. *Li-shih wu-ai*: the non-obstruction between the absolute and the phenomenal;
2. *Chuan-shih shuang-hsing*: the simultaneous exercise of the provisional and the true.
3. *Erh-t'i ping-ch'eng*: the compatibility of the Two Truths.
4. *Tsing-hsiang jeng-chi*: the interpretation of nature and characteristics;
5. *T'i-yung tsu-tsai*: the free interaction of essence and function.
6. *Kung-yu hsiang-ch'eng*: the mutual complementarity of emptiness and existence;
7. *Cheng-chu chien-hsiu*: the simultaneous cultivation of the primary and auxiliary practices;
8. *Tung-yi yi-chi*: the one-realm of the identical and the different;
9. *Hsiu-hsing pu-erh*: the non-duality of the acquired and natural, and
10. *Yin-kuo wu-ch'a*: the non-differentiation of cause and effect.[13]

The first of these ten pairs is regarded as the "general" (*tsung*) and the other are "particular" (*pei*). Because of his Hua-yen orientation, Yung-ming adopted the familiar theme of the harmonious identity of the absolute (*li*) and the phenomenal (*shih*) from the Hua-yen philosophy as the foundation of his syncretism. Thus, he said that if one wishes to simultaneously cultivate various practices, one must completely follow *li* and *shih*. When *li* and *shih* are non-obstructive, one can benefit both oneself and others, perfecting compassion for beings who are of the same nature as oneself.

Applying this ontological *li-shih* identity to religious life, Yung-ming emphasizes the unity of the theory (*li*) and practice (*shih*) for soteriology. The principle guides the practice, and the practice manifests the principle. However, because of the discriminative tendency of human nature, some make too much of theory while others make too much of practice. Moreover, in the world of realities (*shih*), practices often go against one another. Consequently, the religious experience becomes one-sided. Confrontation and antagonism, instead of harmony, arise. If an individual, Yung-ming says, clings to the theory without applying it in practice, he falls into the foolishness of the Śrāvakas, and if he engages in practice without basing it on the understanding of the theory, he falls into the attachment of mortals. Thus, as the *Vimalakīrti Sūtra* says, in order to implement the non-obstruction of the theory against practice, although a Bodhisattva attains insight into the meaning of emptiness, he plants virtuous roots; although he practices non-form, he liberates sentient beings; although he understands the theory of non-activity, he manifests himself in various bodies to help others; and although he practices non-arising, he gives rise to all good deeds.

In summary, Yung-ming's Ch'an–Pure Land syncretism has involved four aspects: (1) In the light of idealism, Yung-ming interpreted Pure Land as "mind only Pure Land," (2) Yung ming explained away the contradiction between self-power and other-power by rejecting the possibility of salvation through the reliance on other-power solely, (3) Yung-ming found the common ground between *nien-fo* and Ch'an meditation from the theory of one-mind *nien-fo*, (4) Yung-ming built his syncretism on the Mahāyāna doctrine of non-duality of any polarity. The purpose of Yung-ming's syncretism of these two practices was to show that, basically and ultimately, not only do they not contradict each other, but also the dual practice of both ensures salvation.

The Evaluation of Ch'an–Pure Land Syncretism

From as early as the time of the fifth Ch'an patriarch, the trend of Ch'an–Pure Land rapprochement and synthesis had gradually developed. It culminated at the time of Yung-ming, and remains in the mainstream to this day in the form of *nien-fo kung-an*.[14] In the course of its development, the syncretic trend encountered little resistance from either the Ch'an School or Pure Land School. However, it was mainly championed by Ch'an monks rather than Pure Land teachers. Thus some questions arise. Does this effort of syncretism indicate that the Ch'an School has traditionally "read its presuppositions into the Pure Land tradition so as to synthesize Pure Land teachings with its own,"[15] as one scholar points out? Or is the syncretism a remolding of traditional Pure Land doctrine and practice which has transformed Pure Land into an "inferior" form of Ch'an?

A close study of the historical and doctrinal interaction between the two traditions shows negative answers to these questions. As we have already seen, although the *nien-fo* practice incorporated into the Ch'an

School represented only a certain form of *nien-fo*, namely the mediative type, this type of *nien-fo* is by no means a "remolded" traditional Pure Land practice. In fact, it is the earliest form of *nien-fo* from which the more popular invocational *nien-fo* developed. This meditative *nien-fo* functions the same way and produces the same effect as Ch'an meditation, and this is exactly why both traditions can be practiced simultaneously and harmoniously.

However, it is true that those who advocated Ch'an and Pure Land syncretism emphasized only one aspect of the Pure Land teaching, and that when they tried to rationalize the joint practice, they dealt little with, or often overlooked and ignored, the differences between the two traditions. They simply explained away the differences or contradictions by denying any differences from the point of view of enlightenment (Ultimate Truth).

Furthermore, Yung-ming and other syncretists were not interested in dialectics; rather, they were soteriologically oriented. That is to say, to them all disciplines with the same religious goal were valid and could be practiced together regardless of their differences, which existed only on the level of conventional truth. Moreover, to the practical minds of the Chinese, the dual practice of Ch'an and *nien-fo* were a "double insurance":[16] If a practitioner failed in one (more likely Ch'an), he was sure to succeed in the other. The Chinese syncretists sincerely believed in the compatibility of the diverse schools. They had the practical religious goal in their minds when they advocated the simultaneous use of meditation and *nien-fo*, and did not care to maintain the "purity" of the distinctions of different sects. Thus, the Ch'an–Pure Land harmonization was not a conscious attempt of one school to denigrate the other, but an effort to insure the co-existence of both disciplines so that the sectarian confrontation could be avoided and the religious goal could be more quickly reached.

However, in spite of the positive intention on the part of the syncretists, we will want to ask what kind of impact, positive or negative, the syncretism of Ch'an and Pure Land had upon Chinese Buddhism on the whole. Did it cause the deterioration of the quality of Ch'an as some opponents claimed? Did the Pure Land School lose the distinctive features of its teachings, such as devotion and faith when it was allied with Ch'an? And did the syncretism contribute to the decline or the survival of Chinese Buddhism?

The main criticism of the indiscriminate mixture of disparate elements of Ch'an meditation and *nien-fo* is that it makes Ch'an practice impure and degenerate. In other words, the incorporation of the devotional elements of the Pure Land contaminates and dilutes the vitality of Ch'an meditation, which is essential for a profound, direct, unique "break-through" experience. However, when we examine closely the way that the Ch'an followers practice *nien-fo*, we find that they understand and practice it in monistic-idealistic terms. Buddha Amitābha no longer represents a transcending being, but rather the self-Buddha in every sentient being. As such, the *nien-fo* exercise is nothing but another form of meditational device, which aims at the realization of the Buddha-nature as Ch'an meditation does. Since the devotional *nien-fo* is understood and practiced in this fashion, it should be free from the criticism of causing deterioration in the quality and purity of Ch'an practice.

If the *nien-fo* adopted in the Ch'an fashion does not necessarily devitalize the essence of Ch'an as we have argued, then we want to raise the question as to whether this Ch'an-fashioned *nien-fo* has altered the fundamental Pure Land doctrines or re-located the emphasis of its teachings. The main concern of the Pure Land devotees with regard to the *nien-fo* Ch'an is that it de-emphasizes the essential teachings of faith in the "other-power" of Buddha Amitābha and the desire for the birth in the Pure Land after death, and in some cases, it even denies the existence of the Buddha and his Pure Land under the slogan that "the Pure Land is mind-only, and the self-body is Amitābha." According to Pure Land devotionalism, if the faith in the Buddha is not strong and the desire for birth in the Pure Land is not earnest, its ultimate religious goal, the realization of birth in the Pure Land, cannot be achieved. Superficially, it seems that the devotional aspect of faith in the Pure Land teachings is not stressed when *nien-fo* is practiced in a Ch'an fashion. Actually, faith is not totally ignored; rather, its dimensions are widened. The Ch'an monk Yung-chueh Yun-hsien interpreted it in the following way:

> There are two aspects with regard to the faith in the Buddha. One is the faith in the "principle" (*li*); the other is the faith in the "phenomenal" (*shih*). The faith in the "principle" means to believe that one's mind is the Pure Land and one's nature to believe that the Pure Land is in the Western Region, and there exists Buddha Amitābha. From the aspect of the "principle," the aspect of "phenomenal" manifests; it is like the Ocean-seal's being able to manifest myriad phenomena. From the aspect of "phenomenal, the aspect of the "principle" manifests, for the myriad phenomena are inseparable from the Ocean-seal. These two aspects of faith are both one and two, yet neither two. To have faith in this manner is called true faith.[17]

The argument is that from the viewpoint of the principle, the Pure Land and the Buddha do not go beyond one-mind, and from the viewpoint of the phenomenal, the mind-only Pure Land and the Buddha exist. Yet the idealistic and realistic views do not contradict each other. To have faith in both aspects is to have true faith in the Pure Land teaching.

Aside from the harmony of seemingly contradictory elements of both traditions, which is justified by the doctrinal interpretation, there is also the psychological affinity between them that leads to their ultimate identification. The pronouncing of the Buddha's name starts with a feeling of dualism in the devotees who, as is usually assumed, are people of inferior capacities, and thus do the *nien-fo* not to attain samadhi, but to express their devotion with the purpose of attaining birth in the Pure Land after death. Nevertheless, without the devotees' awareness, the *nien fo* works in some mysterious manner in the consciousness in which the barrier of all distinctions—"other-power" versus "self-power," the Buddha versus the self, the Pure Land versus this *Saha* world—break down.[18] Understanding the mysticism and psychology of *nien-fo*, the syncretists did not find it necessary to put much effort into rationalizing the disparate elements between *nien-fo* and Ch'an. To them, as long as one entered the house, it did not matter from which door one entered.

Another factor that harmoniously united Ch'an and Pure Land is that they represent two indispensable pillars of Buddhism, wisdom *parjñā* and compassion *karuṇā*, which constitute enlightenment. Pure Land is more inclined to emphasize compassion, whereas in Ch'an there is a stronger tendency to emphasize wisdom. Being too demanding and too independent, Ch'an often ignores the emotional side of life, and disregards the need for an intimately spiritual relationship between mortals and the object of their devotion. This is why, if carried to the extreme, Ch'an is described as "dried up Ch'an." On the contrary, Pure Land devotionalism, which is based on the compassion of Buddha Amitābha, provides a hopeful, secure, and complacent religious life, which can psychologically smooth and compensate the strict life of Ch'an. It is because of this complementarity of Ch'an and Pure Land, or *parjñā* and *karuṇā*, that Suzuki once said, "Buddhism produced the two schools of Zen (Ch'an) and Shin and the future development of Mahāyāna over the whole world will come from the synthesis of these two."[19] Actually, the synthesis of the two has already been existing in China for many centuries.

Now we come to the question whether Ch'an–Pure Land syncretism left a positive or negative impact upon post-T'ang Buddhism. From a sectarian viewpoint, the answer may be negative, but in terms of Chinese Buddhism on the whole, it has left a positive impact. The main reason is that Ch'an and Pure Land contributed to each other with their own strengths and eliminated each other's weaknesses.

By the time of Sung Dynasty, Ch'an had already lost its originality and vitality due to the loss of great masters and the great religious persecution in late T'ang. The systematized *kung-an* was then developed in order to regain its inner strength. Because of its systematized approach and accessibility to all enlightenment seekers, *kung-an* was regarded as a reviving stimulus to the weakening Ch'an tradition. However, some undesirable features of Ch'an developed in the post-golden period which undermined the essence of the earlier Ch'an tradition. One of them was the tendency toward intellectualism. The *kung-an* Ch'an, if not rightly practiced, turned from a striving for intuitive enlightenment to an intellectual interpretation and analysis of the *kung-an*, which at best resulted in an imitation of genuine experience of enlightenment.

The other feature was that post-T'ang Ch'an became more iconoclastic and anti-scriptural. It showed little reverence toward images or rituals and it discouraged sutra-study and neglected the exercise of traditional Buddhist disciplines. All these caused the most disastrous results, not only to the individual who had no genuine enlightenment or had only partial enlightenment, but also to Buddhism on the whole. Another development of the post-T'ang Ch'an was the approach to Ch'an championed by the Ts'ao-tung sect. It was called the "silent illumination Ch'an" characterized by a preference for quiet meditation. Although the practice of total quiet meditation was not without merit, it was often accused of leading the mind to passivity and stagnation (*hun-ch'en*), which was a great hindrance to enlightenment.

It is the incorporation of *nien-fo* into Ch'an that corrects these shortcomings to some extent. The devotionalism of the Pure Land counters the intellectualism in the *kung-an* practice, for devotional practices make the religious experience more personal and intuitive than intellectual. Moreover, broadly speaking, *nien-fo* is a kind of mental and moral discipline. When the mind concentrates exclusively on the Buddha, this is a state of innocence, morally speaking, since there is no room for thought of avarice or hatred, nor for any thought of discrimination. Together with *nien-fo* exercise, other moral disciplines are also emphasized in *nien-fo* Ch'an, for as we have shown, the Pure Land School in Chinese Buddhism has never totally disregarded other religious practices.

Ch'an–Pure Land syncretism has also left a positive impact on the Pure Land Buddhism. As indicated in the *Smaller Sukhāvatī vyūha Sūtra*, the focal point of the *nien-fo* exercise is the "undisturbed single-mindedness" (*i hsin pu luan*). It is through the uninterrupted mindfulness on the Buddha (either by invocation or by meditation) that the Pure Land practitioner reaches the state of undisturbed mindfulness. This is where Ch'an meditation can help. On the one hand, when the Ch'an meditation is associated with *nien-fo*, it deepens and accelerates the spiritual development of the nien-fo practice itself. On the other hand, by synthesizing with *nien-fo*, Ch'an was able to avoid further quietism, intellectualism, and moral degeneracy, which could have caused a total loss of the essence of Ch'an. As for Pure Land Buddhism, although the adoption of *nien-fo* by the Ch'an school might have shifted emphasis from some of its characteristics, it enriched, rather than impoverished, the Pure Land practice. It is for these reasons that we conclude that Yung-ming's Ch'an–Pure Land syncretism has made positive contributions to Chinese Buddhism.

NOTES

1. Yung-ming was recognized as the third Patriarch of the Fa-yen sect of the Ch'an school and also the sixth Patriarch of the Pure Land school.
2. Tsung-mi, a T'ang Ch'an monk, was the most distinguished representative of Ch'an-chiao syncretism. Yung-ming was much influenced by his thought.
3. According to the *Chih-cheh ch'an-shih tsu-hsing-lu*, Yung-ming engaged himself daily in 108 practices, including recitation of sutras and dharmas, performance of repentance, releasing lives (fang-sheng), etc.
4. Yung-ming's lifetime coincided with the period of the Five Dynasties (907–960), an age of extreme political and social disorder.
5. The Chinese philosophy of harmonizing is best reflected in the amalgamation of the three religions of Buddhism, Confucianism, and Taoism. The Chinese believe in the universality of truth.
6. *T.* 47, 271b.
7. *T.* 48, 342b. The English translation is cited from Philip B. Yampolsky, *The Platform Sūtra of the Sixth Patriarch*. New York: Columbia University Press, 1967, 157–158.
8. *T.* 47, 79A. For a discussion and an English translation of the *Ching-t'u Shih-yi lun*, see Leo Pruden, "A short Essay on the Pure Land," *Eastern Buddhist*, new series, vol. 8, no.1, 1975, 74–95.
9. *T.* 40, 844a.
10. See D.T. Suzuki, "Zen and Jodo. Two Types of Buddhist Experience," *Eastern Buddhist* 3(1924–25), 102–105.
11. *T.* 48, 967a-b.
12. *T.* 48, 506a.
13. *T.* 49, 992a.
14. *Nien-fo kung-an* is practiced in the fashion of a *kung-an* when one meditates on the question "Who is it that does the *nien-fo*?" Chih Ch'e is said to have originated the practice.
15. Paul O. Ingram, "The Zen Critique of Pure Land Buddhism," *Journal of the American Academy of Religion*, XLI/2, June 1973, 185.
16. The Chinese dual practice of Ch'an and *nien-fo* was criticized by the Japanese Zen Monk Hakuin. See Winston L. King, "A Critique-Interpretation of Pure Land Practice and Experience (Hakuin Zenji: 1685–1768)," *Asian Religion*, 1971, 56.
17. Quoted from the *chiao-hu chih*, *Wan-tsu hsu-tsang-ching* vol. 109, 538.
18. The story of Enjo is one of the best examples that illustrates a Pure Land practitioner's insight into the iden Dokuto and asked, "To which sect do you belong?" Enjo replied, "The Pure Land School." "How old is Buddha Amitābha?" Dokutan asked. Enjo answered, "The same age as I." "And how old are you?" Dokutan asked again. "The same as Amitābha," Enjo replied. "Then where are you right at this moment?" Enjo clenched his left hand and raised it a little. Dokutan was startled and said, "You are really a true practitioner of the Pure Land doctrine."
19. Suzuki, "Zen and Jodo," 98.

PART 2

7

INTEGRATION OF SŪTRA AND TANTRA

Masao Ichishima

IT IS A WELL-KNOWN FACT that the founding leaders of Japanese Buddhism, Saichō (766–822) and Kūkai (774–835), were very much interested in integrating Sūtra and Tantra. Kukai established Shingon or Mantra-yāna Buddhism on Mt. Kōya around 816 A.D., while Saichō founded Tendai or Eka-yāna Buddhism on Mt. Hiei in 806 A.D. Saichō is also responsible for integrating the Vairocana Esoteric Teaching and *śamatha-vipaśyanā* meditations, Chinese T'ien-t'ai doctrine based upon the *Lotus Sūtra*, while Kukai emphasized the attainment of Buddhahood in this lifetime (*sokushin jōbutsu*) manifesting the non-dual awareness of "diamond-realm" (*vajra-dhātu*) and "womb-realm" (*garbha-dhātu*). The latter exclusively advocated Shingon Esoteric Buddhism.

Saichō established the Ichijō Shikanin (One Vehicle, Samatha Vipaśyanā) Temple on Mt. Hiei and advocated the One Buddha Vehicle rather than the traditional Three Vehicles of Hossō or Yogacara School at Nara, the capital of Japan at that time. He tried to institute the Mahāyāna Ordination Platform on Mt. Hiei so that anyone who seeks the Buddha-dharma can be a Bodhisattva by simply keeping the Mahāyāna precepts based upon the *Brahmajāla-sūtra*. When Saichō tried to institute the Mahāyāna Ordination Platform at Mt. Hiei, he found that the ordination had to be performed according to precepts accepted at one of the temples among Tōdaiji at Nara, Yakushiji at

Kozuke (Tochigi Prefecture), or Kanzeonji at Tsukushi (Kyūshū). Saichō first accepted 250 precepts in order to be ordained as a monk at Tōdaiji, Nara. Then he renounced them in order to establish the Mahāyāna Ordination Center at Mt. Hiei for the laity and monks who sincerely follow the Mahāyāna form of Buddhism. His dream came true seven days after he died in 822.

According to his curriculum for the students on Mt. Hiei,[1] there were two major courses: one is the *śamatha-vipaśyanā* course and the other the Vairocana course. In other words, both Sutra and Tantra courses were integrated to establish Japanese Tendai Buddhism on Mt. Hiei. He argues that there is no difference between Tendai teachings and Esoteric doctrines, saying:

> Ekayāna correct teaching transmitted by Vajra-bodhi, Amoga-vajra, and Prajña Master agree with the Tendai Doctrine; it is not the same doctrine as "Rough Food Eater" (Tokuitsu, Yogācāra Monk 822-842ca). If you want to trace the sources, you should read...the commentary the *Tajih ching i shih* by I-hsing (683–727).[2]

This commentary says that Secret Ekayāna Doctrine, introduced into China by those esoteric masters Vajra-bodhi, Amoga-vajra, and Prajña was not different from the esoteric doctrine of the *Lotus Sūtra*. I-hsing, who wrote the commentary to the *Tajih ching i shih*, interpreted the *Lotus Sūtra* as the secret Ekayāna generating inner awareness that manifests *chi* (the external traces of the Buddha) and reveals *pen* (the fundamental doctrine of the eternity of the Buddha).[3] The *Lotus Sūtra* consists of 28 chapters. The first 14 chapters are called *chi-men* because they expound the nature of things as they are, while the last 14 chapters are called *pen-men* because they discuss the Revelation of the Eternal Life of the Tathāgata.

In other words, the views of the Buddha-kāya of both the *Lotus* and the *Mahāvairocana* are identical in terms of skillful means (*upāya-paryavasāna*) as the final goal. According to Chih-i (538–597), the Chinese founder of T'ien-t'ai, the body of the four means of attaining joyful contentment (*szu an-lo-hsing*)[4] represents the proper direction of deeds of the body, the words of the mouth, the thoughts of the mind, and the resolve or the will to preach the *Lotus Sūtra* by relying on the following three kinds of practices: calmness, discernment, and compassion. They are essential factors to save other sentient beings. It can be said that the first half of the *Lotus* discusses the calmness and discernment, and the latter half the compassion of the Eternal Buddha. In the first half of the *Lotus*, the calmness and discernment are discussed as *upāya* or skillful means and the compassion of the Eternal Life of

Tathāgata is expounded in the latter half of the Sutra. These doctrines are in agreement with the basic *Mahāvairocana* doctrine. Thus we can see that the *Lotus* has esoteric implications. According to the Tendai interpretation, the Eternal Life of Tathāgata Śākyamuni-Buddha is identical with the *Mahāvairocana-tathāgata*.

Amoghavajra

Amoghavajra (705–774), a disciple of Vajrabodhi (671–741), is known as a Tāntric master who translated the *Tattvasaṃgraha* into Chinese. It is said that Amoghavajra was born in Central Asia, and being the son of an Indian father and a Chinese mother, he was proficient in Sanskrit as well as Chinese. He lost his father when he was a child, and his uncle took him to China when he was ten years old. He met Vajrabodhi in Changan when he was fourteen. When he became twenty, he was ordained as a monk by Vajrabodhi. After the death of his master, Amoghavajra went to India and brought back with him a number of Mahāyāna sūtras and Tāntric texts to China. He tried to integrate Mahāyāna sūtras and tantras. He translated into Chinese the Tāntric ritual text of the *Lotus* called the *Yogatantra visualizing wisdom ritual to accomplish the Lotus Sūtra*.[5]

There are four categories mentioned in this ritual text to introduce the *Lotus* into the esoteric way: 1) to approach a spiritual master, i.e., Tāntric Acarya; 2) to listen to righteous Dharma, i.e., the *Lotus Sūtra*; 3) to discipline one's mind according to the truth, i.e., Yogatantra visualizing wisdom; and 4) to practice Dharma according to *śamatha* and *vipaśyanā*. It is believed that if you patiently follow these items, you will accomplish unexcelled enlightenment.

In the Maṇḍala formation, it says that there is an eight-petaled Lotus Maṇḍala in the center. The *Stūpa* is placed on the embryo of the eight-petaled flower. Then there are the drawings of Śākyamuni-tathāgata and Prabhūta-ratna-tathāgata sitting together on the same seat in the *stūpa*. There is an opening in the west gate of the *stūpa*. On the eight petals, the following Eight Great Bodhisattvas are made to take their seats clockwise from the east-north petal, i.e., Maitreya, Mañjuśri, Bhaiṣajyarāja, Gaḍgaḍaśvara, Nityavīrya, Akṣayamati, Avalokiteśvara, and Samanthabhadra.[6] In this Maṇḍala, you will see Śākyamuni and Prabhūta-ratna *tathāgatas* sitting on the same seat. These two *tathāgatas* are, in other words, the expression of non-dual enlightenment of both *vajra* (phenomena) and *garbha* (noumena) in the esoteric tradition. This non-dual Buddha represents the Eternal Life of the *tathāgata* in the *Lotus Sūtra*. That is to say, the first 14 chapters of the *Lotus Sūtra* mainly discuss *śamatha-vipaśyanā* practices intended to bring about the realization of the nature of things as they are, and the last 14 chapters present the revelation of the Eternal Life of the *tathāgata* from an esoteric way of expression. Thus, it can be said that this ritual text is the example of integration of both Sūtra and Tantra.

Wu t'ai shan in China

Amoghavajra was also the founder of Chin-ko-sze Temple on Mt. Wu t'ai in China. At the end of the T'ang dynasty around 958 A.D., there lived Tao-tuan at the Chin-hosze, one which was most probably the same temple as the one founded by Amoghavajra. The names of the temples on Wu t'ai shan were changed sometimes due to political reasons. At that time, when Tao-tuan was active at Chin-hosze, many Tibetan and Mongolian Lamas resided there. Tao-tuan also emphasized the integration of Sūtra and Tantra in his work.[7] The Yellow Hat School of Tibetan Buddhism, which was founded by Tson Kha Pa (1357–1419), is the typical example of the integration of Sūtra and Tantra. He wrote the *Lam rim*, the basic text for exoteric Buddhism which discusses the practice of *śamatha* and *vipaśyanā*. Tson Kha Pa said that those who had studied the scriptures well and practiced them well, based upon calmness, (*śamatha*), and discernment (*vipaśyanā*) can enter into the Tantric practices based upon the *Guhyasamāja* or *Hevajra*. He maintained that the value of the result of meditative actualization of both Sūtra and Tantra is the same, but the Tāntric approach provides a quicker means to attain enlightenment. Tao-tuan, the author of the *Hsien Mi Yuan tung chen fu hsin yao chi*, outlined the essential points of attaining enlightenment through the integration of Exoteric and Esoteric Buddhism at Mt. Wu t'ai, quoting various scriptures of Exoteric Mahāyāna-texts and Esoteric-mantras, introduced by Amoghavajra, as well as the famous Tibetan Buddhist Mantra, "Om Maṇi Padme Hum."

Taimitu Lineage

The Japanese master Ennin (798–864) spent ten years in China, visiting Ch'ang-an and Wu t'ai shan and studying the Chinese Esoteric Buddhist tradition in order to improve the esotericism of the Japanese Tendai founded by Saichō. Following Saichō's intention, Ennin devoted himself to the study of the so-called "One Great Perfect Teaching" (*ichidai-engyō*). *He maintained that the Shingon esoteric path (mantra-mārga*) was identical with the teachings expounded by Śākyamuni Buddha. Writing a commentary to the *Tattvasaṃgraha*,[8] he explained the *ichidai-engyō* as follows: "The teachings of the three vehicles is an exoteric teaching, and the teachings of the *Flower Ornament Scripture*, *Vimalakīrti-nirdeśa-sūtra*, *Wisdom Sūtra*, and the *Lotus Sūtra*, etc., belong to esoteric teaching, i.e., one vehicle." He further said that those "one vehicle" scriptures are esoteric in principle. However, they do not mention the ritualistic and practical side of scriptures. According to his commentary on the *Susiddhi*, the *Mahāvairocana*, *Tattvasaṃgraha*, and *Susiddhi* combine both theory and practice.[9]

Another Great Master, Enchin (814–891), who founded the Jimon sect of Tendai at Miidera Temple, classified those esoteric texts as belonging to the Fifth Period among T'ien-t'ai Four-fold Teachings.[10] Ennin also spent six years in China visiting Ch'ang-an and Mt. T'ien-t'ai in order to assist the integration of Sūtra and Tantra in Taimitsu Esoteric Buddhism. The author of the *T'ien-t'ai Fourfold Teaching*, Chegwan, says: "The Great Master T'ien-t'ai Chih-che (538–597) used the classification of the Five Periods and Eight Teachings to arrange and explain, in a complete and exhaustive way, the sacred teachings of Buddha which were flowing east (from India to China)."[11]

The five periods are:

1. The period of the Hua-yen (Buddha expounded the *Flower Ornament Sūtra*).
2. The period of the Deer Park (in which the four Āgamas were taught).
3. The period of Expanded (*vaipulya*) Teaching (in which the *Weimo*, *Szu-i*, *Leng-chia*, *Leng-yen san-mei*, *Chin-kuang-ming*, and *Sheng-man Sūtras* were taught).[12]
4. The period of wisdom (in which the various Wisdom Sūtras were taught, such as the *Mo-hopojo*, *Ching-kang-po-jo*, and *Ta-p'in-po-jo*.
5. The period of the *Lotus* and *Nirvāṇa* (*sūtras*).

And four methods of conversion are mentioned as follows: sudden, gradual, secret, and variable. Another four doctrines of conversion are Tripiṭaka, shared, distinctive, and complete. It goes without saying that the esoteric texts such as the *Mahāvirocana*, *Tattvasaṃgraha*, and *Susiddhi* were later productions than those sūtras mentioned in the classification of sūtras into the five periods. Therefore, the problem is how to incorporate all these esoteric sūtras into the five periods. Ennin included them in the fifth period. Later, Annen (841–?) rearranged them as the fifth doctrine added to the four doctrines of conversion mentioned above.

Integration of Sūtra and Tantra by Ennin and Enchin

Enchin further tried to integrate the doctrines of Tendai and esoteric teachings. For instance, he considered the *śamatha* and *vipaśyanā* as the pre-*upāya* gate entering into the "secret," and the triple views of T'ien-t'ai[13] as the pre-*upāya* entering into the letter A[14] in the esoteric teaching. According to the "Oral Transmission relating to the View of Fire Ritual" by Ennin, the *Lotus Sūtra* consists of the ideas of *śamatha* and *vipaśyanā*. The *śamatha* is equivalent to Vajra, while *vipaśyanā* corresponds to Garbha Dhātu in the esoteric sense. That is to say, the first 14 chapters of the *Lotus* represent *śamatha* or Vajra and the last 14 chapters relate to *vipaśyanā* or Garbha Dhātu. Enchin attributed this arrangement to Ennin. Enchin tried to maintain more of a balance between exoteric and esoteric Buddhism than did Ennin. Ennin and Annen evaluated esoteric Buddhism as being superior to exoteric Buddhism. Thus, Enchin followed Saichō's attempt at harmonizing exoteric and esoteric Buddhism.

Integration of Sūtra and Tantra in India and Tibet

When we trace the history of the development of Mahāyāna Buddhism in India and Tibet, it becomes evident that Tāntric Buddhism emerged there following the *bodhisattva* ideal of Mahāyāna Buddhism. Kamalaśīla (750–794) introduced the Indian theory of gradual stages of meditative actualization into Tibet around the end of the 8th century. According to his conception of meditative actualization in terms of *śamatha* and *vipaśyanā*, the first five perfections (from *dāna* to *dhyāna*) among the six perfections of the *bodhisattva* ideal comprehend the skillful means (*upāya*) and the sixth is insight (*prajñā*). The *upāya* is identical with calmness (*śamatha*) and *prajñā* is equivalent to discernment (*vipaśyanā*).

Tson Khapa (1357–1419), the founder of the Gelukpa Yellow Hat School of Tibet, followed the meditative actualization introduced by Kamalaśīla around 794. In his great work, *Lam rim*,[16] Tson Khapa quoted the *Bhāvanākrama*[15] more than 58 times. Kamalaśīla insisted that the perfect liberation of mind could be obtained when the practitioner practiced the balanced training of both śamatha and *vipaśyanā* which were equivalent to *upāya* and *prajñā*. This idea in fact was the product of the later development of Mahāyāna Buddhism up to the 9th century A.D. in India. The cultivation of the calmness (*śamatha*) and discernment (*vipaśyanā*) is, in other words, the actualization of means (*upāya*) and insight (*prajñā*). The perfect liberation (*mokṣa*) is the result of the meditative actualization of calmness and discernment.

Tson Khapa claimed that those who are well trained in calmness and discernment can begin with Tantra or esoteric practices. Then, he wrote the *Snags-rim*, which is the basic text of the Tāntric teaching in the Yellow Hat School. From the linguistic point of view, the last vowel "a" of *upāya* denotes masculine gender and the last vowel "a" of *prajñā* represents feminine gender. The relation of *upāya* and *prajñā* therefore can be compared to father and mother. The Mahāyāna text, *Vimalakīrti-nirdeśa*, says: "The mother is transcendental wisdom, while the father is the skill in liberative technique. The leaders are born of such parents."[17] In Part II of his *Bhāvanākrama*, Kamalaśīla quoted the sūtra that equates perfection of wisdom with the mother and skillful means with the father. Tson Khapa also quoted the same passage in his *Lam rim* exactly the same way as Kamalaśīla did. According to Tibetan tradition, *upāya* is called Father Tantra and *prajñā* is Mother Tantra. The *Guḥyasamāja-tantra* is the basic text of the Father Tantra lineage and the *Hevajra-tantra* represents the Mother Tantra ritual text. In this case, the *Guḥyasamāja* is the text for *upāya* and the *Hevjra* is for *prajñā*. His Holiness Tenzin Gyatso, the 14th Dalai Lama, and his followers were invited to Naritasan Shinshoji Temple, one of the leading Shingon Chisan Mantrayāna schools in Japan, in May 1984. They performed the traditional "fire burning ritual of the increase of the deity Śri Guḥyasamāja," based upon the *Guḥyasamāja*, on the occasion of the consecration of the Stūpa at the Temple.

Fortunately, I had a chance to translate the text into Japanese. It is very interesting to compare the differences between the fire rituals described in Tibetan and Japanese esoteric ritual texts. Though the materials dedicated to the main deity are somewhat different, there are many similarities in their rituals. The ritual fire service of the Tibetan tradition emphasizes *upāya* based on the *Guḥyasamāja-tantra*. According to their rituals, first of all, in the preliminary rites, a practitioner practices enough to be a main deity Akṣobhya himself. This preliminary practice takes long hours of procedure, i.e., they have to follow their traditional precepts and practice of *śamatha* and *vipaśyanā*. After they have fully accomplished the preliminary rites, they can enter into the "fire burning rituals." That is to say, the practice for the sake of saving other sentient beings.

In the case of Japanese esoteric rituals, the attainment of Buddhahood in this lifetime is emphasized in the process of the rituals. The preliminary rites in terms of the process of *juhachidō (precepts), kongōkai (śamatha)*, *taizōkai* (*vipaśyanā*) are for self-training so that the practitioner can attain Buddhahood, and the last Goma (compassion), the fire ritual, is for the sake of sentient beings.

Esoteric Texts in China and Japan

Japanese esoteric Buddhism, Tōmitsu (Shingon) and Taimitsu (Tendai) use the two *maṇḍalas* for their objects of meditation. They are also called *ryokai maṇḍalas*, namely, *kongōkai* (*vajra-dhātu*) and *taizōkai* (*garbha-dhātu*). In the case of Taimitsu, *kongōkai* is for *śamatha* and *taizōkai* is for *vipaśyanā*. And non-dual awareness of "*kon*" and "*tai*" is *mokṣa* (release). This idea is common to both Tōmitsu and Taimitsu so far as non-dual awareness is concerned. The *kongōkai* ritual is based upon the *Vajraśekhara-sarvatathāgatatattva-saṃgraha mahāyāna-pratyutpannābhisambuddha-mahātantrarāja sūtra*, or in short, the *Tattvasaṃgraha* which was introduced to China in 720 by Vajrabodhi (671–741) and translated into Chinese by Vajrabodhi and Amoghavajra (705–774). Taizōkai is based upon the *Mahāvairocana-abhisambodhi vikurvitādhiṣṭhānavaipulya-sūtrendra-rāja-dharma-paryāya*, or in short, the *Mahāvairocana-sūtra*, which was brought to China by Subhākarasiṃha (637–735). Subhākarasiṃha and his disciple, I-hsing (687–722), translated the sūtra into Chinese in 716. The *Mahāvairocana-sūtra* was introduced into China through central Asia from north-west India, while the *Tattvasaṃgraha* came through the southern sea routes from south India. The Vajrayāna tradition of Vikramaśilā monastery, together with the *Tattvasaṃgraha* was also introduced to Java approximately around the 7th century. The Buddhist monument Barabudur must have been influenced by the idea of *maṇḍla* derived from the *Tattvasaṃgraha*. Another monument which was inspired by Barabudur is Angkor Thom (12th century) of Cambodia. The *Tattvasaṃgraha and Mahāvairocana* are the most essential and influential of the esoteric texts in Japan.

A famous *gathā* in the *Mahāvairocana* reads: "*tad etat sarvajña-jñānaṃ karuṇāmūlaṃ bodhicitta-hetukaṃ upāyaparayavasānaṃ,*"[18] which means "That omniscient wisdom is the basis of compassion, the seed of the thought of enlightenment, and the goal of the means." So far, we do not have the original Sanskrit manuscript of the Mahāvairocana text except for some fragments. The above quotation is from the *Third Bhāvanākrama* by Kamalaśīla. In the case of the Chinese and Tibetan versions, the order of *karuṇā* and *bodhicitta* is reversed when compared to the Sanskrit quotation, i.e., *bodhicittāhetukaṃ* comes before *karuṇā-mūlaṃ*. Kamalaśīla quoted the *Mahāvairocana* in the *First and Second Bhāvanākrama*. He used the above *gathā* of the *Mahāvairocana* to compile the *Bhāvanākramas*. He emphasized the importance of compassion, saying that our exhaling and inhaling take place prior to the functioning of heart or life faculty, and likewise the compassion of the *bodhisattva* must come first before the thought of enlightenment (*bodhicitta*). There probably were different manuscripts in Sanskrit before the Chinese and Tibetan translations were made.

Bodhicitta, Karunā, Prajñā and Upāya

According to the *Mādhyamikavṛtti*,[19] Nāgārjuna spoke of both *upāya* for *karuṇā*. Hence, *upāya* is considered to have the same connotation as *karuṇā*. Furthermore, *bodhicitta* was interpreted as *prajñā*. Hence, the *bodhisattva* ideal expounded in the *Mahāvairocana*. In the Buddhist *tantra*, *bodhicitta* developed as the pure consciousness (*vijñaptimātratā*) which was the non-dual nature of *śūnyatā* and *karuṇā*. And this pure consciousness became the *dharma-kāya* (one of the trinity of *buddha-kāyas*, i.e., *dharma-kāya*, *sambhoga-kāya*, and *nirmāṇa-kāya*).

Śiva, Śakti Interpreted as Prajñā, Upāya

The relationship between *upāya* and *prajñā* can be compared to that which holds between *śiva* and *śakti* in the Hindu Tantra. Śiva is a male god who has static nature, and Śakti represents the dynamic female. Śakti is considered a destroyer. However, when she is married to Śiva, the world becomes peaceful. Hindu Tantra says that perfect bliss is obtained by the union of Śiva and Śakti, and they consider this union to be the highest non-duality. From an ultimate standpoint there is neither Śiva nor Śakti.[20] In the Buddhist Tantras, their sexes are reversed. That is to say, *upāya* (Śiva) becomes male, and *prajñā* (Śakti) becomes female. Therefore, *upāya* is dynamic form and *prajñā* is static. *Upāya* in general has missionary activities in the form of preaching the truth among lay people to remove their veil of ignorance and to enable them to realize the truth through the processes of opening, revealing, awakening to, and penetrating.[21] The *Mahāvairocana* emphasizes that *upāya* is the most important in realizing the super knowledge of Tathāgata saying: "the ultimate accomplishment is achieved by means (*upāya parayavasāna*)."

In most religions, compassion and wisdom are like a pair of carts or two wings of a bird. This is especially so in Mahāyāna Buddhism. *Bodhicitta* is the non-dual nature of both wisdom and compassion. Thus according to the Buddhist Tantras in India, the *bodhicitta* is identical with *dharma-kāya*.

Śākyamuni and Mahāvairocana

Shingon tradition of esoteric Buddhism in Japan stresses that the *dharma-kāya* is the embodiment of the highest Buddhist truth. And Vairocana Buddha is considered to be of higher rank than Śākyamuni Buddha, since Mahāvairocana is in the center of the matrix of the *maṇḍala* as the central Buddha, and all other Buddhas are considered to be incarnations of Mahāvairocana. Therefore, in Shingon, Mahāvairocana is looked upon as *dharma-kāya*, as is evident from the description: *hōsshin dainichi nyōrai* (*dharmkāya-mahāvairocana-tathāgata*). Thus they considered even the historical Buddha Śākyamuni as the manifestation of Mahāvairocana. Mahāvairocana is always expounding *dharma* to us, sentient beings, according to Shingon esoteric doctrine. So, they say that anyone can attain Buddhahood in this lifetime as Śākayamuni did. Many of the Taimitsu and Tōmitsu temples in Japan enshrine the two *maṇḍalas* at their temples.

The way these two *maṇḍalas* (*vajra dhātu* and *garbha dhātu*) are displayed is also important. As you face them on your left, there is *kongōkai* (*vajra dhātu*) *maṇḍala* and on your right, *taizōkai* (*garbha dhātu*). It can be said that these two *maṇḍalas* originally represented *upāya* and *prajñā* of the Indian Buddhist Tantras. The Chinese and Japanese *maṇḍalas* are painted flat on the scroll, hence they are two-dimensional *maṇḍalas*, while in South and South East Asia, they are considered as three dimensional *maṇḍalas*. For instance, Barabudur stupa of Java is the best illustration of the three dimensional *maṇḍalas*, and this is influenced by the Vajrayana tradition of India. There are two types of Tathagatas on the top of the stupa representing Sākyamuni and Prabhūta-ratna of the *Lotus maṇḍala*. In the center of Guyasāmaja *maṇḍala*, there is a non-dual image, Yab and Yum. In Tibetan Buddhism, Yab indicates Father Tantra and Yum is the Mother Tantra. In the context of Mahāyāna, these represent the non-dual form of *upāya* and *prajñā*. Japanese *kongōkai* (*vajra dhātu*) *maṇḍala* has Mahāvairocana in the center of *maṇḍala* manifesting Chiken-in *mudrā* (wisdom-fist hand gesture).

Getty maintains that the symbol of the index finger of the right hand of Mahāvairocana is the diamond element corresponding to the spiritual world while the other five fingers of the left hand symbolize the matrix element corresponding to the material world.[22] In other words, the left index finger denotes consciousness and the right five fingers manifest the elements of the world: namely, earth (little finger), water (ring finger), fire (middle), wind (index finger), and space (thumb).

These hand gestures also show us the non-dual form of *vajra* and *garbha*. The Yab-yum form of the Guḥyasamāja *maṇḍala* is an expression that appeals to the Chinese and Japanese since it resembles the *yin-yang* principle that serves as the foundation of Confucianism. The *chiken-in mudrā* is a milder expression of the Yab-yum theory. Thus, Japanese esoteric Buddhism interpreted or understood the "wisdom-fist hand gesture" of Mahāvairocana as the symbol of the non-dual form of *upāya* and *prajñā*.

Japanese Tendai Buddhism, founded by Saichō (766–822) following the *Lotus*, interpreted Vairocana as being in the same rank as Sākyamuni Buddha. As such, Sākyamuni and Prabhūta-ratna sit together on the same seat in the stupa of the *Lotus maṇḍla*. The *Lotus Sūtra* emphasizes the conception of ultimate reality. In his *Mo-ho chih-kuan* the Chinese T'ien-t'ai Master, Chih-i (538–597), explained this reality by saying that "even a single color or a fragrance is nothing but the dynamic awareness of the Middle truth."[23] Japanese Tendai followed his teaching and Saichō accommodated esoteric Buddhism in explaining the *Lotus* teaching. This is because esoteric Buddhism was very popular when he was studying the T'ien-t'ai lineage in China around 804. Thus Saichō established Japanese Tendai Buddhism on Mt. Hiei on January 26, 806, integrating both exoteric and esoteric forms of Buddhism. When Saichō established Japanese Tendai Buddhism on Mt. Hiei, he petitioned the Emperor Saga to establish the Mahāyāna Ordination Center on Mt. Hiei. He also requested the government to have two ordinant students to follow *shikango* (*śamatha-vipaśyanā* exoteric course) and *shanago* (Vairocana esoteric course). Therefore, the Japanese Tendai curriculum for students contained two major courses, namely, *shikango* and *shanago*. The *shikango* students specialized in calmness and discernment (*śamatha*, *vipaśyanā*) based on exoteric Mahāyāna scriptures, while *shanago* students practiced the esoteric way of meditative actualization based on the *Mahāvairocana Sūtra*.

Subsequently, other esoteric texts such as the *Tattvasaṃgraha* and *Susiddhikaramahātantra sādhanopāyikapāṭala sūtra* of Taimitsu were added by his successor, Ennin (789–864). Taimitsu (Japanese Tendai esoteric Buddhism) recommended the *Susiddhi* for *juhachido* (eighteen paths to initiation following two *maṇḍlas*, i.e., *sila* or precepts), the *Mahāvairocana* for *taizōkai* (*garbha-dhātu*), and the *Tattvasaṃgraha* for *kongōkai* (*vajra-dhātu*), and finally *goma* (fire burning ritual) was recommended as a means for the practice of compassion, that is, to cultivate merit transference to all sentient beings.

Hence, Tendai students receive training in these curricula on Mt. Hiei, and this is considered to be their shortest course to monkhood. They must spend at least two months on Mt. Hiei. During the first month, they study *shikango* (exoteric course), and they devote the last 35 days for the practice of *shanago* (esoteric course in terms of *shidōkegyō*, i.e., *juhachidō*, *taizōkai*, *kongōkai*, and *goma*).

The Threefold Training in Esoteric Buddhism

Buddhism recognizes a three-fold training relating to precepts, meditation, and wisdom. They are the core curriculum for Buddhists. If this threefold training is to be related to the four kinds of initiations (*shidōkegyō*), *then juhachidō will stand for precepts, kongōkai* for meditation, and *taizōkai* for wisdom. The final *goma*, or fire-burnt ritual, is for the sake of transferring merit toward sentient beings (compassion). In the case of *bodhisattva* ideal, i.e., the six perfections, the *dāna* and *sīla* represent precepts; *kṣānti*, *vīrya*, and *dhyāna* stand for meditation and final *prajñā* is wisdom. This is how esoteric Buddhism relates itself to the Mahāyāna conception of *bodhisattva*. If we follow the expression of the *heart sutra*, "emptiness" (*śūnyatā*) can designate exoteric Buddhism and "form" (*rūpa*) can represent esoteric Buddhism. The famous stanza of the *Heart Sūtra* says "Form is identical with emptiness, emptiness is identical with form." When we go beyond these two truths, "emptiness and form," there is non-dual formless-form. In such manner the integration of Sutra and Tantra developed throughout India, Tibet, China, and Japan.

Finally, a word about the explanation of the Tantric doctrine in *Lam rim* by Tson Khapa (1357–1419), the founder of the Yellow Hat School in Tibet. Tson Khapa was a reformer of Tibetan Buddhism. He mastered exoteric doctrines of the Mādhyamika, Yogācāra, traditional discourses as well as the esoteric teachings of the Tantras. He maintained that the value of meditative actualization in both traditions is the same, but the Tantric approach to the main deity is quicker than that of the exoteric approach. However, those who are involved in Tantra practices cannot interrupt their daily rituals. If they do, they are destined to hell. This indeed is a very severe injunction. Quoting from the *Ārya-ākāśagarbha-sūtra*,[24] Tson Khapa, in his *Lam rim*, states that "by depending on wisdom (*prajñā*) suffering is completely eliminated, and by depending upon *upāya* a *bodhisattva* never forgets the suffering of all sentient beings."

It is very clear that the *upāya* involves the missionary activity of saving all suffering sentient beings. In other words, *upāya* is identical with *karunā*, as explained in the *Mādhyamikavṛtti* referred to earlier. The *Lam rim* further says that "insight and means" represent the Mahāyāna. This is also stated in the *Āryagayāśīrsa-sūtra*: "The path of the *bodhisattvas* in short amounts to two. The path of means, and the path of insight." It is also proclaimed in the *Āryatathāgataguhya sūtra* that "The whole path of the *bodhisattvas* is comprised by these two, i.e., means and insight."

The above explanation in the *Lam rim* follows Kamalasīla's *Bhāvanākrama III*, especially the chapter on the thesis of Hva san. At the end of the eighth century, religious debates took place at Sam-yas in Tibet between the Chinese Zen Master Hva san and the Indian Master Kamalasila in the presence of King K'ri sron lde bstan (718–780). Hva san stood for the Sudden Zen, and emphasized that *prajñā* was the most efficient way to enlightenment. He rejected the other perfections saying, "it is only for the sake of the ignorant people that giving and the other wholesome practices are taught."

Kamalasīla responded as follows: "By insisting that giving and the rest is to be repudiated, the Great Vehicle consisting of insight and means is also repudiated. As the *Gayāśīrṣa* says, briefly stated there are two paths of the *bodhisattvas*. What are the two? Insight (*prajñā*) and means (*upāya*). And the *Tathāgataguhya-sūtra* says: "This insight and means constitute the cultivation of all perfections by the *bodhisattvas*."[25]

Kamalasīla is said to have won the debate. As a result, Tibetan Buddhism came to be influenced by the Indian version. Tson Khapa followed Kamalasīla and emphasized that *śamatha-vipaśyanā* practices are essential for *bodhisattvas*, and only those *bodhisattvas* well trained in such exoteric Buddhism can proceed to the Tantra. That is the reason why he wrote the *Lam rim* and *Snags rim*.

The Threefold Buddha-kaya and Fivefold Wisdom

The idea that *upāya* and *prajñā* are non-dual is also expressed in the commentary on the *Tattvasaṃgraha*. The *Tattvāloka* says "The wisdom of equality of Tathāgata is the non-dual method of *upāya* and *prajñā*, and it is the wisdom of the universal that can be tasted in the *dharmadhātu*." In the Chinese version of the *Bhāvanākrama*, there is a final section outlining the relationship between the three-fold *buddha-kāya* and the five-fold wisdom of the Tathāgatas. The five-fold wisdom of Tathāgatas are *dharmadhātu-svabhāva*, *ādarśa*, *samatā*, *pratyavekṣaṇa*, and *kṛtyānusthāna*. Each type of wisdom is associated with five Buddhas, i.e., *dharmadhātu-svabhāva* with Mahāvairocana, *ādarśa* with Akṣobhya, *samatā* with Ratnasambhava, *pratyavekṣaṇa* with Amitāyus, and *kṛtyānusthāna* with Amoghasiddhi. Kamalasīla further explains that the first two forms of wisdom (*dharmadhātu svabhāva* and *ādarśa*) belong to *dharma-kāya*, *samatā* and *pratyavekṣaṇa* to *sambhogakāya*, and the last *kṛtyānusthāna* to *nirmāṇakāya*. The theory of the five-fold wisdom and its relation to the Buddha-*kāya* was originally formulated in the *Buddhabhūmi-sūtra* and the *Buddhabhūmi-vyākhyāna* by Śīlabhadra.

Anyway, the non-duality of *upāya* and *prajñā* is considered to be the third form of wisdom, i.e., *samatā*. *Samatā* is also identical with the second *ādarśa* when *samatā* becomes the non-duality of *upāya* and *prajñā*. Kamalasīla concluded that the first five perfections correspond to the *upāya* and the last to *prajñā*. When *upāya* and *prajñā* are perfectly united, then *mokṣa* or perfect liberation of mind will result. Because the *bodhisattva* has great compassion, he does not want to dwell even in the state of perfect liberation or Nirvana. By his use of skillful means (*upāya*) he attempts to save all the people who are suffering. *Upāya*, thus, represents dynamic activity in Mahāyāna Buddhism. This explains the final statement of the *Mahāvairocana-sūtra*: '*upāya-parayavasāna*' ("the Perfect Accomplishment is achieved by the Means"). Thus, the idea that "Emptiness is the Form" expressed in the *Heart Sūtra* is realized through the integration of *upāya* and *prajñā*. According to the non-dual theory, the exoteric Buddhism alone does not make sense. When exoteric Buddhism is integrated with esoteric Buddhism, then the non-dual reality is realized.

NOTES

1. The Collected Works of Saichō, *Dengyō Daishi Zensū* vol. 1, 12.
2. Ibid, vol. 2, 44.
3. The *Commentary to the Mahāvairocana Sutra*, in *Dainichikyō-gishaku, Jyushinbon* by I-hsing, *Manjizokuzōkyō* vol. 36, 281.
4. Kentoku Sasaki, *Study of the Esoteric Lotus, Hokkemikkyō no Kenkyū*, Ryūkoku University, 1943, 181.
5. Amoghavajra, *Chen-chiu Miao-fa lien-hua-ching wan Yu-Ch'ieh kuang-chi-i-kuei T.* vol. 19, No. 1,000.
6. Ibid, *T.* 19, 595c.
7. Tao-tuan, *Hsien-mi yuan-tung chen-fu hsin-yao-chi*, *T.* 46, 989.
8. Ibid, *T.* 61, 16b.
9. Ibid, *T.* 61, 393b.
10. *Chishō Daishi Zenshū*, B. 676.
11. David W. Chappell & Masao Ichishima, *T'ien-t'ai Buddhism: An Outline of the Fourfold Teachings*, Tokyo: Daiichi Shobo, 1983, 53–54.
12. Ibid, 53.
13. *Chishō Daishi Zenshū*, C. 937.
14. Ibid.
15. Masao Ichishima, *Lam-rim ni ataeta Bhavanakrama no eikyō*, in *Tendai Gakuhō* No. 27, 1985, 65.
16. Alex Wayman, *Calming the Mind and Discerning the Real, Buddhist Meditation and the Middle View*, New York: Columbia, 1958.
17. Robert A.F. Thurman, The *Holy Teaching of Vimalakirti*, Philadelphia: Pennsylvania State University, 67.
18. Masao S. Ichishima, "Relationship between the *Bodhicaryavatara* and the *Sutrasamuccaya*," *The Memoirs of Taishō University*, Tokyo, No. 72, 1986, 498.
19. S.B. Dasgupta, *An Introduction to Tantric Buddhism*, Calcutta: University of Calcutta, 1958, 92.
20. Ibid, 100–101.
21. D. Chappell & M. Ichishima, *T'ien-T'ai Buddhism*, 80.
22. Alice Getty, *The Gods of Northern Buddhism*, Tokyo: Charles E. Tuttle, 1962, 32.
23. Chih-i, *Mo-ho chih kuan*, *T.* 46, 1c.
24. M. Ichishima, *Tendai Gakuhō*, No. 27, 68.
25. M. Ichishima, "An English Translation of the Third Process of Meditative Actualization by Kamalasila," *Annual of the Institute for Comprehensive Studies of Taishō University*, No. 1, 1979, 221.

8

THE MAHĪSĀSAKA VIEW OF WOMEN

Cheng-mei Ku

Introduction

ACCORDING TO VASUMITRA, the Mahīsāsakas, as a Buddhist sectarian school, branched out from the Sarvāstivāda in the third century after the Buddha's ***parinirvāṇa***. Vasumitra records this chronological order of both the Sarvāstivāda and the Mahīsāsakas in his ***abhidharma*** work, ***Yibu zhonglun lun (hereafter Yibu)***.[1] Vasumitra's historical knowledge of the Sarvāstivāda and the Mahīsāsakas is different from that of the Pali tradition.[2] Nalinaksha Dutt explains this anomaly in the following way:

> A reference to the doctrines of this school reveals that there were two Mahīsāsaka schools, one earlier and the other later. Vasumitra missed the earlier Mahīsāsakas while enumerating the sub-sects. He, however, points out the earlier Mahīsāsakas agreed more with the Theravādins while the later with the Sarvāstivādins. It may be that the Pali tradition was aware of the earlier division only of the Mahīsāsakas, and so naturally placed their origin before the Sarvāstivādins.[3]

So far, we still have difficulty deciding which school should come first. But where their views of women are concerned, the writer of the *Sūtra Spoken by Buddha on the Girl Nāgadatta* (hereafter, *Nāgadatta*) uses a suggestive description (father-and-daughter relationship) to help us identify which view comes first. According to him, the Mahīsāsaka view of women comes before that of Sarvāstivādins.[4] The writer of the *Nāgadatta* uses Māra to represent the Mahīsāsakas and the daughter of Māra to represent the Sarvāstivādins or the Vātsīputriyavādins.[5] The *Nāgadatta* is a Vātsīputriyavāda work. If this father and daughter relationship is not the actual historical demonstration, the writer of the *Nāgadatta* would not have placed the Sarvāstivādins in the daughter's position.

The *Nāgadatta* was translated into Chinese at the beginning of the 3rd century A.D. by a Yuezhi translator, Zhi Qian. This was the time that the Early Mahāyāna (A.D. 100–250) began to decline in north-western India.[6] Many of the Early Mahāyānic works belonging to the Śūnyavāda school were translated into Chinese at this time or slightly later. These early Chinese translations show that the issue of women, i.e., whether a woman can gain Buddhahood, had become an important issue and was debated among the sectarian schools.[7]

The Sarvāstivāda view of women was developed before the rise of the Early Mahāyāna. This is evident in the earliest extent *Prajñāpāramitā* work, the *Aṣṭasāhasrikāprajñā-pāramitā-sūtra* (hereafter, *Aṣṭa*). The *Aṣṭa* was translated into Chinese in 179 A.D.[8] As one of the earliest Mahāyānic works, the *Aṣṭa* had adopted the Sarvāstivāda view of women as one of the Early Mahāyānic teachings. Even though the Early Mahāyānists had established their own view of women before the 3rd century A.D. and denounced the Sarvāstivāda view of women, yet from the fact that Zhi Qian translated the *Nāgadatta*, we know that both the Sarvāstivāda and the Mahāyānic views of women were still flourishing side by side in north-western India after the 3rd century A.D. In other words, the Sarvāstivāda view of women did not disappear nor was it replaced by the Early Mahāyānic view of women.

According to the suggestion given by the author of the *Nāgadatta*, the Mahīsāsaka view of women comes before that of the Sarvāstivāda. Since the Sarvāstivāda view of women was flourishing before the rise of the Early Mahāyāna, the Mahīsāsaka view would have come some time before the 2nd century A.D.

The Early Mahāyānists may not have felt that the Mahīsāsaka view of women was a threat to them, for that view is hardly mentioned in their literature. The Mahīsāsaka view of women came to be introduced into the Mahāyānic literature after the decline of the Early Mahāyāna (ca. 250 A.D.). Some of the Mahāyānic works written after the period of decline has adopted the Mahīsāsaka view of women as the second or third view. For instance, in the *Saddharmapuṇḍarīka-sūtra* (hereafter, *Saddharma*) the Mahīsāsaka view of women is adopted as the second view[9] and in the *Sūryajiḥmikaraṇa-prabhā-sūtra* (hereafter, *Surya*) the Mahīsāsaka view of women is the third.[10] The Mahīsāsaka view of women did not exert any influence on the northern tradition before the 5th century A.D. But this situation changed after the Chinese began introducing the sectarian *vinaya* literature in the 4th century A.D. The establishment of the Chinese Female Saṅgha at the beginning of the 5th century, as a matter of fact, was influenced by the Mahīsāsaka view of women.[11]

The Traditional View of Women

Women were first mentioned in the discussion of the monks' practice of *brahmacarya*. The Mahīsāsakas, like the other early sectarian schools, also thought that *brahmacarya* was the most important course that a man leading the homeless life (*bhikṣu*) has to observe in his practice of monkhood. A *bhikṣu* believes that if he constantly observes the *brahmacarya*, he will consequently purify his verbal, mental, and physical behavior. Therefore, the *brahmacarya* is also called the path of purification. When a *bhikṣu* observes the *brahmacarya*, he may face all kinds of obstacles. Among these obstacles, the most difficult to conquer is sexual temptation. In the *Forty-two Sections* (hereafter, *Forty-two*) and other places, we read of *bhikṣus* who, because of their failure to control carnal desire, cut off their penises with axes.[12]

The *Mahāsāṅghika Vinaya* (hereafter, *Mahas. V.*) clearly enjoins that a *bhikṣu* should not enjoy lust for sex.[13] For as soon as his carnal desire is aroused, his pure mind becomes polluted. With a polluted mind, a *bhikṣu* will not be able to realize the truth. The *Mahas. V.* says:

> The so-called 'carnal desire' is a pollution of the mind, which changes the condition of a mind. 'Change' means that the original condition of a mind no longer exists. Therefore, 'change' means that the condition which enables a person to realize the truth is no more existent. The mind (in this context) refers to human consciousness.[14]

In order to prevent a *bhikṣu* from falling into a polluted state, almost every sectarian *vinaya* recommends that if a *bhikṣu's* mind is polluted, he has to receive the punishment of *saṅghādisesa* (separation)[15], and if he enjoys lust with women or even animals, he has to face the punishment of *pārājika* (cutting off one's head).[16] The early Buddhist monks took these *dharmas* (punishments) seriously.

Many incidents recorded in the early *āgama* literature relate how a *bhikṣu* handles his problem when he faces the problem of arousal of carnal desire. According to these records, he usually chooses to give up the practice of *brahmacarya* and leave the *saṅgha*. For instance, the *Sūtra Spoken by Buddha on Ananda's Fellow Students* (abbreviated *AFS*) informs us that monk Gupta, after failing to control the fire burning in his body, decided to give up the practice of *brahmacarya*.[17] It is obvious that enjoying carnal desire not only causes a Buddhist practitioner to pay the price but harms the *saṅgha* as well. The early monks therefore set up all kinds of means to prevent such things from happening. The author of the *Mahas. V.* shows his concern for this problem and mentions various means to deal with it. He says:

> You (Yasa) ought not to enjoy lust with women. O Yasa, haven't you heard that I often use all kinds of means to rebuke enjoyments of lust? An enjoyment of lust will make a person intoxicated. It is just like a flaming fire, which burns out one's good sense. Therefore an enjoyment of lust is a great obstacle (for monks to observe the *brahmacarya*). Therefore I often use all kinds of means to praise a person who is detached from such enjoyment, who ceases to be involved in such enjoyment, and who goes beyond such enjoyment.[18]

In order to help their fellow monks to overcome this problem, the early monks recommended various means. The most common means seen in the texts include the simple practice of good conduct and meditation. For instance, the *Forty-two* encourages monks to practice good conduct and meditate on impurity. The text says:

> Not to look at women, when you see them, not to talk to them. If you talk to them, you should control your thoughts and should say thus to yourself: 'I am living in an impure world. I should behave myself like a lotus flower which grows in dirty pond and yet is not polluted. Therefore I should consider those who are older than I as my mother and elder sisters, and younger as my younger sisters and daughters, and should respect every one of them. If I feel my mind is about to be polluted, I should meditate on their bodies, head and toes. I shall realize that inside these bodies there is only filthy discharge and impure organs and thereby release my mind.'[19]

The practice of good conduct, "not to look at women" and "not to talk to women" will make monks avoid actual or direct contact with women. The early monks really believed that the less they have contact with women, the less their problems would be. The *Mahīśāsaka-vinaya* (hereafter, *Mahis. V.*) even suggests that their monks "do not say more than five to six words to women."[20]

The *Ekottarāgama* (hereafter, *Ekottara*) points out that the polluting forces come from two sources, one from women and the other from the mind. Therefore, controlling one's thought is also very important. The *Ekottara* refers to an example of how a monk struggles with his carnal desire, and how important it is to control one's thought when one faces the problem:

> Now my carnal desire is burning like a fire in my body. If I see a beautiful woman, I will tell myself that I like to enjoy lust with her. But after saying this to myself, I also tell myself that this is not the right *dharma* to observe. I know that I should not give way to my carnal desire.[21]

Therefore the author of the *Ekottara* asks the monks to fight carnal desire like warriors fighting their enemies.[22] We see two different practices of meditation mentioned in *Ekottara* too. They are the meditation upon impurity and the meditation upon impermanence. These meditations are mental disciplines, and the early Buddhists believed that through such meditations the monks could solve problems of carnal desire and control their thoughts. In *yuan* 27 of the *Ekottara* the author gives a very detailed description of how to practice the meditation on impurity:

> When Duoquishe saw the woman smile, he immediately generated the thought: 'Your (referring to the woman) body is supported by bones and wrapped up in skin. Although it looks like a beautiful vase, in fact all kinds of impure elements are contained in it. (Your physical appearance) deceives people and makes them crazy.' At that time, Duoquishe looked at the woman from her head to feet and felt nothing worth being attached to. (He therefore meditated on) the impurities of thirty-six elements inside the body.[23]

The *Ekottara* also gives the method of the meditation upon impermanence. The author of *yuan* 12 says:

> Our desires are impermanent. If one does not realize that our desires are impermanent, he will suffer greatly.... Now suppose you see a kṣatriya's daughter, a brahmin's daughter, an elder's daughter who is about 14, 15, 16 years old, who is not too tall, not too short, not too plump, not too skinny, not too fair, not too dark, and looks the most beautiful among all. When one just sees her, he will experience the desire for sensual pleasure. This desire is called the desire for form (*rūpa*). This so-called desire (for form or a woman's body) is (the cause of suffering) to be understood thus: Supposing you meditate upon the same women, in her eighties, nineties, or even a hundred years old. Her skin complexion is changed. She has no teeth, with little white hair. Her body looks dirty and is with wrinkles.... After meditating on the beautiful woman you meditate on the old one, don't you think that the desire for a woman's body is (a cause of) suffering? Supposing you meditate on the same old woman who is sick in her bed again. Lying there she cannot control her excretions, nor can she move around. After meditating on the beautiful woman, you meditate on the sick woman, don't you think that the desire for a woman's body is a great suffering? Supposing you meditate on the same woman who is dead....[24]

The two types of mental disciplines are used very often. Usually a monk only chooses one of these types of meditation to ward off his carnal desire.

Monks take women as objects of meditation in the two kinds of mental exercises. This is the context where the early monks talk about women. In order to help their monks ward off carnal desire, the early Buddhist teachers encouraged their monks to conceptualize the impure and polluting image of a woman, usually a woman's dirty or impure body, to be meditated upon. Therefore in their literature, they often liken a woman's body to excrements, woman's speech to confusion and woman's mental activities to evil and poisonous snakes.[25]

Some scholars still argue over whether Buddhist prejudice against women was due to internal factors, or caused by some external influence. Many of them suggest that the prejudice may have been imposed from outside. Misu Nagata is one of them. He suggests that the Kusanas' promotion of Brahmanism (or caste discrimination) in the beginning of the Mahāyānic movement may have influenced Buddhist practitioners into taking action to change their attitude towards women as well.[26] We are informed that in the Buddha's day, women enjoyed equal treatment in the *saṅgha*.[27] But nobody knows when the situation changed so that women no longer enjoyed equal treatment and worse still, were condemned everywhere in the early literature.

It took several centuries for Buddhism to become a common culture of Asia. During its development, Buddhist practitioners, especially elites, confronted all kinds of problems, doctrinal and practical, in the context of different cultures and different people. In the process of maintaining the tradition of *brahmacarya*, the early monks may have been responsible for gradually transforming the conceptualized image of women utilized at the disciplinary level into reality. The process of transformation may have taken a while. At the end of it, women came to be held in prejudice in both social and religious circles. Although this prejudice is contrary to the Buddha's "original"[28] teaching, yet a prejudiced view of women did emerge in the Buddhist tradition due to the development of sectarian ideas. However, we should not be unmindful of the context in which such a prejudice emerged, namely, the need for the *bhikṣus* to practice the *brahmacarya* without generating carnal desires, through the practice of good conduct and meditation.

The Mahīsāsaka View of Women

It seems that when sectarianism emerged in the Buddhist tradition, every practitioner accepted the view that women are impure and polluting. During the early period, women were not regarded as an issue, for according to the records, we don't see anyone arguing over the impurity of women. But the situation changed when the sectarian Buddhists came to argue whether women can attain enlightenment (Buddhahood). According to the *Nāgadatta*, when the sectarian Buddhists disagreed with each other over the issue, women's welfare became the center of debates. In the Chinese records, we notice at least three sectarian schools involved in the debates. These are the Mahīsāsakas, the Sarvāstivādins, and the early Mahāyānists (the Śūnyavādins).

The Mahīsāsaka was the only school which stood against the idea that women can attain Buddhahood. Their opinions over the issue can be found in both the Sarvāstivāda and the Mahīsāsaka literature. But why in the Sarvāstivāda literature as well? Two reasons may be adduced: (1) In the Buddhist history, the Sarvāstivādins may have held direct debates with the Mahīsāsakas over the issue; and (2) the Sarvāstivāda view of women could really emerge as a result of the criticism of the Mahīsāsaka view, as is evident from the *Nāgadatta*. Therefore, from the Sarvāstivāda literature, such as the *Nāgadatta*, we get a glimpse of the Mahīsāsakas' view of women as well. The *Mahis. V.* and the *Sūtra Spoken by Buddha on the Prophecy of Gautami* (hereafter, *Pro. Gautami*)[29] are the two representative works of the Mahīsāsakas. In these two texts, the Mahīsāsaka view of women is very clearly defined.

In the *Nāgadatta*, Māra, who represents the Mahīsāsakas and takes the disguise of Nāgadatta's father, holds a debate with Nāgadatta over the issue. Through the contents of the debates, we can see the views of the two schools on women. Let me cite the core of the debates here:

> Māra therefore took the disguise of Nāgadatta's father and said thus to Nāgadatta: 'Your thought is too serious. Buddhahood is too difficult to attain. It takes a hundred thousand *niyutas* of *koṭis* of *kalpas* to become a Buddha. Since few people attain Buddhahood in this world, why don't you attain Arhathood? For the experience of Arhathood is the same as that of *nirvāṇa*: moreover, it is easy to attain Arhathood....' Nāgadatta said: 'It is not as father tells me. Although an Arhat and a Buddha attain the same *nirvāṇa*, yet their achievements in regard to enlightening living beings are different. A Buddha's wisdom is like empty space of the ten quarters, which can enlighten innumerable people. But an Arhat's wisdom is inferior.... Māra said: 'I have not even heard that a woman can be reborn as a *cakravartin*, how can you be reborn as a Buddha? It takes too long to attain Buddhahood, why not seek for the Arhathood and attain *nirvāṇa* soon?' Nāgadatta replied: 'I also have heard that a woman cannot be reborn as a *cakravartin*, a Sakra, a Brahma, and a Buddha, and yet I shall make the right effort to transform any woman's body (*strīkāya*) into a man's. For I have heard that those respectable ones, by the practice of *bodhisattvacaryā* for a hundred thousand *niyutas* of *koṭis* of *kalpas* diligently attain Buddhahood.'[30]

In this debate, the Mahīsāsakas uphold the theory that women have the five obstacles and therefore cannot attain Buddhahood. The Mahīsāsaka conception of women's five obstacles is posed against the theory of the Sarvāstivādin which holds that through the practice of transformation of the body, women can attain Buddhahood. These two conflicting theories over the issue as to whether women can attain

Buddhahood, are in fact established upon two contradictory sets of doctrines. These doctrines are recorded in Vasumitra's treatise, *Yibu*. On each of these doctrines, these two schools hold contradictory views. The set of doctrines belonging to the Mahīsāsaka is listed as follows:

1. There is nothing which can transmigrate from one existence to another.
2. There is no intermediate state of existence (*antārabhāva*).
3. No heretic can gain the five supernatural powers.
4. Good *karma* cannot become the cause of existence.[31]

The Vātsīputriyas, like other Sarvāstivādins, believe that the existence of *pudgala* (I or me) is real. Influenced by the Sarvāstivādin belief in the existence of *pudgala*, the Vātsīputriya advocated that "one (*pudgala*) can transmigrate from one existence to another."[32] If a *pudgala* can transmigrate from one existence to another, the form (*rūpa* or *kāya*) can be transformed while the transmigration takes place. With this understanding, the Vātsīputriya suggested that women can change their sex and attain Buddhahood when they transmigrate from one existence to another. This is what I call the theory of the transformation of the body (*kāya-vivarta*). The Vātsīputriya belief in the transformation of the body is also based upon another of their views, that is, "a heretic can gain the five supernatural powers."[33] The Vātsīputriya include women in the category of "heretic," and say that women can also attain the status of Buddha, Sakra, Brahma, universal monarch, and Māra along with the five supernatural powers. The Vātsīputriyas also upheld that if a woman has a great initial religious commitment, such as the ability to generate *bodhicitta* or to perform a religious suicide, (as the *Nāgadatta* states[34]), as her foundation for practicing *bodhisattvacaryā*, she can definitely transform her body or sex in a future life. For this reason, they advocated that "good *karma* can become the cause of existence."[35]

The Vātsīputriyas also recognized the existence of *antarābhāvaa (intermediate existence)*.[36] Therefore the author of the Nāgadatta maintains that the transformation of a woman's body takes place during the antarābhāva. The antarābhāva is a period of existence between the immediate post-death and rebirth. The author of the Nāgadatta uses a very suggestive description to convince his readers how Nāgadatta goes through the *antarābhāva* and takes the exercise of transformation of the body. He thus writes:

> Now I (Nāgadatta) shall seek refuge in you. O Great Lord, I shall offer this body as I offer flowers to you. Having thus said to the Buddha, she jumped

> from the (seventh) floor of the building to commit suicide. Before she reached the ground, and when she was still in the air, she transformed her woman's body (*strīkāya*) into a man's body.[37]

Nāgadatta's religious suicide is suggested in the act of "jumping," and the existence of *antarābhāva* is indicated by the period "before she reached the ground, and when she was still in the air." During that time the author says, "she transformed her woman's body (*strīkāya*) into a man's."

The Sarvāstivāda (the Vātsīputriya) theory that women can attain Buddhahood through the practice of transformation of the body, as the *Nāgadatta* states, is completely refuted by the Mahīsāsakas. The Mahīsāsakas hold a set of doctrines which are completely contrary to those of the Sarvāstivādins. First of all, by including women in the category of "heretic," they deny the idea that women can obtain the powers of a Buddha, a Sakra, a Brahma, or a universal monarch.[38] From this the theory of women's five obstacles is derived. In both the *Mahis. V.* and the *Pro. Gautami* we hear the Mahīsāsakas talking very loudly about this theory:

> A woman cannot gain the five supernatural powers. She cannot be reborn as a Tathāgata who has no attachment and has attained full enlightenment. She cannot be reborn as a Sakra, a Māra, a Brahma, or a *rājā-cakravatin*. But a man can gain the five supernatural powers. He can be reborn as a Tathāgata who has no attachment and has attained full enlightenment. He can also be reborn as a *rājā-cakravatin*, a Sakra, a Brahma, or a Māra.[39]

The author of the *Pro. Gautami* states very clearly that women cannot gain the five supernatural powers. Therefore, the belief that women cannot be reborn as the Tathāgata who has no attachment and has attained full enlightenment is derived from the above mentioned theory of women's five obstacles. Because of the refutation of the Sarvāstivāda doctrines cited and discussed above, the Mahīsāsakas subsequently denied the existence of *antarābhāva* (doctrine 2) and the theory which says, "one can transmigrate from one existence to another" (doctrine 1). Since the Sarvāstivāda theory of the transformation of the body is basically established upon the beliefs in the existence of *antarābhāva* and possibility of transmigration, the Mahīsāsakas, in opposing these two doctrines, also deny the idea that a woman can attain Buddhahood and advocate the theory that women have five obstacles.

When the Mahīsāsakas put women in the category of "heretic," they include nuns also. This is evident in the story of the establishment of the first female *saṅgha*, as stated in both the *Mahis. V.* and the *Pro. Gautami*. In the story, the authors of these two texts mention women's five obstacles at the end of their description of the Buddha's granting Mahāpajāpati permission to establish the first female *saṅgha*.[40] The reference to these five obstacles coming at the end of the report regarding the establishment of the female *saṅgha* implies that the Mahīsāsakas discouraged women from leading a homeless life. This attitude of the Mahīsāsakas can be verified by the practices of the eight extra rules (*gurudharma*) which is also stated in both the *Mahis. V.* and the *Pro. Gautami* as part of a nun's ordination.[41]

In the story of the establishment of the first female *saṅgha*, the Buddha's stepmother Mahāpajāpati is said to have received the ordination only after requesting the Buddha three times to grant her and her fellow women practitioners permission to lead a life of the homeless. Although the Buddha finally granted her request, yet he asked women to observe the eight extra rules or the eight chief untransgressable rules as part of their ordination. These eight rules are:

1. *Bhikṣunis* have to ask for the disciplinary methods from monks every half month.
2. *Bhikṣunis* cannot have their rainy-season (*vassa*) retreat in a place where there are no monks.
3. *Bhikṣunis* should hold (*pavāraṇa*) in front of the same *saṅgha*, with regard to the three matters (namely, what has been seen, what has been heard and what has been suspected).
4. When a *bhikṣuni*, as a novice, has been trained for two years, she should ask for higher ordination (*upasampadā*) from both *saṅghas*.
5. A *bhikṣuni* cannot revile or abuse a *bhikṣu*, nor can she talk about a *bhikṣu's* offenses or perversions in a layman's house.
6. The official admonition by *bhikṣunis* of *bhikṣus* is forbidden, whereas the official admonition of *bhikṣunis* by *bhikṣus* is not forbidden.
7. A *bhikṣuni* who has been guilty of a serious offense has to observe the *mānatta* (confession) discipline for a half month under the supervision of the two *saṅghas*. When the observance of the *mānatta* penalty is over, she has to ask for pardon from the two *saṅghas* consisting of twenty members in each group.
8. A *bhikṣuni*, even of a hundred years standing, should make salutation to, and should rise up, in the presence of a monk, even if he is newly ordained.[42]

The unequal treatment of the female *saṅgha* is another sign of the Mahīsāsakas' prejudice against women. The eighth rule is an obvious discouragement of the nuns from adopting a homeless life and practicing the Buddhist way of life. It is a suggestion that even if a nun has spent a long time practicing Buddhism, her effort in the practice of *brahmacarya* is in vain for her religious achievement is considered to be less than that of a newly ordained monk. The eight extra rules are seen scattered in many othdr sectarian *vinaya* literature, such as, the *Buddhabhāṣita-mahāprajāpati-bhikṣunī-sūtra* (hereafter, *Buddhabhāṣita*)[43] and the *Dharmaguptaka-karma* (hereafter. *D.K.*)[44] but it is only in the *Mahis. V.* that the reason why nuns have to observe the eight extra rules is explained. In the *Mahis. V.*, the Buddha, in explaining why Mahāpajāpati has to observe rules, such as the eighth one, says thus to Ānanda:

> The reason that I ask women to observe rules, such as the eighth one, is that it is difficult for women to practice Buddhism for they have five obstacles. They cannot be reborn as a Sakra, a Māra, a Brahma, a *rājā-cakravatin* and a *dharma*-king of the three realms (Buddha). Should I have not bestowed the ordination the Buddhist *dharma* could have lasted for a thousand years. Now I let them go forth to the homeless, the Buddhist *dharma* can only last for five hundred years.[45]

It is very obvious that the Mahīsāsakas did not believe that a woman can change either her nature or her physical existence by the practice of Buddhism.

The fourth doctrine attributed earlier to the Mahīsāsakas explains their denial of a nun's ability to practice Buddhism. According to that doctrine the Mahīsāsakas disagreed with the Sarvāstivāda belief that "good karma can become the cause of existence." According to the Sarvāstivādins, a woman's unusual religious commitment, such as generating *bodhicitta* or performing suicide, can become a healthy cause in determining her next existence. Basically the Mahīsāsakas also accept the law of *karma*, like the other sectarian schools. That means they also believe that whatever kind of seed a man sows, that sort of fruit he will reap. But, this kind of Buddhist law of *karma* is only applied to men, or more specifically to the male Mahīsāsaka practitioners. The third doctrine attributed to them exclude the "heretic" from the category of people who can obtain the five supernatural powers. Since women are included in the category of "heretic," certainly a nun's religious effort does not count and is excluded from the law of *karma*. For this reason, the fourth doctrine applied only to women and other "heretics."

The Mahīsāsaka prejudice against women is based upon the traditional view of women. Like some of the other early Buddhist practitioners, they did not trust women, even nuns. This explains why they restricted the nuns' social and religious activities in the *saṅgha*. Sometimes they liken the nuns' existence to hail which damages a good harvest. The *Pro. Gautami* says:

'I shall not let women go forth to lead the homeless life, O Ānanda. If I allow them the practice of *brahmacarya* will exist no more. It is just like a family which has more women than men. As such, will the family become prosperous?' (Ānanda) said: 'No, My Lord.' 'So it is, O Ānanda, if I let women go forth to the homeless, the *brahmacarya* will not last long. It is just like hail dropping in the paddy-fields. The grains, like rice and wheat, will be destroyed completely.[46]

Should the issue of women not have become an important one in the history of Buddhism, the sectarian schools would not have debated it again and again. The Mahīsāsakas' view of women is the most conservative and prejudiced among those of the debating schools. Many contemporary scholars fail to realize that the issue of women in Buddhism is a debatable one, and therefore their interpretations of the theory of women's five obstacles and the theory of transformation of the body vary. For instance, Diana Y. Paul classifies the Mahāyānic *sūtras* into three types. According to her, these three types of texts depict the women's role as a *bodhisattva* as follows:

1. denial of a woman's entrance into Buddhaland,
2. acceptance of women as lower-state *bodhisattva*,
3. acceptance of women as advanced *bodhisattvas* and imminent Buddhas.[47]

She gives the *Pure Land Sūtra*[48] as the most notable work of the first type and suggests that "the famous thirty-fourth vow of the text does not preclude the possibility of women's progress in the bodhisattva vehicle. Even so, the implication points to the necessity of a male nature for such progress. In order to be born in the land of Amitābha, one must have a male nature. Because of the *bodhisattva's* vow, there was the acknowledgment that women could be reborn as men in the next life and then realize spiritual growth."[49]

Concerning the second type of sūtra, she notes:

The majority of Mahāyāna sūtras fall into the second category. While women are acknowledged as spiritual assistants to the Buddha, on the one hand, they are relegated, on the other hand, to a lower stage of development than their male counterpart. This subordination of the woman's authority to that of man's reflects both the social order of India at that time and the monastic hierarchical structure of the community wherein even the most senior nun must be deferential to the youngest novice monk. The majority of *sūtra* literature is representative of this group, but one concession is made, however, to those advocating an egalitarian view toward all human beings. A narrative known as the 'transformation of sex' (*parivṛttavyañjana*) plays an important role in advocating a more equitable sociopolitical order.[50]

When Diana Paul gives the *Pure Land Sūtra* as an example of the first type of *sūtras*, she mentions that "Because of the *bodhisattva's* vow, there was the acknowledgment that women could be reborn as men in the next life and then realize spiritual growth." It seems that Paul does not realize that the *Pure Land Sūtra* is also an example of her second category of texts. The view that "women could be reborn as men in the next life and then realize spiritual growth" is a Sarvāstivāda view of women which advocates the idea of transformation of sex (or body), an idea that she mentions as a main theme of her second type of *sūtras*. In fact, Paul does not explain the first type of text for us.

If the first type represents a "denial of a woman's entrance into Buddhaland," that literature should reflect the Mahīsāsaka view of women. It is true that the Mahīsāsaka view of women does not appear as frequently as that of the Sarvāstivādins. The Mahīsāsaka view appears in Mahāyānic texts, such as the *Saddharma* and the *Surya*. However, they do not identify the view as that of the Mahīsāsakas.

The Sarvāstivāda view of women was adopted by the Early Mahāyānists at the beginning of their movement. This is witnessed in the *Pure Land Sūtra* and the *Aṣṭa*. But the view was refuted by the Śūnyavādins during the more advanced stage of Mahāyāna (ca. 150 A.D.) In many works compiled during this period, we can see that the Early Mahāyānists (Śūnyavādins) create many female *bodhisattvas* to take care of the Sarvāstivāda theory of transformation of the body. These female *bodhisattvas* use the method of *upāyakauśalya* (skill in means) to refute the Sarvāstivāda view of women. For instance, in the *Vimalakīrtinirdeśa-sūtra* (hereafter, *Vim. Nir.*) the *devi* (a created or transformed female *bodhisattva*) uses both perfect eloquence and magical power to debate with the Sarvāstivāda representative, Śāriputra, over the issue of transformation of the body.[51] The *devi's* major argument used to criticize the Sarvāstivāda view of women is that, since every existence is unreal or empty (*śūnya*), the existence of a woman or a man too is unreal.[52] The Mahāyānists upheld an entirely different view of existence from that of Sarvāstivādins. They therefore denied the idea of transformation of the body as well as of the existence of a woman or a man.

Upholding a philosophy which considers every existence (*dharma*) to be unreal, these Mahāyānists certainly could not accept the Sarvāstivāda view of women based on the belief that the existence of *pudgala* is real. We notice that many Mahāyānic works were altered after the decline of the movement (ca. 250 A.D.), and in these altered texts, the Sarvāstivāda view or the Mahīsāsaka view of women appears, and these represent the second view or the third view of women listed by Diana Paul.

Although Diana Paul notices the juxtaposition of views of women in these altered texts, yet she does not think that such juxtaposition stands in the way of women's welfare. Instead, she suggests that, "some texts represent a dualistic system of beliefs and values, in which women are excluded from the fulfillment of their religious conviction. Others reflect a nondualistic system in which women are included as fully human and religious."[53]

It seems that Diana Paul believes that a sectarian school, such as the Early Mahāyāna or the Śūnyavādins, could advocate more than one view of women, and that these views could even be contrary to each other.

The fact that the Early Mahāyānists upheld a view of women only after the mature period of their movement may be confirmed by the following evidence: (1) the Early Mahāyānists had no reason to accept a view that was contrary to their teaching, which they themselves refuted. (2) Not every text written in the mature period by the Early Mahāyānists upholds the second view of women.[54] That means some of the Early Mahāyānic texts, not altered by later hands, show that the Early Mahāyānists recognized the view that a *dharma* is neither male nor female. (3) We have much evidence to show that the Early Mahāyānic teachings were given new interpretations after its decline. The Early Mahāyānic texts were altered either by inserting the sectarian doctrines, such as those of the Sarvāstivādins,[55] or by reinterpreting the Early Mahāyānic concepts by giving sectarian meanings. For instance, the concept of *upāyakauśalya* was altered mechanically to the sectarian meaning of *upāya*.[56]

Thus, a Śūnyavādin appears just like a Sarvāstivādin or a Mahīsāsaka who upholds only one view of women. The juxtaposition of views of women found in the Mahāyānic texts demonstrate that the texts were altered. For this reason, I doubt whether we can classify the Mahāyānic texts in terms of the roles they assign to women, as Diana Paul does in her book *Women in Buddhism*.

We indeed can find three types of women depicted in the Mahāyānic texts, but these views do not all belong to the Mahāyānic school. Only one of them belongs to the Early Mahāyāna and the rest belong to the Mahīsāsakas and the Sarvāstivādins. Diana Paul's classification of the Mahāyānic *sūtras* gives the misleading impression that the Mahāyāna more specifically, the Early Mahāyāna or the Śūnyavādins, upheld three different views of women.

The only set of rules which deals with the interaction between the male *saṅgha* and the female *saṅgha* belongs to the Mahīsāsaka. Therefore, many sectarian schools adopt the rules in their *vinaya* literatures. But not every sectarian school which adopts these eight rules agrees with the contents of the eight chief rules recorded in the *Mahis. V.* We notice that in some *vinaya* literature, the eighth rule, which says that "A *bhikṣuni*, even of a hundred years standing, should make salutation to and should rise up in the presence of a monk, even if he is newly ordained," is not adopted. For instance, the rule is not adopted by the author of the *Mahas. V.*[57] Many schools adopt the fourth rule but disagree with its content recorded in the *Mahis. V.* Such is the rule recorded in the *Mahas. V.*,[58] the *Caturvaggavinaya*[59] (hereafter, Catur. V.) translated by Zhu Fonian and Buddhayasas in A.D. 408, and the Dharmaguptaka-karma[60] (hereafter, D.K.) translated by Tan Wuti in 254 A.D. The rule recorded in the *Mahas. V.* agrees with that of the *Mahis. V.*, while the rule recorded in both the Catur. V. and *D.K.*, has a different statement on the *upasampadā* initiation. According to the *Mahis. V.*; a *bhikṣuni* has to ask for the *upasampadā* initiation from both *saṅghas*. But the rule adopted by the *Catur. V.* and the *D.K.* says that "a *bhikṣuni*, as a novice trained for two years, should ask for the *upasampadā* initiation from the male *saṅgha*." The *Catur. V.* and the *D.K.* are the Dharmaguptaka works, and are consistent with the statement of the fourth rule. The author of the *Mahas. V.* accepts the fourth rule of the *Mahis. V.*, yet rejects the imposition of the eighth rule. Therefore, the adaptation of the eight rules vary from school to school.

The disagreements on the contents of the eight chief rules practically caused a serious problem for the Chinese Saṅgha, especially after the first Chinese Female Saṅgha was established in 375 A.D. According to the *Biographies of Buddhist Nuns* (hereafter, *BBN*), a Kasmiri monk called Dharmagupta ordained the first four Chinese nuns in the year of 357 A.D. and established the first Chinese Female Saṅgha on the basis of the Mahāsaṅghika *vinaya*, i.e., the *karma* and the *Mahāsaṅghika-bhikṣuni-vinaya*.[61] It is said that the newly established Chinese Female Saṅgha was rejected by some members of the Saṅgha at that time.[62] The main reason given in the Chinese records for the disapproval of the establishment of the Chinese Female Saṅgha is that "the ordination of the four Buddhist nuns by Dharmagupta was not complete."[63] Contemporary scholars, such as Zhiqing Lin, argue that the "incompletion of the ordination" is due to the fact that, "the four Buddhist nuns did not ask for the *upasampadā* initiation from both *saṅghas*."[64]

It is true that the first four Buddhist nuns, even though they followed the Mahāsaṅghika *vinaya* and *karma*, did not actually observe the rule which says that, "A *bhikṣuni* should ask for the *upasampadā* from both *saṅgha*." However, before the establishment of the first Chinese Female Saṅgha, the Chinese did not have a concrete idea about a woman's ordination. What they could follow at that time was the inadequate conception relating to the eight chief rules recorded in the Mahāsaṅghika texts and the controversial contents of eight chief rules recorded in the Dharmaguptaka *karma*.

The establishment of the first Chinese Female Saṅgha and its rejection by some certainly instigated the study of sectarian *vinayas* at that time. Not long after the establishment of the first Chinese Female Saṅgha, Fa Xian left China for India seeking for the sectarian *vinayas*.[65] He brought back the *Mahāsaṅghika-vinaya* and the *Mahīsāsaka-vinaya*.[66] Before both the *Mahas V.* and the *Mahis. V.* were translated into Chinese in 418 A.D. and 423 A.D. and *Sarvāstivāda-vinaya* was also translated by Punyatara in 404 A.D.[67]

It seems that the question whether a *bhikṣuni* should ask for the *upasampadā* initiation from two *saṅghas* has also become an issue debated by the members of the Saṅgha after the establishment of the first Female Saṅgha in China. Approaching the thirties of the 5th century A.D., because of the translation of the *Mahis. V.* and communication with Sri Lanka,[68] the Chinese Saṅgha with the assistance from the emperor Wen of the earlier Song Dynasty 420–479 A.D. decided to hold the second official ordination for the Chinese Buddhist nuns and settle the issue.

It is said that under the recommendation of *brāmaṇas* Hui Guang and Hui Zhong, the emperor Wen invited Gunavarman to come to China.[69] Gunavarman was a native Kasmiri, yet he spent many years studying Buddhism in Sri Lanka before he came to China in 431 A.D.[70] After Gunavarman's arrival in China, the Chinese *Saṅgha* decided to re-establish the Chinese Female Saṅgha with his help. Gunavarman therefore asked the ship owner Nandi to transport eleven Sri Lankan nuns for the purpose of forming the Chinese Female *Saṅgha*.[71] Since Gunavarman died before the ritual actually took place in 433 A.D., the second Chinese Female Saṅgha was established under the guidance of Saṅghavarman.[72] It is said that on the occasion more than three hundred Chinese Buddhist nuns were re-ordained.[73] The second official ordination of the Chinese nuns took place about 76 years after the first.

Fa Xian's obtaining of the *Mahis. V.* from Sri Lanka and Gunavarman's contact with that country explain why the Chinese Saṅgha at that time agreed to bring Buddhist nuns from Sri Lanka, and also the fact that the Mahīsāsaka teaching was prevalent in that country between the second half of the 4th century A.D. and the first half of the 5th century A.D. The translation of the *Mahis. V.* and the arrival of Gunavarman in China suggest that the Mahīsāsaka teaching was also an important part of Buddhist studies in China at that time. The Chinese interest in the Mahīsāsaka teaching directly influenced the Chinese view on the Buddhist nuns' observance of the eight chief rules. Under the influence of the Mahīsāsaka view of women, the Chinese Saṅgha, at that time, had valid reasons to re-establish the Female Saṅgha. This is the reason why the issue as to whether a *bhikṣuni* should ask for *upasampadā* initiation from both *saṅghas* is said to have been settled in the year 433 A.D.[74]

Before the re-establishment of the Chinese Female Saṅgha, we notice that many Buddhist nuns were very active in both the royal courts and intellectual societies.[75] Their activities indicate that even though members of the Chinese Saṅgha were debating over the issue, yet they did not have any authority to control Buddhist nuns' social and religious activities. However, the situation changed after the second Chinese Female Saṅgha was established in 433 A.D. for we notice that the Chinese nuns were not as active as before. This, of course, is due to the imposition of the eight chief rules of the Mahīsāsakas on the Chinese Female Saṅgha. The imposition of the eight chief rules directed the Buddhist nuns in China to live a restricted and dependent life in the *saṅgha*.

Conclusion

The Mahīsāsakas finally won the debate over the issue of ordination in China. Although this is the case, it does not mean that the Mahīsāsaka view of women that got entrenched in the practice of Buddhism is better than those of other sectarian schools. For a sectarian attitude towards women is determined by the teachings (doctrines) of the particular school, and this is clarified by the analysis of the Mahīsāsaka view and the Sarvāstivāda views of women mentioned above. Certainly the mere adaptation of the Mahīsāsaka view of women embodied in the eight chief rules does not mean that this view of women or view of nuns is more comprehensive than those of other sectarian schools. This explains why the author of the *Mahas. V.* did not accept the eighth rule.

However, the rejection of the first Chinese Female Saṅgha as an illegitimate one or its establishment as an "incomplete act" is indeed very questionable. Ever since the imposition of the eight chief rules on the Chinese Female Saṅgha, the Chinese Buddhist nuns have observed these rules faithfully and without any questions. Even today, they follow the eight chief rules because of their observance of the *Catur. V.*

The Mahīsāsaka view of women is only a sectarian view of women, which is the most unkind and conservative view ever established in the history of Buddhism. After considering the evidence presented above one wonders whether we should be as pessimistic, as Nancy Auer Falk, regarding the damage inflicted by these rules. Nancy A. Falk thus says:

> The discriminatory provisions meant that women would never be leaders in the life of the whole community or have any decisive voice in shaping its direction.[76]

NOTES

1. The *Yibu zhonglun lun* was translated by Xianzhuang in the 7th century A.D. The work is said to have been composed by the Sarvāstivādin scholar, Vasumitra, in the first century A.D. The earliest Chinese translation was done by Zhen Ti in the Cheng dynasty (557–589 A.D.). Concerning the chronology of the Sarvāstivādins, see *T*. 2031, vol. 49, 15b.
2. Nalinakasha Dutt, *Buddhist Sects in India* (Delhi: Motilal Banarsidass, 1978), 121.
3. *Ibid*.
4. The *Sūtra Spoken by Buddha on the Girl Nāgadatta* was first translated into Chinese by Zhi Qian in Wu dynasty (220–280 A.D.). The second Chinese translation done by Zhu Fahu or Dharmaraksa of the Western Jin dynasty (265–316 A.D) is composed in the form of verse and has a prelude placed in front of the text that is not found in Zhi Quian's version composed in prose. See *T*. 556, vol. 14, 909–11.
5. According to the *Yibu zhonglun lun*, the Vātsīputriyavāda branched out from the Sarvāstivāda. The doctrines listed under the Vātsīputriyavāda are: (1) because of the existence of *pudgala* every one can transmigrate from one existence to another, and (2) a heretic can also obtain the five supernatural powers... etc. See *T*. 2031, 16c. Since the idea that "good *karma* can become the cause of existence" is upheld by the Sarvāstivādins as a general belief, the Vātsīputriyavāda advocates the theory, too. See, the *Yibu*, ibid. In the first translation of the *Yibu*, under the doctrines of the Vātsīputriyavāda, also mentions that "a *bodhisattva* is born in the *antarābhāva*," see *T*. 2034, vol. 49, 22a. Therefore, what are recorded in N. Dutt's *Buddhist Sects* concerning the doctrines of the Sarvāstivādins and identical with the doctrines mentioned in the *Nāgadatta*, are the Vātsīputriyavāda beliefs. See N. Dutt, *Buddhist Sects*, 125 and 170. See also *T*. 556, 909–911 and the detailed discussion later.
6. 100–250 A.D. set as a period of the Early Mahāyānic movement is used by many contemporary scholars, such as Masao Shizutani and Lewis R. Lancaster. See Masao Shizutani, *Shoki Daijo Bukkyo no Seritsu Kotei* (Kyoto: Hyakkaen, 1974), 47–49. See also, Lewis R. Lancaster, "An Early Mahāyāna...Sermon about the Body of the Buddha and the Making of Images," *Artibus Asia*, vol. xxvi, 1/2, (1974), 278.
7. See the *Aśokadatta-vyākaraṇa sūtra*, translated by Zhu Fahu, *T*. 337, vol. 12, 88c; the *Buddhasaṅgiti sūtra* translated by Zhu Fahu, *T*. 810, vol. 17, 768b, 14ff; the *Candrottara-dārikā-vyākaraṇa-sūtra*, translated by Jñānagupta in 591 A.D., *T*. 480, vol. 14, 620b; the *Manjuśrī-vikrīḍita-sūtra*, translated by Zhu Fahu, *T*. 817, vol. 17, 818c, 13, and 223a; the *Ratnastrī paripṛcchā-sūtra* translated by Zhu Fahu, *T*. 339, vol. 13, 460b, 11ff; the *Strīvivarta-vyākaraṇa sūtra 2*, translated by Zhu Fahu, *T*. 563, vol. 14, 914a, 9; the *Sūtra on Sumati*, translated by Zhu Fahu, *T*. 334, vol. 12, 78a, 13ff; the *Upāyakauśalya-sūtra* or the *Strīvīvarta-vyākaraṇa-sūtra 1*, translated by Zhu Fahu, *T*. 565, vol. 14, 927b; the *Vimaladatta-paripṛcchā-*

sūtra, translated by Zhu Fahu, *T*. 338, vol. 12, 96c; the *Vimalakīrti-nirdeśa-sūtra*, translated by Zhi Qian, *T*. 474, vol. 14, 964b, 11ff; the *Sutra Spoken by Buddha on Yantizhe's Perfect Eloquence*, translator unknown, *T*. 580, vol. 14, 278. See also Cheng-mei Ku, the *Mahāyānic View of Women*, (a dissertation submitted to the University of Wisconsin, 1984), 1–15.

8. The *Aṣṭa* is said to be translated into Chinese by Lokaksema or Zhi Lojiaqian in A.D. 179. See the *Kaiyuan shijiao lu*, *T*. 2154, vol. 55, 479a.
9. The *Saddharmapuṇḍarīka-sūtra* was first translated into Chinese by Zhu Fahu. The Mahīsāsaka view of women is mentioned in the text as the second view of women, see *T*. 263, vol. 9. 106a. A different edition called *Satan fantuoli jing* was translated into Chinese around the same time of Zhu Fahu's translation of the text. In the latter's version, the Mahīsāsaka view of women is not mentioned. See *T*. 265, vol. 9, 192.
10. The *Sūryajiḥmīkaraṇa-prabhā-sūtra* was translated into Chinese by Nie Chengyuan of the Western Jin dynasty. The Mahīsāsaka view of women is the third view of women placed behind the Mahāyānic view and the Sarvāstivāda view, in the text, see *T*. 638, vol. 15. 541.
11. See discussion later.
12. The *Forty-Two Sections* is said to be the earliest Chinese Buddhist text edited by two Central Asian monks, Zhu Falan and Kāśyapa Mātanga. See the *Kaiyuan lu*, *T*. 2154, vol. 55, 478. Chinese Buddhologist Yongtong Tang suggests that the contents of the *Forty-two S*. are identical with many of the Pali texts. See Yongtong Tang, *Han Wei Liangjin Nanpeicao Fojiao Shi* (Taipei: Commercial Publication, 1961), 31–46. See also the *Forty-two S*., *T*. 784, vol. 17, 723b, 27ff.
13. The *Mahāsaṅghikavinaya* was translated into Chinese by Buddhabhadra and Fa Xian in A.D. 418. In the text, the author, in telling Yasa's story, says that "you ought not to enjoy lust with women." See *T*. 1425, vol. 22, 229b, 15.
14. The *Mahas, V*., 267a.
15. See the *Mahas, V*., *T*. 1425, 235c. See also Munetada Suzuki, *Kompon Daijo* (Tokyo: Gannando Shoten, 1977), 35.
16. Ibid., 233–38.
17. The *Sūtra Spoken by Buddha on Ananda's Fellow Student* is an elaboration of the version recorded in *juan* 27 of the *Ekottarāgama*, *T*. 149. vol. 2, 874–875, and was translated by An Shigao in the second half of the second century A.D., see *T*. 125, vol. 2, 700c.
18. The *Mahas. V*., 229, 25.
19. The *Forty-two*, 723b, 27ff.
20. The *Mahīsāsakavinaya* was translated by Buddhajiva and Fa Xian in 423 A.D. The rule see *T*. 1421, vol. 22, 38.
21. See *E.A*., *T*. 125, 700c, 4.
22. The *E.A*., 687a, 9ff.
23. *Ibid*., 701b.

24. *Ibid*., 605b–606a.
25. See the *AFS*., 874–75.
26. Mizu Nagata, "The View of Women in the Mahāprajñā-pāramitā śāstra," *JIBS*, vol. xxviii, no. 2 (1980), 200–203.
27. See Meena Talim, *Women in Early Buddhist Literature* (Bombay: University of Bombay, 1972). See also I.B. Honer, *Women under Primitive Buddhism* (London: George Routledge and Sons, 1930).
28. *Ibid*.
29. The *Sūtra Spoken by Buddha on the Prophecy of Gautamī* was translated into Chinese by Hui Jian of the Earlier Song dynasty (A.D. 420–479), *T*. 60, vol. 1, 856–58. The part talking about the Mahīsāsaka view of women is consistent with what we see in the *Mahis. V*. I therefore codify the text as a work of the Mahīsāsakas.
30. The *Nāgadatta*, *T*. 557, vol. 14, 909–10.
31. The *Yibu*, *T*. 2031, vol. 49, 17a. See also N. Dutt, *Buddhist Sects*, 125.
32. See footnote 5.
33. *Ibid*.
34. *Ibid*. See also the *Nāgadata*, 909–10.
35. See footnote 5.
36. *Ibid*. See also Cheng Lu, *Introduction to the Chinese Buddhist Thought* (Taipei: Tienhua Publication, 1982), 82.
37. See the *Nāgadatta*, 910a.
38. The *Pro. Gautami*, 858, 1ff.
39. *Ibid*. See also the *Mahis. V*., 186a.
40. *Ibid*.
41. The *Mahis*. V. 185–86.
42. The eight chief rules often arranged differently in different sectarian *vinaya*. The one recorded here is taken from the *Mahis. V*., 185.
43. The *Buddhabhāṣita-mahāprajāpatī-bhikṣuni-sūtra* is collected in the Record of the Northern Liang dynasty (A.D. 397–439). The translator's name is unknown. This text comprises two sections. The first section talks about the story of Mahāpajāpati's ordination, where the Mahīsāsaka belief of women's five obstacles and eight rules are mentioned as the prelude of the Sarvāstivāda view of women, i.e., the idea of transformation. The writing style in this section is similar to that of the *G. Nāgadatta* and can be considered as a *sūtra* literature. The second section talks about the practices and rules that a Sarvāstivādin nun ought to follow. Among these practices the practice of self-introspection is considered as the most important. A nun is asked to observe the practice of self-introspection all the time. She has to watch herself very carefully and tell herself that she is the obstacle of the monks' practice of *brahmacarya*. The writing style of the second section can be considered as a *vinaya* literature. This text is collected in the *Vinaya Piṭaka*, *T*. 1478, vol. 24, 945–55. According to Dutt, the Sarvāstivādins had a tendency to mix up the *vinaya* and *sūtra* literatures, while the Theras kept them separate. N.

Dutt, *The Spread of Buddhism and the Buddhist Schools* (New Delhi: Rajesh Publications, 1925), 156. This text is one of the examples of what N. Dutt means by the "case of mix up."

44. The *Dharmaguptaka-karma* was translated by Dharmasatya or Tan Ti in A.D. 254, *T.* 1433, vol. 1, 1057a.
45. The *Mahis. V.*, 186a, 7ff.
46. The *Pro. Gautami*, *T.* 60, vol. 1, 856-c.
47. Diana Y. Paul and Frances Wilson, *Women in Buddhism* (California: Asian Humanities Press, 1979), 169.
48. *Ibid.*
49. *Ibid.*, 170.
50. *Ibid.*
51. The *Vimalakīrtinirdeśa-sūtra* was first translated into Chinese by a native translator called Yan Fodiao in A.D. 184. But the version is lost. The present version (first) was translated by Zhi Qian. The debate over the issue of whether women can transform their female bodies into the male is recorded in *T.* 474, vol. 14, 523a, 14ff.
52. *Ibid.*
53. Diana Y. Paul, *Women in Buddhism*, xv.
54. For instance, in the *Manjuśrī-vikrīḍita-sūtra*, the *Ratnastrī-paripṛcchā sūtra*, the *Vimalakīrti-nirdeśa-sūtra* and the *Sutra Spoken by Buddha on Yantizhe's Perfect Eloquence*, we don't see the second view of women listed. These four texts are codified by me as the Early Mahāyānic products. See *T.* 817, *T.* 339. *T.* 474, and *T.* 580. See also Cheng-mei Ku, the *Mahāyānic View of Women: A Doctrinal Study* (A thesis submitted to the Graduate School of the University of Wisconsin, Madison, 1984), 1–18.
55. See the texts mentioned in footnote 7. See also Cheng-mei Ku, the *Mahāyānic View of Women*, 10.
56. Cheng-mei Ku, the *Mahāyānic View of Women*, 15–18, and 134–151.
57. See the *Mahas, V.* 514b, 533a, and 541c. The author of the text did not accept the entire set of the eight chief rules.
58. *Ibid.*, 514b.
59. The *Catur. V.*, *T.* 1428, vol. 22, 764a.
60. The text is also called *Karma*. The contents of the eight chief rules of the text basically are consistent with that of being recorded in the *Catur. V.*, *T.* 1433, vol. 22, pp. 1056c–1057a.
61. See the *Biography of Jin Jian* recorded in the *BBN*, *T.* 2063, vol. 50, 934c.
62. See the *Biography of Hui Go* recorded in the *BBN*, *T.* 2063, 937 b-c. See also the *Biographies of the Buddhist Monks* (hereafter, *BBM*) edited by Hui Jiao of the Liang dynasty (A.D. 502– 557), *T.* 2059, vol. 50, 341a-b. See also Zhiqing Lin, "Transmission of Sila," *Chinese Buddhist* (Peking: Zhishi Publication, 1981, vol. 2, 335–36).

63. *Ibid.*
64. Zhiqing Lin, "Transmission of Sila," 336.
65. Fa Xian left China in 398 A.D. (or 399, A.D.). In Central India he obtained the *Mahas. V.* and the *Sarvāstivāda vinaya*, and in Ceylon he obtained the *Mahis. V.* See the *Biography of Fa Xian*, recorded in the *BBM*, 338A.
66. *Ibid.*
67. See the *Biography of Punyatara* recorded in the *BBM*, *T.* 2059, 333a. According to the record, Punyatara specialized in the *Sarvāstivāda-vinaya*. He was asked to recite the text, and Kumārajīva translated the text into Chinese.
68. Before Gunavarman came to China there were some Sri Lankan Buddhist nuns in China already. Apparently the communication with Sri Lanka was quite a phenomenon at that time. See *Biography of Gunavarman* recorded in *BBM*, *T.* 2059, 341b. See also the *Biography of Hui Go*, *T.* 2063, 939c, and the discussion later.
69. See the *Biography of Gunavarman*, *T.* 2059, 340c.
70. *Ibid.*, 340–341.
71. See the *Biography of Sanghavarman* recorded in *BBM*, *T.* 2059, 342b.
73. See the *Biography of Hui Go*, *T.* 2063, 939c.
74. *Ibid.* See also Zhiqing Lin, "Transmission of Sila," 336.
75. See the *Biography of Dao Xin* recorded in *BBN*, *T.* 2063, 936c. Dao Xi specialized in the *Sad. Pun.*, the *Vim. Nir.* and the *Aṣṭa*. Who gave public lectures on these texts in the Eastern Temple of Lo Yang. See also the *Biography of Dao Ron* recorded in *BBN*, *T.* 2063, 936b. Dao Ron was well respected by the emperor Ming of the Jin dynasty and the emperor Jian Wen, because of her ascetic power. According to the record, she performed Buddhist rituals very often in the courts.
76. Nancy Auer Faulk and Rita M. Gross, *Unspoken World* (San Francisco: Harper and Row, 1980), 216.

9

THE SIGNIFICANCE OF PARITTA AND ITS APPLICATION IN THE THERAVĀDA TRADITION

Hammalawa Saddhatissa

Three Aspects of Religion

IT IS AN UNDENIABLE FACT that in every religion in the world, followers have developed many aspects beyond the original teachings and practices, such as the philosophical, moral, and benedictory aspects. For over 2,500 years, various Buddhist traditions spread over many parts of the world as a practical religion fulfilling the religious needs of many millions. Along with meditation and other practices, the aforementioned three aspects were gradually developed in various cultures.

The benedictory aspect is the apotropaic phenomenon which has affinity with enchantment and charm against evil influences. It is concerned with the important events of the world such as illness and health, drought and rain, calamity and tranquility, danger and security, famine and prosperity. It is commonly accepted that there are ghosts, demons, and evil forces in the world who could adversely influence and harm human beings and their environment.

Therefore, in order to avoid these situations, recourse has been sought in various forms of benedictions. The chanting of *paritta*[1] falls into the category of benediction along with invoking the blessings of the Triple Gem, the Buddha, Dhamma, and Sangha. Paritta is regarded as a safeguard against dangers and through it security is sought. Like incantation and invocation, as well as blessings in other religions, *paritta* is apotropaic, and it is chanted to extricate the believer from any calamity which befalls him, or to avert potential calamities and dangers. Although adherents use sufficient naturalistic techniques for all the problems of life, it is customary to resort to apotropaic rituals like chanting *paritta*, *bodhipuja*, and the like. It originated during the Buddha's lifetime, but the method of chanting underwent a gradual transformation. After the introduction of Buddhism to Sri Lanka in the 3rd century B.C., a book entitled the *Catubhāṇavarapāli*[2] was compiled by the monks of Mahāvihāra at Anurādhapura, containing appropriate texts gleaned from the Suttā-piṭaka for the purpose of chanting.

From time immemorial most of mankind has thought that there was a sense and a power in sounds and in the composition of selected syllables in the form of words, hymns, or verses. Accordingly, the tradition of chanting verses and prayers, and the uttering of mantras on occasions of happiness, joy, and sorrow is widely prevalent in diverse traditions.

The Buddhist believes that there is a great power in the words that came out of the mouth of the Buddha, who was totally free from all defilements such as desire, anger, and ignorance. It is said, "The word which the Buddha speaks, a sure, safe guide to nibbāna, puts an end to all ill will, that is the word supreme."[3] "Yet one sentence of the Dhamma is better which, if a man hears, he is at peace."[4] Attentively listening and following the words of the Buddha (*Buddhavacana*), one could obtain happiness in this life and in the next and would be able to attain the ultimate, everlasting bliss of *nibbāna*. Those of his sayings which have been formalized for chanting by the Theravāda tradition are known as *paritta*.

Paritta means "protection," "safeguard," or "safety." It is a collection of texts which is recited mainly on special occasions. They are still widely used by Buddhists in Burma, Thailand, Cambodia, Laos, Sri Lanka, and other Theravāda countries for warding off evil influences or to bring about fortune or prosperity. It is primarily used for invoking blessings and benediction, but in some cases has become a formula for exorcism. The *paritta* ceremony is used on all possible occasions, i.e., before the building of a new house, at the house-warming, when embarking on a journey, inaugurating any project, and also in times of illness, epidemic, drought, famine, flood, and other disasters. Newborn babies and newly married couples are also blessed by the chanting of *paritta*. The *dhāraṇī* is the counterpart of *paritta* in Mahāyāna. They are also designed for averting various evils or securing certain desired blessings.

The *dhāraṇīs* or protective "spells" constitute a large and important part of Mahāyāna literature.[5] *Dhāraṇī* is a synonym of *rakṣā* and Pali *paritta*. The need for benediction in very early times was fulfilled by Brahmans with Vedic *mantras*, especially those of the Atharvaveda. It played an important part in the religious life of the people.

We have already seen how the Buddhists in Sri Lanka and other Theravāda countries used *paritta* for similar ends. In the same way, Mahāyāna Buddhists transformed some *sūtras* into magical formulae. There are numerous invocations of deities of both Buddhist and Hindu origin. Generally speaking, in the daily life of the Buddhist, the benedictory and apotropaic aspects are very much present, as in other great religions.

Buddhist philosophy teaches a theory of *kamma* (action) and *vipāka* (consequences). *Vipāka*, however, could be mitigated by various methods which are again stipulated in the teaching.

There is a common belief that most of the afflictions and misfortunes that men suffer are due to the anger of malignant beings or forces. It is therefore believed that the anger of these spirits can be appeased by chanting *paritta*. The *paritta* ceremony is professed to have sanctity in the surroundings as well as among the listeners, but its effect may be reduced or negated by the effects of grave *kamma*, by the presence of mental defilements in the listeners, or by lack of faith.

Paritta text (in Sinhalese: *pirit-pota* and *piruvāna-potvahanse*) consists of four parts. According to the Theravāda tradition in Sri Lanka, it should be memorized by all *bhikkhus* before completion of their *nissaya* period.[6]

The word *paritta* first occurs in the *Cullavagga*[7] and the Aṅguttara-nikāya[8] in connection with the Khandha-paritta as a protection for oneself. The occasion for the delivery of this discourse was the death of a monk by snake-bite. When the Buddha was asked why the monk died, he said, "It was because he did not show loving-kindness (mettā) towards the four tribes of snakes, namely: Virūpakkha, Erapatha, Chabyaputta and Kaṇha Gotamaka. If he had practiced *mettā*, he would not have died." Rhys Davids comments on this as follows:

> "The profession of amity, according to Buddhist doctrine, was no mere matter of petty speech. It was to accompany an express psychic suffusion of the hostile man or beast or spirit with benign, fraternal emotion—with *mettā*. For strong was the conviction, from *sutta* to Vinaya to Buddhaghosa's Visuddhimagga,

that 'thoughts are things,' that psychical action, emotional or intellectual, is capable of working like a force among forces. Europe may yet come round further to this Indian attitude."[9]

The *Mahāmaṅgala-sutta*[10] is often recited as a means of protection. It deals with auspicious signs or blessings. From ancient times all sorts of objects and events were regarded as good or bad omens which could bring about good luck or misfortune. Maṅgalas, or auspicious signs such as benedictions, feeding of Brahmans and ascetics, garlands of flowers, music, and singing of the birds were regarded as blessings. In the Mahāmaṅgala-sutta, however, thirty-eight entirely different and practical blessings have been elucidated. These include avoidance of bad company, association with the wise, honoring those worthy of honor, rendering service to parents, and to wife and children, giving alms, patience, obedience,etc. This *sutta* was preached by the Buddha in response to a god who asked about auspicious signs. It is similar to the *Śvastyāyana gāthā*[11] and also occurs in the Mahāmaṅgala-jātaka,[12] thus showing the great antiquity of these blessings.

The Ratana-sutta[13] is one of the finest lyrics in early Pali poetry. It contains charming hymns of praise of the Buddhist Holy Triad – Buddha, Dhamma, and Saṅgha. It is recited to ward off dangers and to secure prosperity. Vaiśali, a prosperous city of the democratic Licchavi people, was plagued by drought, famine, and an epidemic of a contagious disease called "snake-breath" (ahivātaka); non-human beings were attracted to the city due to the stench of the corpses. The Licchavis requested the Buddha to come from Rājagaha. When the Buddha came, he stopped at the city gate and addressed the Venerable Ānanda, "Learn this 'Jewel Sutta' and with the Licchavi princes perform a safeguarding ceremony (paritta) in procession around the city, taking with you materials for making ceremonial offerings." Then Ānanda took water in the Buddha's begging bowl and walked around the city sprinkling the water and reciting the *sutta*. The demons fled on hearing the sutta and the sickness of the people abated. The Buddha then entered the city hall (*santhāgāra*) and preached the same *Ratana-sutta* to the assembly. In the time of King Upatissa (370–412 AD), in Sri Lanka, the island was afflicted by a drought, and on the advice of the monks this *sutta* was recited and the calamities disappeared. The king issued a decree advising the use of the same ceremony in the future.[14]

The *Karaṇīya-mettā-sutta*[15] was preached by the Buddha to some monks who had complained that they were being harassed by evil forces while they were meditating in the forest. The Buddha taught them the Karaṇīya-mettā-sutta and told them to cultivate the meditation on loving-kindness. He instructed them to return to the same forest grove assuring them that those beings would wish them well. The rest of the suttas selected for inclusion in the category of *paritta* were chosen mainly for two reasons. One is diffusing the benedictory nature of ethical and moral teaching. The other is that some suttas are pleasing to deities. For clarification of this, a brief review of the *suttas* follows.

The *Catubhāṇavara Pāli* opens with the *saraṇāgamana* (taking refuge with the Buddha, Dhamma and Saṅgha),[16] *dasasikkhāpada* (the ten precepts),[17] *dvattiṃsākāra* (meditation on the 32 types of bodily impurity),[18] and the *paccavekkhaṇa* (introspection on the use of the four requisites).[19] Then the *suttas* begin; the first one being the *Dasadhamma-sutta,*[20] which contains the ten virtues which should be often recollected and practiced by Buddhist monks. After this they invoke the blessings with asseveration. Then follow the three main *suttas*: *Mahāmaṅgala*, *Ratana*, and *Karaṇīyamettā*, which in turn are followed in sequence by the *Khandhaparitta* (cultivation of loving-kindness towards snakes),[21] the *Mettānisaṃsā* (on the benefits of friendship and loyalty),[22] the *Mora paritta* (a short verse said to have been recited by a peacock to secure protection by praising the sun god, the Arahants, and the Buddhas).[23] These are followed by the *Candaparitta*[24] and the Suriyaparitta,[25] which are connected with the virtues of the Buddha and to the relief of affliction that comes from Rahu (eclipse) by paying homage to and reflecting on the Buddha. Next are the Dhajagga sutta (the crest of banner),[26] which embodies the noble qualities of the Triple Gem and is a specific remedy against fear, the three Bojjhaṅga-suttas, recited by Cunda to the Buddha,[27] by Buddha to Mahākassapa,[28] and by the Buddha to Mahā-Mogallāna,[29] respectively, on the occasion of illness. These contain the seven factors of enlightenment. Then there is the *Girimānanda-sutta*,[30] which contains a list of different ailments and constitutes a meditation on the impurity of the body taught by the Buddha to Ānanda for the benefit of Girimānanda who was grievously sick, the *Isigili-sutta* (an enumeration of Paccekabuddhas),[31] and the *Aṭānāṭiya-sutta*[32] which was approved by the Buddha on the recommendation of four guardian deities for protection from demons. On one occasion, the Buddha was staying on the Vultures' Peak near Rājagaha, and the Four Great Kings, the guardian deities of the four quarters of the celestial regions, came to tell the Buddha that there were many demons in the land who neither believed in the Buddha nor abided by the five precepts, and who would frighten and attack monks and lay devotees who retired to lonely places for meditation.

Therefore the great King Vessavana (or Kuvera) wanted to present the Āṭānāṭiya paritta to the Buddha so that it might be recited to make the displeased demons pleased; and consequently the monks, nuns and lay devotees would be at ease, guarded, protected, and unharmed. It mentions gods and yakkhas (or demons) who are not pleased with the Buddha. The Buddha gave his consent by remaining silent so King Vessavana recited this *paritta-sutta*. Then the four guardian deities departed. When the night had passed, the Buddha addressed the monks and requested that they learn the *Aṭānāṭiya-sutta* by heart and to recite it constantly. It is regarded as pertaining to the welfare of the disciples and as a saving chant (*rakkha manta*) to get rid of evil forces. The *Dhammacakkha-sutta*[33] was the first sermon of the Buddha to the five ascetics who were his companions. Because many thousands of deities assemble to listen to this discourse, people believe that on occasions of reciting it deities are pleased and so protect the listeners. Māhasamaya-sutta (Celestial Retinue of the Buddha),[34] mentions some gods who are found on this earth, and also in the regions above. It gives us a long list of gods. The Parābhava-sutta[35] is the antithesis of the *Maṅgala-sutta*. It was taught by the Buddha to a god who visited him and asked about the cause of one's downfall. To put it in a nutshell, the Buddha told him, that the love of Dhamma leads to progress, hating Dhamma leads to downfall.

Āḷavaka-sutta[36] consists of the answers given by the Buddha to a demon, Āḷavaka, who asked a number of questions. The Aggikabhāradvāja or Vasala-sutta[37] explains the true meaning of an outcast. The Buddha explained to Aggikabhāradvāja that by deeds alone one becomes an outcast or a noble man, and not by birth. The Kasībhāradvāja-sutta[38] contains a conversation with a Brahman on ethics and moral principles. The Saccavibhaṅga-sutta[39] explains the Four Noble Truths in detail. The Āṭānāṭiya-sutta[40] is recited at the conclusion of paritta ceremonies. It is regarded as having influence which pervades a hundred million world systems and is therefore recited with great fervor. It opens with salutations to the seven Buddhas beginning with Vipassi and is followed by the names of other gods and super-human beings. This sutta is considered most powerful in exorcism. The recipient should take the five precepts in the company of the congregation, and then the *paritta* is recited. If the evil forces do not leave, the *paritta* recitation is repeated, beginning with the *Maṅgala-sutta*. The evil force should be told that if it leaves the victim, the merits of the offerings will be transferred to him, and he should leave out of respect for the Saṅgha. After declaring that the evil force must obey the word of the Buddha, the *Aṭānāṭiya-sutta* is once again recited.

The Paritta Ceremony

Any social function, religious festival, or ceremony is incomplete without the recital of *paritta*. It could be a simple ceremony or an elaborate one as the occasion demands. A special pavilion (*maṇḍapa*) is constructed and gaily decorated with flowers and leaves. The text of a palm-leaf manuscript is brought together with the sacred relic casket, which is installed on the altar. First, the Buddha *puja* (offering to the Buddha) is performed followed by casting of flowers, fried grain, mustard, broken rice, jasmine, and a special kind of grass (heleropogon hirtus). Then the *paritta* thread (*pirit nūla*) is twisted around a new clay pot filled with water, and the thread is hung around the interior of the pavilion and tied around the *paritta* text and the relic casket, and is then held by the monks and by all the congregation. The sponsor then invites the monks to recite *paritta* with the following *gāthā*:

Vipattipaṭibāhāya sabbasampattisiddhiyā,
Sabbadukkhavināsāya parittaṃ brūtha maṅgalaṃ,
Sabbabhayavināsāya parittaṃ brūtha maṅgalaṃ,
Sabbarogavināsāya parittaṃ brūtha maṅgalaṃ.
In order to ward off all calamities, to fulfill all fortunes,
For the destruction of all sufferings, please recite the *parittas*,
For the destruction of all fears, please recite the *parittas*,
For the destruction of all diseases, please recite the *parittas*.

Then the leading monk invites the devas as follows:

Samantā cakkhavālesu
Attrāgācchantu devatā
Saddhammaṃ munirājassa
Suṇantu saggamokkhadaṃ.
In all the world systems
May all the devatās come to listen to
The good law of the king of sages
Which gives divine and nibbānic bliss.

Then the assembled monks chant the three *suttas*, *Maṅgala*, *Ratana*, and *Karaṇīyametta, concluding with the Jayamaṅgala gātha*, and thereafter chant the whole text of the *paritta* from beginning to end. The period of chanting can be as little as one hour or as much as one week, depending on the occasion. In the case of the ceremony lasting a whole day or a whole week, after the preliminary ceremonies are over, the chanting is done by two monks who are replaced by another pair every hour. This takes care of the continuity in chanting. When the chanting continues for several days, the whole group of monks assembles three times a day to chant the three main *suttas*, and on the morning of the last day a grand procession is organized to send a messenger of the gods (*devadūta*) to the neighboring monastery. The messenger conveys messages to the guardian deities, who are invited to attend the ceremony prior to its conclusion so that they may partake of its benefits. Until the messenger returns, the officiating monks remain seated, but the chanting is suspended. Then when the messenger returns with the *devatās* the *parittas* are chanted more energetically than ever. An admonition (*anusāsana*) is delivered to the assembly, and the *Āṭānāṭiya-sutta* is recited for the last time to bring the ceremony to a close. By then the thread and the water have become sacred, and the sacred water is distributed among the participants who take a sip of it, and the thread is tied around their wrists or necks by the monks. All these observances are regarded as protective measures against danger, and are blessings.

The Buddhists in the Theravāda countries esteem the recital of *paritta* as a means to ward off malignant forces and to promote health and prosperity. The general rule underlying the chanting of *paritta* is to emanate loving-kindness and compassion towards all beings. The chanting of loving-kindness is no mere sentimentality; it is imbued with psychical and emotional power. The reciters must have great love towards the listeners; and the listeners must listen with respectful attention, and thereby contribute toward the realization of the expected result.

Another means of achieving the efficacy of *paritta* is through the Asseveration of Truth (*saccakiriya*) by the monks.

The *paritta* ceremony is not an abberation of Buddhism, but is in perfect harmony with it. Of the forty meditation objects enumerated in the *Visuddhmagga*, one is the recollection of *dhamma* (*dhammānussati*). Therefore, the recital of *paritta* is another way of practicing *dhammānussati*.[41]

Hindu Influence

During the Polonnaruwa period (1017–1235 A.D.), more than during the Anurdhapura period, Hindu elements have been gradually assimilated into the *paritta* ceremony. During the Kandy period (1494–1815), several ritual elements of the ceremony were given prominence, thus making the ceremony more glamorous and devotional, so that Hindu devotees could participate with the Buddhists on such occasions. These include aspects such as the messenger of the deities (*devadūta*), the gateway message (*dorakaḍa-asna*), and the admonition (*anusāsana*).

Rites, rituals, and ceremonies were not the essentials of Buddha's teaching, but these elegant and innocent practices afford inspiration, devotion, unity, goodwill, and friendship among religiously oriented people. In my opinion, however, traditions and superstitions play a big part in the *paritta* ceremony, and these are not totally lacking in practical value.

The Efficacy of Paritta

The *paritta* ceremony is a form of *saccakiriya* (Sk. *satyakriyā*), i.e., the asseveration of the truth of something which is embodied in the *parittas*. It is believed that by the assertion of truth, evil influences and diseases are warded off. This means the establishing of oneself in the power of the truth to gain one's end. The Buddha said, "The truth protects him who lives by it" (*dhammo have rakkhati dhammacārī*). This power of truth is also said to permeate the whole world through the practice of loving-kindness (*mettā*). The power of love is limitless in warding off evil influences, healing diseases, and promoting health.

There are many stories which depict the efficacy of *paritta*, and the following one is well known among Buddhists: Two Brahmins became ascetics, but after practicing austerities together for forty-eight years, one of them reverted to lay life. Some years later he returned with his wife and child to pay obeisance to his former companion. Blessing the man and wife he said "Long life to you but not to the child." When questioned about the reason for this, the ascetic told them that their son had only seven days to live, and suggested that they should see the Buddha to ask him if there was any means of averting the child's death. They did so, and the Buddha told them to erect a pavilion outside their house for the recital of *paritta*. The monks recited *paritta* for seven days, and the Buddha did so all night long. At the end of the seven days, the Yakkha Avaruddhaka, to whom the child had been promised, could no longer claim him. The Buddha declared that the boy would live for 120 years, and he was renamed Āyuvaddhana.[42]

The sounds of chanting are regarded as a penetrating and effective force. The power of good thoughts mixed with the vibration of the sound can be transmitted to beings over great distances. It is believed that the sonorous sounds of *paritta* soothe the nervous system, purify the blood, and produce peace and tranquility of mind, thus bringing about harmony of the physical state.

Again, in the *paritta*, there is the power of virtue. One takes the five precepts at the outset. The *Maṅgala*, *Parābhava*, *Āḷavaka*, and *Vasala suttas* describe the benefits of a virtuous life. Listening with reverence to the Dhamma is also a virtue, and virtue is the basis of mental culture (*bhāvanā*) which purifies the mind from the defilements which cause disease and distress.

C.A.F. Rhys Davids, whom we have quoted earlier, was of the opinion that the *parittas* are not alien to Buddhist doctrine, but are as much in harmony with it, as prayer is with theistic religions. She remarks that the harmful spirits are not, as in other cults, cursed, but are blessed with good wishes and suffused with love. Even the most malignant beings are looked upon not as hopelessly and eternally damned, but as erring unfortunates upon their long upward way. These *parittas* are intended to arrange benign agencies on the side of the patient, and to ward off those that may be harmful. She compares them to prayers like Balaam's inspiration, "Let me die the death of the righteous and let my last end be like his."[43]

In the course of his teaching, the Buddha never precluded the practice of what is beneficial. He said:

Jappena mantena subhāsitena
Anuppadānena paveṇiyā vā
Yathā yathā yattha labhetha attham
Tathā tatha tattha parakkameyya
(By chant and charm, well-worded speech
Gifts or by custom rightly kept, Where and whatever good may gotten be
Just there let him exert himself for that.)[44]

A Bactrian king, King Menander (2nd century B.C.) argued with a monk, Venerable Nāgasena, that if the Blessed One said,

"Not in the sky, not in the ocean's midst
Not in the most secluded mountain cleft
Not in the whole wide world is found a spot
Where remaining one could escape the snare of death,"[45]

then the *parittas* like *Ratana*, *Khandha*, *Mora*, *Dhajagga*, *Āṭānāṭiya*, and *Aṅgulimāla* prescribed by the Buddha for the protection of those in danger must be useless. If the *paritta* ceremony is not useless, then the Buddha's statement that there is no escape from death must be false.

To this Nagasena replied, "*Paritta* verses, O king, are meant for those who have some portion of their life left to run. There is no ceremony or artificial means for prolonging the life of one whose allotted span of life has come to an end. And there are three reasons for the failure of *paritta*: the obstruction caused by past *kamma*, the obstruction caused by present defilements, and the obstruction caused by lack of faith. That which is a protection to beings loses its power through faults of those beings' own making."[46]

The Occasions

The Arahant Aṅgulimāla, on the advice of the Buddha, performed the averment of truth on an expectant mother who was suffering the pangs of labor, declaring that he had not intentionally killed any life from the time he became a noble disciple. Immediately she got relief and delivered the child. In Buddhist countries expectant mothers are blessed by this *Aṅgulimāla-paritta*.[47]

It is an indispensable monastic duty (*vatta*) of the residing monks to chant *paritta* every morning and evening. They assemble in one place, either in the Vihāra or under the Bodhi tree. First of all, each one reveals his minor offenses (*āpattidesanā*), and they chant *paritta* in unison. At the end they pay salutation to their teachers and elders. This monastic observance is known as *Vattaparitta* (Sinhalese: *Vatapirita*).

The chanting of *paritta*, either for blessings or for safety at the outset of auspicious work in the Vihāra or in the homes of devotees, is called *Sāntiparitta* (Sinhalese: *Setpirita*). In some cases, *paritta* is chanted for two or three sessions, morning and evening. All-night *paritta* and seven-day *paritta* are also ceremonially conducted by lay devotees as occasion demands. All-night *paritta*, as well as seven-day *paritta*, begins with chanting of three *suttas*: *Mahāmaṅgala*, *Ratana*, and *Karaṇīya-mettā* along with the *Jayamaṅgala-gāthās*. When the entire assemblage of the monks takes part in the recitation, it is called the Mahāparitta (Sinhalese: *Mahapirita*).

NOTES

1. *Paritta*: "Protection" (cf. Sk. *paritrāna*: neuter, *Mānavadharmaśāstra*, Prākrit, *parittana*, n. *trai*; Pali *paritta*, feminine **tā*: n. *ta* to protect, with prefix *pari*: from all directions = protecting from all directions.) Sinhalese, *pirit*.
2. *Bhāṇavara*: term of recital. A literary work of measure: 8 syllables equals one "foot" or quatrain of a poem or sentence, 4 "foots" or quatrains of 32 syllables equals one verse or part: 250 parts of 32 syllables, term or portion of recital, i.e. 800 syllables constitute a *bhāṇavara*. The book contains four (*catu*) such *bhāṇavaras*. The alternative title of this work is *Parittapotthaka* (Sinhalese: *Pirit pota* or *Piruvāna-potvahanse*). The *Catubhāṇavara pāli* has had the following suttas added to it by the Burmese: 14 stanzas of *Paṭhavijayamangala-sutta*, *Anekājati-udāna-gāthā*, *Yadāhave* (3 stanzas), *Jayohi-udāna-gatha*, *Paccayuddesa*, *Paccaya-niddesa*, *Pubbaṇha-sutta*, *Sammāparibbājanīya-sutta*, *Purābheda-sutta*, *Kalahavivāda-sutta*, *Cūlavyūha-sutta*, *Mahāvyūha-sutta*, *Tuvaṭaka-sutta*, *Abhiṇha-sutta*, *Anattalakkhaṇa-sutta*, *Dhammapada*, *Mahāsatipaṭṭhana-sutta*, *Brahmajāla-sutta*, *Chadisapala-sutta*, *Cakkaparitta*, *Parimittajāla-sutta*, *Up-patasanti-sutta*, *Dhāraṇa-sutta* (Board of Ḅuddhasasana, Rangoon, 1950).
3. *S*. 1. 189.
4. *Dh*. v. 102.
5. See *Saddharmapuṇḍarīka-sūtra*, Ch. XXI; *Prajñāpāramitāhṛdaya-sūtras*; *Saddharmalaṅkāvatara-sūtra*, Ch. IX; *Suvarṇaprabha-sūtra*; *Śikṣā-samuccaya*, etc. *The Sanskrit Buddhist Literature of Nepal* by Rajendralal Mitra, Calcutta, 1892, gives 51 *dhāraṇīs*, 194–5. Extra canonical *parittas* have been appended to the text of *paritta*, such as *Jayamaṅgala-gāthā*, *Mahājayamaṅgala-gāthā*, *Jinapañjara*, *Aṭṭhavīsati*, *Aṇa*, *Angulimāla*, *Jaya*, *Sīvali*, *Aggi* (*gini*), *Vassa*, *Vattaka*, *Bojjhṅnga*, etc. These are akin to *dhāraṇīs*. In Burma Pali *dhāraṇīs* are called *dharanas*.

   Nissaya: under the guardianship of the *ācariya* the *bhikkhu* gets his training in the Dhamma-Vinaya and remains under his guidance until he has completed five years after Upasampadā (ordination). The period of *nissaya* may be extended if the trainee does not prove himself able to live without guidance. The period may be extended even for the whole life if it seems he is unable to live according to the discipline. *Piritkatikāvata* (Disciplinary Code of *paritta*) was drafted and constituted by the Saṅghasabhā, Malvatta, Kandy, in 1906.
7. *Vin* 2. 109; *J*. 2. 146.
8. *A*. 2. 72.
9. *Dialogues of the Buddha*, tr. Rhys Davids, PTS, 3. 186.
10. *Khp*, 2–8; Sn, 46.
11. Verses on well-being; hymns which invoke blessings.
12. *Journal of the Pali Text Society*. No. 453.
13. *Khp*. 3–6; Sn. 222-238.
14. *Mahāvamsa*, 37. 189–198.

15. *Khp*. 8–9; Sn. 143–152.
16. *Ibid*., 1.
17. *Ibid*., 1.
18. *Ibid*., 2.
19. *A*. 3. 388.
20. *Ibid*., 5. 87.
21. *Ibid*., 2. 72; Vin. 2, 109.
22. *Ibid*., 5. 342.
23. *J* 2. 33, No.47.
24. *S* 1. 50.
25. *Ibid*., 1. 51.
26. *Ibid*., 1. 281f. *Miln*, 150.
27. *S*. 5. 81.
28. *Ibid*., 5. 80.
29. *Ibid*., 5. 79.
30. *A* 5. 108.
31. *M* 3. 68.
32. *D* 3. 194.
33. *Vin* 1. 10ff.; *S* 5. 420ff.
34. *D* 3. 253.
35. *Sn* pp. 18–20.
36. *Ibid*., pp. 31–33.
37. *Ibid*., pp. 21–25.
38. *Sn*., pp. 12–16 ; *S* 1. 172.
39. *M*. 3. 248.
40. *D*. 3. 194ff.
41. See the *Path of Purification*, tr. by Nyanamoli, Colombo, 1964, 68–230.
42. *DhA*. 2. 235ff.
43. *Dialogues of the Buddha*, *op. cit*., 186–187.
44. *A* 3. 56, 62; *J*. 3. 205; cf. *Mahāvastu*, 290.
45. *Dh*. v. 127, cf. 128; *Petavatthu* 21.
46. *Miln* 150–151.
47. *M* 2. 97; Miln. *op. cit*., 150–151.

10

THE PARITTA CEREMONY OF SRI LANKA

ITS ANTIQUITY AND SYMBOLISM

Lily de Silva

PARITTA, called *pirit* in Sinhala, is a very popular Buddhist ceremony in Sri Lanka. The Pali word *paritta* comes from the Sanskrit *pari+ tra* 'to protect,' and it means protection; therefore *paritta* can best be described as a prophylactic ceremony performed for banishing evil and ushering in good luck.

The indispensable feature of this ceremony is the recitation of particular discourses from the Pali Canon, which have been collected together in an anthology called *Catubhāṇavarapāli* or the *Piruvānapotvahanse*. The anthology comprises 29 *suttas*, called *parittas*, but the most important *suttas* are called the great *parittas* (*mahāpirit*). They consist of the *Ratana-sutta* dealing with the invocation of blessings by the power of the truth (*sacca*) of the infallible virtues of the *Buddha*, *Dhamma*, and the *Saṅgha*, the *Metta-sutta*, advocating the cultivation of loving kindness (*metta*) towards all sentient beings, and the *Mahāmaṅgala-sutta* describing social ethics. The very core themes of *paritta suttas* comprise truth (*sacca*) and loving kindness (*mettā*). Truth when uttered with deep unswerving sincerity and conviction is considered to possess great miraculous power. Similarly loving kindness when cultivated towards all beings without any reservation acts as a protective cover against all types of harm. These are the two themes which form the efficacy of the *paritta* ceremony.

Occasions and Objectives of Performance

Paritta can be performed with dignified simplicity as well as artistic grandeur on all important occasions, be they private and secular, or social and religious. Occasions such as birth, marriage, illness and death, all can be blessed with *paritta*. *Paritta* is recited for a pregnant woman to ensure safe delivery and protection for both mother and child. The *Aṅgulimāla-sutta* is the special discourse recited on such an occasion, and it is never recited for any other event. Just before a wedding *paritta* is recited to bless the couple assuming new responsibilities. During severe illness *paritta* is recited with the hope of eliminating all malign influences, be they demonic, astrological, physical, or karmic in origin and character. The belief is that medicine will exercise its full effect once these hindrances are removed. When a man lies on his death-bed a couple of monks are customarily invited to recite *paritta* for the purpose of diverting the dying man's thoughts to a wholesome theme, as it is believed that the last thought of a dying man influences his next birth. Significant events and achievements in the life of an individual such as building a new house, undertaking a journey abroad, assumption of duty in a new post for the first time, or outstanding success are blessed by this ceremony. Religious festivals are often celebrated with all-night *paritta* ceremonies. National social events such as the New Year's day observance and important public functions such opening a new school or hospital are also occasions which call for the recitation of *paritta*.

Thus *paritta* is performed on a variety of occasions for a variety of purposes. It plays a vital role in all religious and secular activities in the life of a Sinhala Buddhist. It purports to create a climate of general well-being by warding off all types of dangers and fears. It ushers in all that is good and auspicious. It attempts to replace occultism, astrology, and reliance on Hindu deities, though, of course, it has not fully succeeded in ousting them altogether.

Historicity

The rudimentary beginning of *paritta* can be seen in the *Khanda-sutta* of the *Aṅguttara-nikāya*[1] and the Aṅgulimāla-sutta of the *Majjhima-nikāya*[2]. According to the former, a monk died of snakebite, and the Buddha admonished his disciples to cultivate mettā towards all snakes as a measure of protection from such danger. According to the latter *sutta*, Angulimāla makes an assertion of truth (*saccakiriya*), on the advice of the Buddha, to ease the suffering of a woman who had been in labor for seven days. These two episodes belong to the Pali Canon itself, and they go back to the time of the Buddha himself.

Milindapañha[3], which belongs to the first century B.C., mentions six suttas, namely *Ratana-sutta*, *Khandhaparitta*, *Moraparitta*, *Dhajagga-paritta*, *Āṭānāṭiyaparitta* and *Angulimālaparitta* as *parittas* approved by the Buddha. Moreover, there is evidence in this text to believe that *paritta* had already come to be recognized as a healing ritual. Questions are asked whether *paritta* can avert death, how *paritta* becomes effective, and when it is effective and when it is not. In the *Vinayavinicchaya*[4], which is a text on discipline belonging to about the 4th century A.D., there is clear reference to paritta water and *paritta* thread. It says that *paritta* thread should be moistened with *paritta* water before distributing to lay devotees.

The Pali Commentaries of the 5th Century A.D. make it abundantly clear that *paritta* had been established as a fully developed healing ritual. *Paramatthajotikā*, the commentary on *Kuddhakapāṭha*,[5] describes how, on the recommendation of the Buddha, Ānanda recited the Ratana-sutta along the streets of Vesāli, sprinkling water from the Buddha's alms bowl, in order to save the city from the triple scourge of famine, plague, and demonic influence. It is said that demons fled as soon as *paritta* water touched them, and the epidemic subsided.

Now this episode is related at nearly all elaborate *paritta* ceremonies as the prototype of the present-day ritual. The *Dhammapadaṭṭhakathā*[6] contains the episode of the Brahmin child Dighāyu. It was predicted that this child could live only for seven more days as a demon was due to devour him in seven days. To avert the danger Buddha advised the child's father to construct a pavilion (maṇḍapa) and arrange eight or sixteen seats inside and place the child on a small seat in the center. Monks sat on the seats arranged and recited *paritta* for seven days and nights continuously. On the seventh day Buddha also joined the recitation. The demon found no opportunity to get the child and went away disappointed. The child was saved and he enjoyed longevity. In this episode the construction of a pavilion and recitation of *paritta* for seven days are certainly advanced ritual features not found in the previous Vesāli episode. *Sumangalavilāsinī*, the commentary on *Dīghanikāya*[7], contains evidence of further development of the ceremony with the mention of preliminary rites, food, taboos, and ritual accessories such as incense, garlands, and oil lamps.

Thus it is quite clear that nearly all important features present in the paritta ritual of today had developed by the time of the 5th Century

A.D. There is ample evidence in the chronicles[8] of Sri Lanka that *paritta* was practiced as a ritual by kings of ancient Sri Lanka. King Upatissa I caused *paritta* ritual to be performed when the country was vexed with famine and plague during the 4th Century A.D. That is the first-recorded instance of a *paritta* ritual conducted by a king in Sri Lanka. Aggabodhi IV had *paritta* recited several times during the 7th Century A.D. Sena II inscribed the *Ratana-sutta* on a plate of gold and safeguarded his subjects against plague by having *paritta* recited and *paritta* water sprinkled during the 9th Century. In the 12th Century Parakramabahu I had a permanent building called *Pañcasattatimandira* built for *paritta* ceremonies and distribution of *paritta* water and thread.

Inscriptions of Sri Lanka also mention *paritta* several times; the most important one for our purpose states that *nissankalatāmaṇḍapa* built by Nissankamalla was used for the recitation of *paritta*.[9] What is noteworthy in this maṇḍapa is that it contains a miniature *stūpa* at its center, and it can be proven that this is the historical forerunner of the ritual object called *indrakīla* in present-day *paritta* rituals.

These historical references are very valuable as they reveal the impact *paritta* had made on the kings and people of ancient Sri Lanka. As a ritual *paritta* has been remarkably resilient in that its vitality did not fall into oblivion despite colonial domination of the island for nearly five centuries. It forms an integral part of the religious life of the Buddhist laity and clergy even today, and it is no exaggeration to say that *paritta* has remained the Buddhist ritual par excellence in Sri Lanka for centuries.

Paritta as Practiced in Sri Lanka Today

An attempt is now made to give a brief description of the ritual as it is practiced today. Because *paritta* can be performed with varying degrees of complexity, three broad variants are outlined to represent a fair cross section from the simplest to the most elaborate. They are as follows:

1. Sessional *paritta* (Sinhala *varu pirita*);
2. All-night *paritta* (Sinhala *tis paye pirita*)
3. Seven-day *paritta* (Sinhala *sati pirita*)

The indispensable feature and the common factor which runs through all these various forms is the recitation of the *paritta suttas*.

The sessional *paritta* is generally conducted in three, five or seven sessions each lasting about an hour, with two sessions each day in the morning and evening. Three or four monks are invited to a home where they chant *paritta suttas* at a specially prepared place. A pot of water is placed on a table along with a tray of flowers, a coconut oil lamp, a few incense sticks and white thread twisted in three strands wrapped around a betel leaf. The thread is wound around the pot of water and the monks hold it while reciting. The laymen participating in the ritual also hold the thread with hands clasped in veneration. After the recitation at each session the thread is rolled back and placed on the pot of water. At the concluding session benedictory refrains are recited, and *paritta* water and thread are distributed to the participants.

The all-night ceremony is a more elaborate and expensive undertaking. A temporary pavilion called *pirit maṇḍapa/pirit koṭuva* is constructed out of light wood and artistically decorated with cloth, paper, or tender coconut leaves (*gokkola*). The shape of the *maṇḍapa* may be a square or an octagon. It is considered best to keep the entrance to the *maṇḍapa* facing the east. Inside the *maṇḍapa* a minimum of eight or a maximum of sixteen chairs are arranged, and a table of convenient size is placed in the center. They are all covered with freshly laundered white cloth. A white canopy is drawn over the pavilion supported by a network of twine on which are hung tender betel leaves, ironwood leaves, and arecanut flowers. A row of rings made of tender coconut leaves runs along the periphery of the canopy through which passes the *pirit hūya* (a white cord) when the ceremony begins. The whole *maṇḍapa* is beautifully illuminated. Eight *pun-kalas*, vases of plenty as Coomaraswamy[10] calls them, are placed around the *maṇḍapa*. Each of them consists of a new clay pot in which a coconut flower is placed together with a small coconut oil lamp and a few incense sticks.

Inside the *parittamaṇḍapa* a ritual object called the *indrakīla* is constructed. It is fixed in between the two center chairs called *yuga puṭu* (twin chairs), directly opposite the entrance tied together firmly. The *indrakīla* is made with a straight, freshly cut branch of a *sūriya* tree (*Thespesia Populnea*) about six feet long. It is covered with a white, stiff new cloth pleated lengthwise; the cloth is tied on the branch in a couple of places so as to let the cloth puff out in between the knots. At the top, the cloth opens out to form a sort of 'fan.' Behind this structure stands a small arecanut palm with a fully opened coconut flower tied to it. (It is important to remember that there is a pillar called *indrakīla* in the *stūpa* too; and it is believed that this *indrakīla* gives the *stūpa* its sacred character.)

Five items of ritual import called *lada pas mal* (Pali: *laddhapañcamāni pupphāni*, literally meaning "five kinds of flowers") are sprinkled inside the *maṇḍapa*. They consist of white mustard, panic grass (Sinhala: *ītaṇa*), roasted paddy, jasmine buds, and broken rice. A pot of strained water is placed on the table.

Around 8:00 p.m. monks come in procession and take their seats inside the *maṇḍapa*. They bring with them a casket containing bodily relics of the Buddha, an ola leaf, (*Paritta* text and the *pirit hūya*). The *pirit hūya* is a white cord several yards long wrapped round a large bobbin generally made of sandalwood. It is kept in the temple and is taken to all-night *paritta* ceremonies to which the monks of the temple are invited.

The chief householder offers a tray of betel leaves and formally invites the monks to chant *paritta*. The drummers provide loud drum music in a prescribed beat called *magul bera* or auspicious drumming. Simultaneously with its dramatic conclusion, monks start chanting *paritta*. This goes on for about twenty minutes. This phase is called *pirit pe kirīma*, or preliminary chanting. When it comes to a close, drum music resumes and all monks stand up to tie the *pirit hūya*. It is tied connecting the casket of relics, *paritta* text, the pot of water and the *indrakīla*. It is then taken up to the canopy and passed (in a clockwise direction) through the rings made of tender coconut leaves along the periphery of the canopy. When it has fully encircled the canopy it is brought down and passed through the hands of all the monks before it is finally placed back on the table. The *pirit nūla*, i.e., a three-strand white thread wrapped round the panicle of an arecanut flower, is connected to the *pirit hūya* at some point near the canopy. This thread is taken out of the *maṇḍapa* and given to the devotees who are sitting around. Unwinding the skein, the *pirit nūla* is passed round to all the participants who hold the thread with hands clasped in salutation. They take care not to drop the thread on the ground. Thus by means of this thread all participants in the ceremony are connected with the ritually potent objects and the monks inside the *parittamaṇḍapa*.

When the drums stop beating, the next phase of chanting begins. It is called *mahāpirit*, the great *paritta*. This chorus chanting is very impressive, sonorous, and full of religious fervor. After about an hour of such chanting all monks, except two, leave the *maṇḍapa*. The remaining two continue what is called *yuga pirit*, twin *paritta*, and the monks are relieved in pairs every hour, until 3:00 a.m. Then four monks start chanting the *Āṭānāṭiyasutta* in very loud tones suggestive of one purpose of the ceremony, namely exorcism. Around 5:00 a.m., all the monks assemble again in the *maṇḍapa* and chant for about an hour; the ceremony comes to a close with the distribution of *paritta* water and thread.

The monks then return to the monastery and the morning meal is generally prepared and sent to the monastery. But if it is intended to conclude the ceremony with the morning meal (*hīl dāne*) it is offered to the monks in the house itself. Almost always an all-night *paritta* ceremony is followed by a mid-day offering of alms to the monks.

The seven-day *paritta* ceremony corresponds closely to the all-night ceremony, but continues through a whole week. On the seventh day, a young boy dressed as a prince called *devadūtaya*, messenger to the gods, is sent in a procession to *dēvāla* (a shrine dedicated to a god) close by to invite the gods to come and participate in the *paritta* ceremony. The messenger returns in a procession and announces to the monks that the gods have come. This message is couched in highly ornate Sanskritized rhetorical language, and the delivery of this message is an important, impressive part of the ceremony. After the message a monk starts his admonition to the gods who are requested to rejoice in the *paritta* ceremony and share the merit it produced. After this display of oratorical skill, monks chant the *Āṭānāṭiya*, followed by the *mahāpirit*. The ceremony comes to a close with the distribution of *paritta* water and thread. Usually a *sati pirita* is followed by a great almsgiving, and the procedure is the same as for the all-night *paritta* ceremony.

Ritual Significance and Symbolism

Having thus briefly described the ceremony, we are in a position to consider the ritual significance and symbolism of the ritual appurtenances used in the ceremony.

The special ritual object called the *indrakīla* occupies a prominent place in the *parittamaṇḍapa* and no doubt confers a singularly significant symbolic value to the *parittamaṇḍapa*. After a systematic study of the term *indrakīla* through Sanskrit, Pali, and Sinhala literary works, it has been possible to conclude that the *indrakīla* is a synthesis of four symbols, namely:

1. symbol of the limit;
2. symbol of authority;
3. symbol of stability;
4. symbol of the center.

As the Buddhist commentarial tradition[11] has recommended the use of folk ritual appurtenances for the *paritta* ceremony, the symbolism of the *indrakīla* should also be studied in the context of Brahmanical ritual practices. A comparison of the ground plan of the *parittamaṇḍapa* with that of the Vedic sacrificial hall (*yāgasālā*) makes evident the symmetry of the positions occupied by the *indrakīla* in the *parittamaṇḍapa* and the *yūpa* in the *yāgasālā*. The *yūpa* is the sacrificial post in Vedic rituals. A comparison of the *yūpa* and the *indrakīla* shows that the *yūpa* with its cosmic symbolism[12] is the prototype from which evolved the *indrakīla*. Their similarities go beyond symbolism for both are fashioned out of wood, both are white in color, and both have cloth wrapped around them. The *yūpa* carries a wheel called *casāla* at its top in a horizontal position while the *indrakīla* is adorned with a wheel-like object made of white cloth placed in a vertical position.

In Buddhist art the *yūpa* has enjoyed a transparent process of evolution without a change in its nomenclature. The *Divyāvadāna*[13] states that a stone pillar called yūpa was set up in the interior of the dome of a *stūpa*. These *yūpas* were called *indra-kīlas* in Sri Lanka. Paranavitaṇa[14] observes in his study of the *stūpa* in Sri Lanka that these octagonal pillars must have weighed over twenty tons. These huge pillars served no structural purpose; and the labor entailed in hauling them to great heights and setting them up must have been undertaken because they were considered absolutely necessary, according to the religious beliefs of the times, to give the *stūpas* their sacred character.

Now it is clear how the Vedic *yūpa* has been preserved in Buddhist architecture and ritual and how it has survived up to the present day under the name *indrakīla*. This change of nomenclature also is quite significant, for it seems to have been necessitated by the fact that the term *yūpa* is found inadequate to fully express the symbolism when instituted in a Buddhist setting. Here one is reminded of a fundamental principle operating in the diffusion of cultures, vindicated by an exhaustive study of Jewish symbols by Goodenough,[15] namely: When symbols are borrowed from older customs and traditions the value remains constant, but the symbols themselves are intellectually justified in conformity with the tenets of the borrower.

Therefore the center symbolized by the *indrakīla* is neither Mount Meru of Hindu mythology, nor the World Axis which unites the world with heaven for the Vedic sacrificer, but the *bodhimaṇḍa*, the place where the Buddha attained Enlightenment.

The *bodhimaṇḍa* is said to enjoy universal centrality, for the *Dīgha-nikāyā-aṭṭhakathā-ṭīkā*[16] and the Mahābodhivaṃsa[17] call it the navel of the earth. Therefore the indrakīla with its center symbolism is most appropriate for its representation. The *bodhimaṇḍa* is the only steadfast spot in this whole world of change, for it alone remained unmoved even when the entire earth shook with a tremendous roar at the moment of Enlightenment.[18] Hence the suitability of the stability symbolism. According to the *Pūjāvaliya*[19] the bodhimaṇḍa is a great fortress protected by the rampart of the ten *pāramitās*, extending up to the cupola of the *Brahma* world. Hence the suitability of the symbolism of the limit. Even Māra with his vast array of forces could not get past this formidable barrier of the Buddha's authority. Thus it becomes quite clear that the *yūpa* may have been replaced by the *indrakīla* because of the inadequacy of the former to express this composite symbolism. According to some reports[20] the *indrakīla* has also been an object of worship, thus enhancing its suitability to symbolize the most sacred spot on earth, the place where the Buddha attained Enlightenment.

Therefore the conclusion seems quite reasonable that the *indrakīla* ritually recreates the *bodhimaṇḍa* whether it is in a *parittamaṇḍapa* or in a *stūpa*.

The *Nissaṅkalatāmaṇḍapa* which is a permanent pavilion built by King Nissankamalla in the 12th century for the purpose of chanting *paritta* is distinguished by the presence of a miniature *stūpa* at its center. The *indrakīla* is the feature which confers sanctity to the *stūpa* too and in a permanent *parittmaṇḍapa* it was possible to construct a *stūpa* itself to effect the ritual transformation of the place into the *bodhimaṇḍa*. In temporary ritual enclosures used as *parittamaṇḍapas* it was more convenient to improvise the *indrakīla* alone to ritually recreate the *bodhimaṇḍa*.

The most important features in the *bodhimaṇḍa* is the *bodhi* tree itself (*Ficus Religiosa*). As *bodhi* trees are invulnerable it was not possible to cut the branch of the *bodhi* tree even for a *paritta-maṇḍapa*. Therefore a *sūriya* (*Thespesia Populnea*) branch was used to represent the *bodhi* tree. There is striking physical resemblance between the *Ficus Religiosa* and the *Thespesia Populnea*. Moreover there is ample lexical evidence to show that both trees have been designated by identical or similar names in Sanskrit, Pali, Sinhala, and Tamil. *Asvattha*, *kapiṭzhana*, *plakṣa* and *gardabhaṇḍa* are used to denote both the *Ficus Religiosa* and the *Thespesia Populnea* in Sanskrit. In Sinhala the former is called *asaṭu*, while the latter is called *tel asaṭu*,[22] and in Tamil they are called *aracu* and *puvaracu*[23] respectively. This same linguistic affinity has found its way into English as well, for they are called pipal and parspipal.[24] Therefore it is reasonable to conclude that the *sūriya* branch used in the construction of the *indrakīla* represents the sacred *bodhi* tree in the *parittamaṇḍapa*.

The arecanut tree with the fully opened coconut flower represents the *kalpavṛkṣa*, the mythical wish-conferring tree, which Manasara maintains should be constructed in addition to the sacred *asvattha* tree to distinguish a Buddha image.

The fan-shaped object in the *indrakīla* may be interpreted as the *dhammacakka* which traditionally decorates the seat of the Buddha as is evidenced by Amarāvatī *stūpa* sculptures.[26]

The *parittamaṇḍapa* is made to face the east as the Buddha is said to have attained Enlightenment seated under the *bodhi* tree facing the east. Inside the *parittamaṇḍapa* which is thus the ritual recreation of the *bodhimaṇḍa* the sacred Buddhist trinity is assembled, the *Buddha* is represented by the casket of relics, the *Dhamma* is represented by the *paritta* text and the *Saṅgha* by the monks who participate in the chanting. The *pirit hūya* demarcates the sacred area. Thus the most noble Triple Gem, the *Buddha*, *Dhamma* and *Saṅgha* are brought together within the sacred areas of the *bodhimaṇḍa*.

The other ritual appurtenances utilized for the *paritta* ceremony can be broadly classified as those which ward off evil and those which usher in good luck. White mustard and panic grass (*ītaṇa*) are mainly instrumental in banishing evil, the former is also called *rakṣoghna*,[27] demon-killer, while the latter has an epithet meaning spirit-slayer (*bhūtahantṛ*).[28] The arecanut flower is a ritually potent instrument for the removal and absorption of ritual impurities and for imparting fertility.[29] *Pun kalas* represent the Earth Goddess, and in Indian mythology she is also identified with Sri Lakṣmi, the Goddess of Prosperity.[30] Jasmine buds play the positive role of wish fulfillment as it is said that jasmine (*mālati*) has recourse to Viṣṇu (*Māla*) who is the spouse of the Goddess of Prosperity (*Lakṣmi*).[31]

As water has been used in all manner of Brahmanical rituals in ancient India, Buddhists too may have started using water in their prophylactic and benedictive ceremony of *paritta*. According to Vedic mythology, water derived its ritual efficacy from its association with Varuṇa who is one of the greatest gods in the Vedic pantheon.[32] Varuṇa is a sky god, and he is the lord of waters too. He is the moral guardian of the world and upholder of the law and order. He is divine and omniscient. He witnesses men's truth and falsehood. No creature can even wink without his knowing it. Varuṇa punishes wrongdoers with water, and he uses water for curing the penitent too. Though Buddhists did not believe in the ritual efficacy of water derived from Varuṇa, Buddhists started making holy water (*sānti udaka*) by chanting *paritta* over it. It is then believed to possess healing properties. The use of *paritta* thread is an ancient custom traceable to literature of the 4th century A.D.[33] Just like water it derives its efficacy from the chanting of *paritta*, and when worn round the wrist or neck it is believed to form a potent protective ring.

Thus *paritta* is a ritual with a very long recorded history running into the pre-Christian era. It is rich in symbolism, and it communicates a powerful message of well-being, peace, and prosperity to the Buddhists in Theravāda countries, especially Sri Lanka.

NOTES

For more details, please see Lily de Silva, *Paritta: A Historical and Religious Study of the Buddhist Ceremony for Peace and Prosperity in Sri Lanka*. Spolia Zeylanica, vol. 36, Part I, Bulletin of the National Museums of Sri Lanka, Colombo, 1981.

1. *A* 2.72.
2. *M* 2.97.
3. *Miln* 150.
4. *Vinayavinicchaya*, ed. D.Dharmaraksita, Colombo, 1937, vv. 491–492.
5. *Khp*. 164.
6. *DhA*. 2.235–239.
7. *DA* 3.969.
8. *Cūlavaṃsa*, ed. W. Geiger, 2 vols., PTS, London, 1925.
9. *Archaeological Survey of Ceylon*, Annual Report, 1903, 18–20. *Archaeological Survey of Ceylon*. 1911–1912, *Sessional Papers*, 1915, 100.
10. A.K.Coomaraswamy, *Yaksas II*, Smithsonian Miscellaneous Collection, Freer Gallery of Art, Washington, 1928–31, 61–63.
11. *Khp* 164.
12. M. Eliade, *Images and Symbols: Studies in Religious Symbolism*, tr. P. Mairet, London, 1960, 44–45.
13. *Divyāvadāna*, ed. E.B. Cowell and R.A. Neil, Cambridge, 1886, 244.
14. S. Paranavitaṇa, *The Stupa in Ceylon, Memoirs of the Archaeological Survey of Ceylon*, Vol. V, Colombo, 1946, 38.
15. E.R. Goodenough, *Jewish Symbols in the Greco-Roman Period*, 13 vols., Bollingen Foundation, New York, 1953, Vol. XII, 72–73, 133.
16. *Dīghanikāya-aṭṭakathā-tikā, Linatthavaṇṇana*, ed. Lily de Silva, 3 vols., London: PTS, 1970 vol. II, 28.
17. *Mahābodhivaṃsa*, ed. S. Arthur Strong, London PTS, 1891, 50.
18. *Buddhabhāvasahacalatthanabhūta bodhimaṇḍabhūmi*, *Dīghanikāya-aṭṭhakathā-ṭika*, vol. II, 28.
19. *Pūjāvaliya*, ed. K. Nanavimala, Colombo, 1965, 182.
20. *Saddharma-ratnāvaliya*, ed. D.B. Jayatilaka, Colombo, 1928, 488; A.L. Basham, *Wonder that was India*, London, 1954, 203.
21. *Sanskrit-English Dictionary*, ed. M. Monier Williams, O.U.P., London, 1960, *s.v. asvattha, plakṣa* and *kapiṭhana*. *Abhidhānappadīpika*, ed. W. Subhuti, Colombo, 1921, v. 592.
22. J.M. Seneviratna, "Some Ancient Plants and Trees of Ceylon," in *Ceylon Antiquary and Literary Register*, vol. VII, pt. II, Oct. 102.
23. H. Trimen, *Handbook of the Flora of Ceylon*, 5 vols., London, 1893–1900, *s.v. Ficus Religiosa* and *Thespesia Populnea*.
24. *Abhidhānappadīpikā*, v. 592.

25. *Architecture of Manasara*, tr. P.K. Acarya, O.U.P., 1933, 563.
26. J. Burgess, *The Buddhist Stupas of Amarāvati and Jaggeyyapeta* in the Krishna District, Archaeological Survey of Southern India, n.s.vol. I, Madras Presidency, Plates XII, XXIII, fig. 2, XIV, fig. 1, XL fig. 3.
27. *Nāmaliṅgānuśāsanā* (Amarakosha) with the Commentary (Vyākhyāsūdan or Ramasrami) of Bhanuji Dikshit, ed. Pandit Sivadatta, 4th ed., revised by W.L.S. Pansikar, Bombay, 1915, 307.
28. J.M. Campbell, "Spirit Basis of Belief and Custom," in *Indian Antiquary*, vol. XXIV., 226.
29. P. Wirz, *Exorcism and the Art of Healing in Ceylon*, Leiden, 1954, 51, 58.
30. A.K. Coomaraswamy, "Sri Lakṣmi," in *Eastern Art*, vol. I, Philadelphia, 1928–29, 177.
31. *Śabdakalpadruma*, ed. R. Radhakantadeva, Chowkhamba Sanskrit Series Work No. 93, Varanasi - 1 (India), 1961, S.V. *Malati*.
32. *Rigveda*, tr. R.T.H. Griffith, *The Hymns of the Rigveda*, 4 vols., Benares, 1882–1892, 7.49; E.W. Hopkins, *Epic Mythology*, Strassburg, 1915, 117.
33. *Vinayavinicchaya*, ed. D. Dharmaraksita, Colombo, 1937, 491–2.

11

SIGNIFICANCE OF THE RITUAL CONCERNING OFFERINGS TO ANCESTORS IN THERAVĀDA BUDDHISM

P.D. Premasiri

A MAJOR ASPECT OF THE BUDDHA'S TEACHING was its critique of contemporary religious practices. The Buddha's critique was mainly directed against the over-ritualization of religion leading to the loss of all spiritual and ethical meaning and the degeneration of religion into a mere series of mechanical observances of ritual. The Buddhist attitude towards ritual can be seen from its reference to *sīlibbata-parāmāsa* (clinging to rules and rites), an expression used to signify an attitude of over-dependence on ritual which, from the Buddhist perspective, was considered a hindrance to genuine spiritual upliftment of the individual.

Sīlibbata are reckoned in Buddhism among the foremost fetters to be destroyed by the person who enters into the path of spiritual progress.

In the Buddhist critique of ritual an effort was made to show that some rituals involved immorality as in the case of the sacrificial rituals of the Brahmans leading to the killing of animals, while others involved the mere performance of futile acts diverting people from genuine spiritual upliftment, as in the case of bathing in sacred rivers to wash off one's sins. The Buddhist emphasis was on genuine and effective transformation of the inner spiritual nature of man. Ritual can, from the Buddhist point of view, be justified only to the extent that it contributes to spiritual transformation.

Buddhism appears to have recognized the fact that, especially in the case of the ordinary lay people, ritual can be an effective instrument in guiding their spiritual destinies. For there is a natural tendency in man to ritualize his behavior in the face of the more important and striking activities and events of his life such as birth, death, marriage, etc. Whenever possible Buddhism attached a new meaning and significance to contemporary rituals and admitted them to the Buddhist fold, giving them a novel ethical character. The purpose of this paper is to make some observation on the way in which Buddhism attached a new significance to the pre-Buddhistic ritual concerning ancestor worship and transformed an existing ritual to fit in with the moral and pragmatic outlook of Buddhism.

Ancestor worship is regarded as one of the great branches of the religions of mankind. It is believed that the principles of this practice help to keep up the social relations of the living world. The dead ancestor is usually believed to survive in the form of a deity. He is believed to be in continuing relationship with the living, protecting his own family and himself receiving benefits from the family. There are three major reasons for the wide prevalence of ancestor worship among numerous cultures from very ancient times. First, attachment to the dead and the psychological necessity to feel the continuing presence of loved ones who have departed from this world. Second, expectation of benefits from the dead ancestors, especially in the struggle of primitive man for survival. Third, fear of the dead is also a widespread reason for ancestor worship. In many cultures appeals are often made to the departed spirits, imploring them not to return and vex their friends.

In India a vast literature has grown around the ritual of ancestor worship, indicating the importance attached to this ritual in Indian society. It is admitted that even today it is the most important ceremony of the Hindus. The belief in the existence of departed ancestors and the presentation of offerings to them have always formed a part of the

Hindu domestic religion. In the Vedic period it was believed that the spirit of the dead became a *pitṛ* immediately after the disposal of his corpse. According to the original Vedic religion, the dead ancestors survive in the blissful world of the "fathers" (*pitṛloka*) and, like gods, partake of the sacrificial offerings by the people. In the Vedic funeral hymn, the dead man is urged to "go forth by those ancient paths on which the fathers of old have passed away."

The *pitṛs* were considered in the Vedas as the blessed dead who dwell in the third heaven or highest step of Viṣṇu. They are in companionship with *Yama*, the Lord of the Dead, and take their food with the gods. They enjoy *soma* and desire libations prepared for them at the sacrificial offerings of the living. The *pitṛs* look after their worshippers and are invoked by the living to give riches, children and long life. The following formula is found in the Atharvaveda as one to be recited for the invocation of the *pitṛs*: "Come ye O fathers, delectable, by profound roads that the fathers travel; assigning to us life, time and progeny and do ye attach yourself to us with abundance of wealth."[1]

In the Vedic period the ritual of ancestor worship consisted in the casting of sacrificial materials into the fire, a practice which was known as *agnaukaraṇa*. This was probably the *pitṛyajña* sacrifice known to the Ṛgvedic people. Animal sacrifices such as burning of a goat and a cow along with the dead formed an important part of the sacrificial ritual.

Although the Vedic conception of the *pitṛloka* was one of a world of heavenly and blissful existence, in the Brahmanic period the conception of a woeful world, known as the *pretaloka* into which the dead ancestors pass, emerged. In the Gṛhya period the idea was introduced that a man immediately after his death became a *preta* and subsequently became a *pitṛ*, provided that some rites were performed for his release from the *preta* stage. The time span taken for a *preta* to become a *pitṛ* was believed to be a year. According to the *Purāṇas*, as soon as the gross corporeal body of a dead person is burnt the soul of the person takes a subtle body called the *ativāhikaśarīra*. In this state the person is said to suffer from extreme heat and cold, hunger and thirst. The soul could be released from this stage by performing the rite of the offering of *pūraka* lumps. When the soul is released from the subtle body, it acquires the *pretaśarīra*. Still one does not acquire the full-fledged status of a *pitṛ* entitling one to partake of all subsequent rites of ancestor worship.

In the pre-Buddhist Vedic ritual concerning ancestor worship, the emphasis was on the direct transference of material things to the ancestors through offerings made by the living. The term *śrāddha* was used in the Vedic tradition to refer to the rite of ancestor worship. This rite was also known as the *pitṛmedha* sacrifice. In section XXXV of the

Vajasaneyi Saṃhitā of the *Yajurveda*, which contains some funeral verses, is found a description of a ceremony known as *pitṛmedha*. In this ceremony the burnt bones of the dead were placed in an urn and deposited in the earth. Cakes and grains mixed with sesame were placed on bones. Vessels containing articles of food were buried under stones or bricks with the remains of the dead body. Although in the early stages of the Vedic ritual, the practice was the direct offering of food and other sacrificial items to the dead; later the feeding of Brahmanas was introduced as the essential element.

In Buddhism the term *peta* generally meant "departed one." This term also acquired a special meaning when it began to be used to refer to a special class of beings who dwell in the world of *petas* (*petaloka*). The Buddhists, in accordance with the doctrine of *kamma* and rebirth, conceived of a world of ghostly existence called the *pettivisaya*. *Petti-* in *pettivisaya* has a verbal correspondence to the Vedic *pitṛ*; but unlike the Vedic *pitṛs* the beings inhabiting the *pettivisaya* lead a pitiable and painful existence as a consequence of their bad *kamma* in a previous life. The *petas* belong to the class of *vinipātikas*, those who lead a woeful life in hell. In the *Āṭānāṭiya-sutta* the *petas* are described as beings bent on evil, as backbiters, murderous brigands, crafty-minded rogues, thieves, and cheats.

The Buddhist *peta* belief found its formal expression in the *Petavatthu*, a text in verse included in the *Khuddaka-nikāya*, the fifth collection of the *Sutta Piṭaka*. Reference to the conception of *petas* is found scattered in other sections of the Buddhist canon, as well, suggesting that the earlier Brahmanical ritual found its way into Buddhism at a very early period. The correspondence with the Brahmanical belief comes to light in the Gṛhya list of *mahayājña* and a similar list of five *bali* mentioned in the Buddhist texts. The *pitṛyajña* mentioned in the Gṛhya list corresponds to the *pubbapetabali* mentioned in the Buddhist list.[2] An offering of gifts in honor and for the sake of the dead ancestors was considered as a sacred duty of the Buddhist householder (*petānaṃ dakkhiṇaṃ anuppadassati*). Parents are said to desire sons in the family, expecting that they would perform the duty of making these offerings once the parents pass away.[3] The *Tirokuḍḍa-sutta*, occurring in both the *Petavattthu* and the *Kuddhakapāṭha* included in the *Khuddaka-nikāya*, represents the traditional Buddhist position regarding the *petadakkhiṇā* (offering to ancestors).

According to this *sutta*, *petas* visit their own homes and stay across the walls at cross roads and junctions, unable to receive anything from their kinsmen even when they hold great feasts. Compassionate and grateful kinsmen do not fail to make offerings to the *petas*. When such offerings are made the *petas*, who have no other means available in their woeful state of existence to obtain their requirements than through the offerings made by their living kinsmen, become happy and wish their kinsmen long life and happiness. The living, through gratitude for what their ancestors have done for them, should not fail to make offerings to the latter. The best way in which the interests of one's beloved ones who have departed to the other world can be served is by making such offerings to them, and not by crying, sorrowing, or lamenting over the loss of the loved ones. The effective mode of offering recognized in the *sutta* is not direct offering of material things to the *petas* but making offerings to the virtuous community of *bhikkhus*, dedicating the gifts expressly to the ancestral petas, as a consequence of which the latter are said to be released from their sufferings and pass into a better form of rebirth.

The canonical conception of *petas* and the ritual connected with offerings to them in Buddhism has several distinctive features when compared with the pre-Buddhistic ritual concerning ancestor worship. First, the Buddhist belief is that the living are not dependent on the *petas* for their well being in this world, in that the *petas* are conceived as inferior beings who are in need of the assistance of the living. Second, Buddhism emphasizes, through the practice of offerings to the *petas*, the virtue of gratitude. The *Tirokuḍḍa-sutta* gives expression to this idea thus: "He gave to me, he worked for me, he was my kin, friend, intimate. One ought to give gifts for departed ones, through gratitude for what they have done in the past." Third, the ritualistic aspect of the offerings in Buddhism is comparatively very simple, and Buddhism has got rid of the elaborate forms of Brahmanic ritual connected with the practice. Animal sacrifices are never recommended, and there is a deliberate attempt to moralize the practice. The best and the most efficacious manner in which the *petas* can be helped is said to be by making offerings to spiritually elevated persons. According to the *Tirokuḍḍa-sutta*, "When the offering is given to the well-placed in the community, it can be of benefit to them (the *petas*) for long." By offering alms to the Saṅgha, the laymen come into contact with the spiritual community; they also get an opportunity to eliminate their greed and attachment to wealth and other material things by practicing generosity. Consequently their merit is said to increase. Finally, the Buddhists look upon the *petadakkhiṇā* as a practice conducive to lessening the grief of the living on account of the death of their loved ones by suggesting that there is yet an effective means of caring for loved ones who are dead, giving a considerable degree of consolation for the living. The *Tirokuḍḍa-sutta* emphasizes this point thus: "Neither weeping nor sorrowing nor any kind of lamentation aides the departed ones."

The Pali canonical texts or commentaries do not reveal any details regarding the ritualistic procedure to be followed in making offerings to ancestors. However, the traditionally preserved popular ritualistic practice followed by Theravāda Buddhists of Sri Lanka can be observed at the performance of funeral rites and alms givings. It is customary for Theravāda Buddhists of Sri Lanka to offer alms (*dāna*) to the Saṅgha in their homes, at certain fixed intervals of time after the death of a relative. An alms giving for the sake of the dead relative is invariably held on the seventh day after the death. This is usually followed by one, three months, and another, one year after the death. The current belief is that the living relatives of the dead person make merit by giving *dāna* to virtuous monks. Not less than five *bhikkhus* are invited by the relatives to their home and gifts of food and other requisites of *bhikkhus* are given at these *dāna* ceremonies. On these occasions many friends and relatives of the dead person gather to participate in the meritorious act of making offerings to the Saṅgha.

The alms food is formally offered to the Saṅgha by repeating the usual Pali sentence three times: *Imaṃ bhikkhaṃ bhikkhusaṅghassa dema* ("We offer this food to the community of bhikkhus"). When the monks finish partaking of the meal they are offered other requisites (*pirikara*). Finally a small bowl or dish and a pitcher of water are brought before the *bhikkhus* by the immediate relatives of the dead person. At this moment everyone assumes a reverent posture, and the head of the household slowly pours the water into the dish till it overflows. While this is being done the monks recite together the following verses:

Unname udakaṃ vuṭṭhaṃ yathā ninnaṃ pavattati
evameva ito dinnaṃ petānaṃ upakappati.
Yathā vārivahā pūrā paripurenti sāgaraṃ
evameva ito dinnaṃ petānaṃ upakappati.
("As water showered on high ground flows down to the plain,
similarly what was given here serves the departed ones.
As streams full of water flow to fill the ocean,
similarly what was given here serves the departed ones.")

This water pouring ritual takes place at the funeral itself. Before the body of a dead person is cremated or buried the Buddhist monks perform a simple funeral rite. A white cloth is laid on the coffin, and the funeral gathering repeats three times after the chief monk present the following formula: *Imaṃ matakavatthaṃ bhikkhusanghassa dema* ("We give this clothing dedicated to the dead to the community of monks").

A close relative then performs the ritual of pouring water as at the *dāna*, while the monks recite the same verses recited on that occasion.

The most interesting question that arises with regard to the Buddhist practice of making offerings for the benefit of the dead concerns the Buddhist doctrinal explanation of this ritual. Canonical and commentarial references to the ritual indicate that the ancestors benefit by the offerings made by the living relatives only if they are specifically dedicated to them by the former. According to the *Tirokuḍḍa-sutta*, where we find the classical expression of the Buddhist belief and practice, the *petas* subsist on what is given by their relatives in this world (*ito dinnena yāpenti petā kālakatā tahiṃ*). The commentary to the *sutta* of the *Tirokuḍḍa Petavatthu* mentions the story of King Bimbisāra who gave alms to the Buddha but did not dedicate it to the *petas*. As a result the *petas*, who were expecting the king to dedicate the offering to them, appeared at the king's palace in the night and made a terrifying noise. The king who met the Buddha was advised by him to give alms again and dedicate them to the *petas*. The *petas* are said to have benefitted instantly by the offerings. Pleasant ponds covered with lotuses and lilies, sumptuous food fit for consumption by divine beings and divine clothes and dwelling places are said to have appeared before the *petas* for their benefit.[4]

The current Theravāda Buddhist practice in Sri Lanka of transferring merit to the relatives appears to be directly connected with this conception that the condition of the dead relatives can be improved if the merit acquired by performing a good deed is dedicated to them. After the performance of any meritorious act, it is customary for the Buddhists to transfer the merit acquired to the ancestors uttering the following verse: *Idaṃ me ñātīnaṃ hotu sukhitā hontu ñātayo.* ("May this be for my relatives and may the relatives be happy.")

The current view, and the one which may be said to be the official Theravādin view regarding offerings to ancestors, is that the ancestors who are born in the *peta* world alone can benefit from offerings dedicated to them. The belief that was prevalent among the Vedic people and in many other primitive cultures that ancestors can directly benefit from the material things offered to them is not accepted in Theravāda Buddhism. The canonical position regarding offerings to ancestors is not altogether clear as *suttas* like the *Tirokuḍḍa-sutta* only mention that the *petas* subsist on what is given from this world, but the mechanics of such subsistence is not described at all. The *Kathāvatthu* as well as the commentary to the *Kathāvatthu* expressly reject the view that the *petas* subsist on material things given from this world (*na h'ete ito dinnena vatthunā-yapenti*).

According to the Theravādin view expressed in the commentary to the *Kathāvatthu*, the belief that the *petas* benefit by the very same material items offered by the people of this world is a Buddhist heresy held by some sects like the Rājagirikas and the Siddhatthikas. The *Kathāvatthu* shows that the Theravādin was in agreement with the view that the *petas* approve with joy, rejoice, and are pleased in mind and become happy when someone performs the meritorious deed of giving *dāna* for their sake (*Nanu petā attano atthaya dānaṃ dentaṃ anumodenti cittaṃ pasādenti, pītiṃ uppādenti, somanassaṃ paṭilabhantīti? Amantāti.*)[5] According to this view the *petas* benefit not by the merit acquired by someone being transferred to them, in which case it would contradict the Buddhist doctrine of *kamma*, but by the rejoicing of the *petas* in the good deeds of others. This idea does not contradict the Buddhist doctrine of *kamma*. For the Buddhist doctrine explains *kamma* primarily as the functioning of a psychological law. The moral and rational outlook of Buddhism did not permit it to adopt a primitive practice in its original form. Therefore, it changed its character by reinterpreting the significance of the ritual.

Thus the Buddhist ritual concerning ancestor worship is yet another example of the adaptation of existing ritual to suit the spiritual and moral needs of the Buddhist. As B.C. Law remarks, "The guiding principle of practical Buddhism not to introduce anything which is inconsistent with the existing tradition of the time and not to upset anything which is well established as a custom, the belief itself and the social functions and religious rites based upon it, were recognized as a matter of course."[6] Buddhism gave a moral outlook to the whole ritual focussing attention on the evil consequences of immoral action and the wholesome consequences of good action. As in the case of many other contemporary ritualistic practices, Buddhism changed the character of the ritual by both moralizing and psychologizing it.

NOTES

1. Dakshina Ranjan Shastri, *Origin and Development of the Rituals of Ancestor Worship in India*, 22.
2. *A*, 3.45.
3. *Ibid.*, 3.6.
4. *DhA*, 1.103–104.
5. *Kvu* 2.347.
6. B.C. Law, *The Buddhist Conception of Spirits*, London: Luzac, 1936, 8.

12

A RITUAL OF MAHĀYĀNA VINAYA: SELF-SACRIFICE

Cheng-mei Ku

THE DEVELOPMENT of the Mahāyāna *vinaya* (rules of discipline) was relatively later than the traditional (Hināyānic) ones. Although the Early Mahāyāna (100–250) cared very much about the practice of *bodhisattvacaryā*, the school did not actually formulate any specific regulations for their practitioners to follow. The Mahāyāna *vinaya* was formed after the rise of a Mahāyānic syncretical school called the Mahaparinirvāṇavāda (hereafter, MPV), after the fall of the Early Mahāyāna. The establishment of the Mahāyānic *vinaya* was basically meant for lay Buddhist practitioners of the school, although some regulations and ideas applied to both the lay and monastic practitioners, e.g., the making of offerings.

The MPV was established upon the main teachings of the Sarvāstivāda and the Early Mahāyāna. Like its precursors, the MPV was very much concerned about the practice of *bodhisattvacaryā*, especially items such as the dharma-preaching, alms-offering and cultivation of good will. In fact, cultivation of good will covers the practices of dharma-preaching and alms-offering. Since the cultivation of good will was the most essential practice laid down by the MPV for their practitioners, an early Mahāyāna *vinaya* called the *Śāriputrakṣama-sūtra* (hereafter *SK*), stresses the point in the practices of the five *sīlas* (virtues) and six *pāramitās* (perfections).[1] The Sarvāstivāda believed that cultivation of good will is the most fundamental virtue, in that it contributes to the generation of *bodhicitta* (thought of enlightenment), a necessary condition for the realization of buddhahood.[2] In the Sarvāstivāda work, the *Sūtra Spoken by the Buddha on the Girl Nāgadatta*, the author of the text states that due to Nāgadatta's cultivation of good will in the past, she can henceforth observe the practice of transformation of the body (*strī-vivarta*) in this life as preparation for the attainment of buddhahood.[3] If this is so, then how should one cultivate his or her good will? The SK says that one should be good to the Buddha, the Dharma, and the Saṅgha and, furthermore, one should respect and be good to one's parents, teachers, and good friends.[4] The MPV, in explaining the idea of cultivation of good will, consistently used one term to describe the practice, viz. "making offerings" (*dāna*). To the MPV, "making offerings" does not imply the offering of material things only, but also includes spiritual services such as dharma-preaching.

The teaching of the MPV is based upon the story of the Buddha's *parinirvāṇa*. The school believed that when the Buddha attained his *parinirvāṇa* (death) he, in fact, remained in the state of *nirvāṇa* (a state of enlightenment). The idea of the permanent existence of *dharma-kāya* of a Buddha was also accepted as an important corollary by the MPV. The *Saddharmapuṇḍarīka*, an early work of the MPV, frequently mentions the permanent existence of *dharma-kāya*. For instance, in the chapter called "Apparition of the Jeweled Stupa," the Buddha Prabhutaratna is said to be sitting in the *stūpa* with a radiant image, even after his *parinirvāṇa*.[5]

Along with the belief of the permanent existence of *dharma-kāya*, the MPV also advocated the idea of reincarnation of Buddhas. The authors of the MPV often mentioned the stories of a thousand reincarnated Buddhas who will be born in this world during the period of spiritual prosperity (*bhadrakalpa*).[6] Many of these reincarnated Buddhas are said to be born again and again to this world just for the purpose of enlightening sentient beings by performing dharma-preaching. According to the *Saddharma puṇḍarīka*, the Tathāgata named Sun-and-Moon-Glow is said to have been born eighty times to this world by bearing the same name.[7] Due to this belief in the existence of reincarnated Buddhas, Buddha Maitreya, who is one of the reincarnated Buddhas of *bhadrakalpa*, became the most popular Buddha among authors of the MPV. His story of reincarnation has not only been incorporated into many texts of the MPV, but became the subject matter of an entire treatise.[8]

The function of a reincarnated Buddha is *sūtra*-preaching. The MPV considered that *sūtra*-preaching is in fact a form of protection of the true dharma (*dharmarakṣa*). Buddha Prabhutaratna says very clearly in the addharma-pundarika that he will preach the *sūtra*-dharma to sentient beings of the ten quarters when he is alive, and he will also protect the dharma after his *parinirvāṇa*. Therefore he tells that his *stūpa* will appear wherever the *sūtra*-dharma of the *Saddharma puṇḍarīka* is preached.[9]

Since the story of the Buddha's *parinirvāṇa* was the central theme that the MPV developed in its teaching, the school was very much concerned with the succession and protection of the dharma too. Authors of the MPV all agreed that Māhākaśyapa was the legitimate successor of the Buddha's teaching.[10] But where a dharma-protector was concerned, every text of the MPV had its own ideal candidate. For instance, the *Mahābherihāraka-parivarta-sūtra* (hereafter *MHP*) chose the Boy of Li-che-zi whom-every-sentient-being-enjoys-to-see, as its ideal protector of the dharma. The text says, Māhākaśyapa received the Buddha-dharma from the Buddha, but after forty years of protecting the Buddha's teaching, he could not carry out his duty as a dharma-protector. It is only the Boy of Li-che-zi whom-every-sentient-being-enjoys-to-see who could do the job.[11] Dharma-protectors of the MPV were mostly the reincarnated Buddhas or *bodhisattvas* such as the Boy of Li-che-zi.

After the rise of the MPV in the mid-3rd century A.D. in North-west India, the school was flourishing in the area of Ji-bin (Kasmir), the center of their activities.[12] The school laid down many important doctrines to distinguish its teachings from other schools. Besides doing so, the school also characterized its teaching as consisting of the twelvefold method of exposition which other traditional schools did not fully utilize. These twelve forms are:

1. *sūtra*	7. *jātaka*
2. *geyya*	8. *vaipulya*
3. *veyyākaraṇa*	9. *adbhuta-dharma*
4. *gāthā*	10. *avadāna*
5. *udāna*	11. *upadeśa*
6. *itivuttaka*	12. *nidāna*.[13]

According to the MPV, a traditional sūtra writer would only employ the first nine methods. In order to distinguish their teaching or texts from the traditional ones, the MPV added the last three methods. In fact, the last three methods were very often used and emphasized by the writers of the school. Due to this emphasis on the last three methods, the school called its works vaipulya (*vedalla*) *sūtras*.[15]

The implication of *vaipulya sūtras* may have been changed to apply to all the texts composed by the MPV subsequently, for the term is often used to refer to all kinds of works done by the MPV in the context of employing the twelvefold method of exposition. The *vaipulya sūtras* of the MPV were first introduced into China by Dharmarakṣa of the Western Jin dynasty (265–316 A.D.). Dharmarakṣa was a monk from Dun-huang. Before he went to China, he heard of the Chinese practices of temple-building and image-worship. But the Chinese were still lacking the knowledge of the *vaipulya sūtras*. Therefore, he decided to collect *vaipulya sūtras* from around Central Asia and bring them to China.[16] Dharmarakṣa had translated many other types of Buddhist texts besides the *vaipulya sūtras*. The author of the *Biographies of Monks* (hereafter *BM*), Hui-jiao, and other Buddhist scholars did not realize that a Mahāyānic work translated by Dharmarakṣa could be a work of the Early Mahāyāna and not necessarily a *vaipulya sūtra* of the MPV. Consequently they often mistakenly grouped Dharmarakṣa's translations of the Early Mahāyānic works with his translations of *vaipulya sūtras* and referred to all of them as *vaipulya sūtras*. For instance, Hui-jiao, in the *BM*, lists both the *Aṣṭasāhaśrikāprajñāpāramitā-sūtra* (hereafter *Aṣṭa*) and the *Saddharma puṇḍarīka* and regards them as the *vaipulya sūtras*.[17] However, the *Aṣṭa* is a work of the Early Mahāyāna,[18] and the *Saddharma-puṇḍarīka* is a work of the MPV. These two texts belonged to two different schools which were founded during the different periods of the Mahāyānic tradition.

After Dharmarakṣa's translations of *vaipulya sūtras* into Chinese, the Chinese immediately started their studies on the MPV. But works of the MPV were not systematically studied until the beginning of the 5th century in China. The first systematic study of *vaipulya sūtras* was undertaken for political reasons. Ju-qu-mong-xun (fl. 412–433), a Tokharian ruler of a territory stretching from present-day Lan-chou to Dun-huang, of the Northern Liang Dynasty (412–439), decided to impose a project for the purpose of promoting the Buddhist ideal kingship (*cakravartinship*), after he conquered Dun-huang (around 420).[19] Because of Mong-xun's political project, many important texts of the MPV were selected for translation.

The concept of *cakravartin* is primarily a Buddhist one which can even be traced back to the texts composed before the rise of the Early Mahāyāna (100 A.D.).[20] But the concept was not fully developed until the rise of the MPV. A *cakravartin's* duty of taking care of his subjects and religious belief to attain buddhahood were the two topics that the MPV elaborated upon in the period when the concept of offerings was stressed. Therefore, many texts were composed by the school to promote the idea of *cakravartin*.

For instance, the *Mahāsatyanirgranthaputravyākaraṇa-sūtra* (hereafter *MNPV*) is a text where a *cakravartin's* worldly duty is discussed.[21]

The *Karuṇāpuṇḍarīka-sūtra* (hereafter *KP*) is an important work in so far as a *cakravartin's* religious belief is concerned.[22] The MPV had taken a *cakravartin's* patronage to Buddhism into serious consideration, especially when they were promoting the idea of making offerings. They often suggested that a great king's patronage to Buddhism will make the Buddha-dharma spread more efficiently and widely. Therefore where the concept of *dharmarakṣa*, or protection of the dharma is concerned, a *cakravartin's* patronage is considered the ideal form of making offerings among sentient beings on earth. A *cakravartin*, according to the texts, is the one who is well equipped with all kinds of material facilities and political power, with whom a minor ruler or a rich man cannot compare. Therefore, the MHP calls a *cakravartin* "a *dharmarājika* of *dharmarakṣa* (a righteous monarch protecting the dharma), who is the king of kings."[23] When the MPV promoted the idea of *cakravartin*, the great Indian King Aśoka's story of making offerings to Buddhists was often mentioned as a model. The *Biography of King Aśoka* therefore became an important work through which one could understand the concept of *dharmarakṣa*.[24]

Although the concept of *dharmarakṣa* can be explained in relation to the idea of "making offerings," yet in the teaching of the MPV, making offerings can be understood in terms of two different types of action. One is called the *sūtra*-dharma preaching done by reincarnated Buddhas or great dharma masters; the other is called materialistic patronage provided by the ordinary masses and *cakravartins*. In practicing these two types of making offerings, the reincarnated Buddhas or dharma masters, on the one hand, and the ordinary people or *cakravartins*, on the other, will mutually benefit each other. According to the *Mahaparinirvāṇa-sūtra*[25] and other texts of the MPV, such as the Story of Buddha Maitreya's Reincarnation,[26] the ordinary masses are said to benefit from the reincarnated Buddha's sūtra-preaching, while they make materialistic offerings such as lodging, food, drinks, clothing, or medicine to these reincarnated Buddhas or dharma masters. The *cakravartins* and the ordinary masses provide the reincarnated Buddhas and dharma masters with an environment conducive to spreading the dharma. Therefore *dharmarakṣa* has to be achieved through these two types of making offerings. The *Mahāvaipulya*(*vedalla*) *mahāsannipāta-sūtra* (hereafter *MVS*), in a section discussing these two types of making offerings, provides two different names for them. The sūtra-dharma preachings performed by reincarnated Buddhas and great dharma masters is called the offerings of *dharma-kāya*, while the materialistic offerings performed by the ordinary people or *cakravartins* is called the offerings of *nirmāṇa-kāya*.[27]

From many archaeological reports, we learn that the idea of a *cakravartin* was adopted by many Indian and Central Asian kings around the period from the 4th to the 5th century A.D.[28] When these kings adopted the idea, they constructed many images of *cakravartins* in the Buddhist *caityas* or *stūpas*.[29] Ju-qu-mong-xun was a Little Yeh-zhi by birth and was raised in a city called Zhang-yi on the ancient Chinese silk road.[30] He should have been well equipped with the idea of *cakravartin* because of the cultural environment in which he lived before he conquered the area. After he conquered Dun-huang, he immediately recruited a monk from Kasmir called Dharmakṣema to help him to promote the idea of *cakravartin*. Mong-xun's adoption of the idea of *cakravartin* was no doubt due to geographical and cultural factors.

Dharmakṣema (fl. 421–433) is said to have acquired the abilities of both Kumārajīva (who came to China in 403) and Fo-tu-cheng (fl. 330).[31] In Central Asia he was also known as the greatest master in casting spells. Mong-xun valued him very highly, even though the Emperor Tai-wu-di (406–451) of the Northern Wei Dynasty wanted to recruit him. The latter risked a war with the Emperor Tai-wu-di in not letting him go.[33] The first thing Dharmakṣema did for Mong-xun in the campaign of promoting the idea of *cakravartin* was the translation of the *Mahaparinirvāṇa-sūtra*.[34] This is the most important text from which one can grasp the entire teaching of the MPV. The position of this text in the MPV is as important as the *Aṣṭa* in the Early Mahāyāna. Before Dharmakṣema finished his translation of the *Mahaparinirvāṇa-sūtra*, in urgency, he started translating some important *vaipulya sūtras* that are relevant to the promotion of the idea of *cakravartin*.

These texts include the *MVS*, the *KP*, the *Mahāmegha-sūtra*, the *Suvarṇaprabhāṣa* (hereafter *SVP*), the *Sūtra Spoken by Buddha on the King Mandhātri* (hereafter *Mandhātri*), etc.[35] Many of these texts were retranslated and used by later Chinese emperors for the same purpose. For instance, the Empress Wu-ze-tian (fl. 662–705) of the Tang dynasty, in the first year (690) of her reign, issued a decree to spread the text of the *Mahāmegha-sūtra* in every state of her territory in order to spread the idea that she was a female *cakravartin*.[36] Toward the end of this campaign of promoting the idea of *cakravartin*, in the year 703 Empress Wu-ze-tian again issued a decree asking Yi-jing to translate the *SVP*.

Besides ordering the translation of the chosen texts of the MPV to promote the idea of *cakravartin*, Mong-xun also followed the footsteps of Indian and Central Asian kings in commissioning the sculpting and painting of images of *cakravartins* and reincarnated Buddhas in many caves in the area.[38] The production of images of *cakravartins* and reincarnated Buddhas was also considered a medium for the promotion of the idea of *cakravartin*. Many of these objects of art produced at the command of Mong-xun still remain.[39] The stories depicted by them were taken mostly from the texts that Dharmakṣema translated during this period.

In the process of Mong-xun's popularization of the idea of *cakravartin* in the Northern Liang, the Mahāyānic practice of *bodhisattvacaryā*, corresponding to the teaching of the MPV, were also emphasized by the people who were in charge of the entire campaign of promoting the ideal of *cakravartin*. It is for this reason that the Mahāyānic *vinayas* were introduced during this period by the heir apparent Xin-guo and 500 monks who were involved in the work of translating texts.[40] Dharmakṣema therefore translated two Mahāyānic *vinayas* to serve the purpose. These are the *Upāsakaśīla-sūtra* (hereafter *US*) and the *Bodhisattvaprātimokṣa* (hereafter *BP*).[41]

The *BP* is said to have been preached by Bodhisattva Maitreya.[42] Although this *prātimokṣa* lists four *pārājikā*-dharmas and several *dukkaṭa*-dharmas, due to the emphasis on the concept of *dharmarakṣa* in the school, the penalties imposed upon offenders of these dharmas are consistently judged according to one's practice of making offerings. For instance, the first two *pārājikā*-dharmas are applied to those who do not observe both *sūtra*-dharma offerings and materialistic offerings.[43] Thus, the nature of Mahāyānic *vinaya* turns out to be very different from that of the traditional ones.

The *BP* is a very short text that emphasizes the practice of *bodhisattvacaryā*. In so far as the establishment of regulations is concerned, strictly speaking, the *US* is not so much a *vinaya* text as a *sūtra*. However, the text presents a very clear view of the MPV on human life or human activities, including both religious and worldly activities. The MPV's attitude toward worldly activities is very different from the traditional ones that we have encountered. Under the teaching of the Early Mahāyāna, i.e., the Śūnyavāda, every dharma or every existence is viewed as an illusion or a dream. Nothing is considered to be real, either a religious belief or a worldly activity.[44] The MPV's affirmation of worldly affairs could have been a "shocking attitude" to many Buddhist practitioners at that time, especially when they put down statements such as: long life and fortune are the two goals that a practitioner of the MPV has to pursue in this life. The MPV's argument justifying such a view of life is that a person who is serious about worldly business is surely serious about his religious activities also. Thus the *US* states that, seeking for materialistic achievement is not different from seeking religious achievement.[45] Therefore, in the beginning of the *US*, long life and fortune are said to be the result of practicing the six *pāramitās*.[46]

It seems that, had the materialistic life not been so much emphasized, the practice of making materialistic offerings would have been impossible in the context of ***dharmarakṣa***. Due to an affirmation of worldly value, the MPV paid its attention to human morality as well. In the *US* and other places, they talk about moral practices such as filial piety, respect to elders and dharma masters, friendliness and trust in good friends.[47] Even though a materialistic life was emphasized by the MPV, materialistic achievement after all was not considered to be the essential goal of human life, especially in the practice of ***bodhisattvacaryā***. On the contrary, in making materialistic offerings, one is asked to make offerings of all kinds of material things one may possess, such as one's fortune, country, children, wife, and even one's life[48] in the observance of ***bodhisattvacaryā***. In this sense, the idea of making offerings is a teaching which is in conformity with the Buddhist teaching of non-attachment.

When the author of the *US* says one has to offer his fortune, country, children, wife and even one's life when making offerings for the purpose of ***dharmarakṣa***, he means that one has to perform an absolute offering or sacrifice if necessary. Many instances of the ***bodhisattva's*** self-sacrifice are, therefore, described in the *US* and other places, as the ideal performance of making offerings.[49] We don't actually know whether the practice of self-sacrifice had become a ritual in India or Central Asia when the teaching of the MPV came to be disseminated in these areas. However, it became a ritual of the Mahāyāna in China after Mong-xun's promotion of the teaching of the MPV in the Northern Liang.

Upendra Thakur classifies Indian patterns of suicide into two types: social and religious. In the section discussing the Buddhist case, he suggests that in general Buddhist monks were against the practice of suicide, even for a religious purpose.[50] He does not notice that some sectarian schools in fact permitted suicide for a religious purpose. The Sarvāstivāda was one of them. The Sarvāstivādins regarded suicide as a religious discipline, and stated the idea in their work, the ***Sūtra Spoken by the Buddha on the Girl Nāgadatta***. In this text it is said that the girl Nāgadatta, in order to attain Buddhahood, performs a religious suicide while practicing ***dharmarakṣa***. Before she jumps from a high building to commit suicide, she says to herself that she will offer her body to the Buddha like offering him flowers.[51] Nāgadatta's practice of self-sacrifice is therefore considered a religious discipline, by which she shows her determination to attain Buddhahood. The text says that it is only after having undergone such a discipline that she is able to change her sex in the next life.[52] The MPV inherited this discipline from the Sarvāstivāda and permitted the practices of killing and self-sacrifice.

The *Mahaparinirvāṇa* tells a story about a king who, because of protecting a dharma teacher who guarded the right dharmas, was killed.[53] The text also states that if necessary, killing is allowed, even though it constitutes a violation of the five *śīlas*.[54] Since killing is permissible in the practice of *dharmarakṣa*, a religious suicide or self-sacrifice is permissible too.

After the teaching of the MPV was introduced to the people of the Northern Liang, self-sacrifice was treated as a ritual relating to the performance of *dharmarakṣa* by monks in China. A very familiar and moving story about a monk of the Northern Liang performing self-sacrifice is related in the *BM*. The monk's name was Fa-jing. In a year when the Northern Liang encountered a serious drought, many people died of hunger. Monk Fa-jing tried to persuade the central government to release some grain to the hungry, but failed. One day, he purified himself, took off his clothing, went among a group of hungry people and said to them, "Cut me off, so that you can eat my flesh with salt and sustain yourselves for some more days." None could bring themselves to do that. He therefore cut the flesh from his own two thighs and distributed it to them.[55]

The *bodhisattva's* story of cutting himself up to feed the hungry tigress is mentioned very often in *vaipulya sūtras*. So too is the story of the King Shibi. The *US*, in a section mentioning the *bodhisattva's* self-sacrifice, also mentions these two cases.[57] Monk Fa-jing's self-sacrifice is therefore quite familiar to the people of the Northern Liang. According to the MPV, self-sacrifice can be performed in different ways. The *Records of Transmission of the MPV* (hereafter *RT*) mentions three types of self-sacrifice performed by the *bodhisattva*. These are jumping from a cliff, self-immolation, and cutting oneself into pieces. In the text, these practices of self-sacrifice are said to be for the purpose of enlightening sentient beings to realize Buddhahood.[58]

After the Chinese had adopted the practice of self-sacrifice as a ritual of the Mahāyāna, they were particularly in favor of the practice of self-immolation. Self-immolation is mentioned in the *Saddharma-puṇḍarīka*, where it is extolled as the best form of making offerings.[59] The practice is explained thus: "In the practice of making offerings to the Buddha Sun-and-Moon-Glow, the Bodhisattva whom-every-sentient-being-enjoys-to-see told himself that the most thorough practice of making offerings is an offering of one's body. After Bodhisattva whom-every-sentient-being-enjoys-to-see decided to perform the utmost ritual of making offerings, he purified himself with all kinds of perfumes, and drank perfumed oil for 1200 years. Finally, in front of the Buddha Sun-and-Moon-Glow, he wrapped himself with heavenly clothing soaked with all kinds of perfumed oil, and by his magical power, burned himself.[60] The Chinese must have been very much inspired by this story, for, in the period when the teaching of the MPV was flourishing in China around the 5th century A.D., many monks performed the ritual of self-immolation as a way of making offerings. The self-immolation of six monks is recorded in the *BM*, showing that the practice was an important cultural phenomenon of the period. These six were Fa-yu, Hui-shao, Hui-yi, Seng-qing, Fa-guang and Seng-yu.[61] One common feature of the self-sacrifice on the part of the six monks was that they were all reciting the section of the *Saddharma-puṇḍarīka-sūtra* which describes the immolation of the Bodhisattva whom-every-sentient-being-enjoys-to-see until they died.[62]

Conclusion

The ritual of self-sacrifice can be traced back to the period before the rise of the Early Mahāyāna, but the practice of making this offering was developed only after the rise of the MPV. Chinese practice of the ritual was influenced by the teaching of the MPV which was popularized in the northern Liang for political reasons. Should the idea of *cakravartin* not have been popularized in the Northern Liang, the practice of self-sacrifice would not have become a Chinese Buddhist ritual. Therefore the establishment of the ritual of self-sacrifice in China can be considered a by-product of a political ideal in the northern Liang.

The early Chinese practitioners of the ritual of self-sacrifice had viewed the ritual as being an observance of Mahāyāna *vinaya*, and due to this belief, monks performed the ritual without any regret. The practitioners of the ritual never thought that the ritual violated any rules that they had to observe in the practice of *bodhisattvacaryā* in the Mahāyāna tradition.

The ritual of self-sacrifice had in fact spread to places where the Mahāyāna teaching was prevalent. Thus, many Vietnamese monks performed the ritual of self-immolation during the Vietnam War in the 1960s. Without knowing the philosophical background of the ritual, we would certainly feel that the practice of immolation observed by the Vietnamese monks was cruel and meaningless. The *MUS*'s description of making materialistic offerings is very convincing, for, after all, the practice of self-sacrifice is a *dāna* (offering) of *nirmāṇa-kāya* (the physical body).

NOTES

1. According to the Taisho, the *Śāriputra-kṣama-sūtra* is said to be translated by An-shi-gao of the Eastern Han dynasty, who came to China in 147 A.D. But, judging from the contents of the text, it should be codified as a later work of the MPV, or a work of the Sarvāstivāda. See *T*. 1492 vol. 24, 1090–91.
2. See the *Yi-bu-zhong-lung lung*, translated by Xuan-zhuang of the Tang dynasty, the section discussing the doctrines of the Sarvāstivāda, *T*. 2031 vol. 49, 16c, where it says that good will is the cause.
3. See the *Sūtra Spoken by the Buddha on the Girl Nāgadatta*, translated by Zhi-qian of the Wu dynasty, *T*. 557 vol. 14, 909c–910a.
4. See the *Śāriputrakṣāma-sūtra*, 1090c–91a.
5. See the *Saddharmapuṇḍarīka*, translated by Kumārajīva, *T*. 263 vol. 9, 103–04.
6. See the *Bhadrakalpika-sūtra*, translated by Dharmarakṣa, *T*. 425 vol. 14, 50a.
7. See the *Saddharmapuṇḍarīka*, *T*. vol. 9, 65.
8. See the *Mahākaruṇā-sūtra*, *T*. 380 vol. 12, 953c, and the *Maitreya-vyākaraṇa-sūtra*, translated by Dharmarakṣa, *T*. 453 vol. 14, 421–23, etc.
9. See the *Saddharmapuṇḍarīka*, *T*. 263 vol. 9, 102c.
10. See the *Transmission of the Dharma of the MPV*, translated by Ji-jia-ye and Tan-yao of the Northern Wei Dynasty (386–534), *T*. 2058 vol. 50, 297–301, and the *Maitreya-vyākaraṇa* (The Story of Buddha Maitreya's Reincarnation), *T*. 453, etc.
11. The *Mahābheribhārakaparivarta-sūtra*, translated by Gunabhadra of the Sung Dynasty (420–79), T. 270, vol. 9, 298–99.
12. See the *Mahāparinirvāṇa-sūtra*, translated by Dharmakṣema of the Northern Liang Dynasty (397–439), *T*. 374 vol. 12, 422b, and the *Padmamukha-sūtra*, translated by Narendrayaśas in 584 A.D., *T*. 386 vol. 12, 1075, etc.
13. See the *Mahaparinirvāṇa-sūtra*, 390–91a.
14. *Ibid*., 383.
15. *Ibid*., 405a.
16. See Hui-jiao, the *Biographies of Monks*, *T*. 2059 vol. 50, 326, the Biography of Dharmarakṣa.
17. *Ibid*.
18. See Cheng-mei Ku, *The Mahāyānic View of Women*, a dissertation submitted to the University of Wisconsin, Madison, 1984, 5.
19. The Biography of Ju-qu-mong-xun collected in the *History of the Northern Dynasties*, the Juan 81; see also my forthcoming book, *Buddhism in the Northern Liang Dynasty – A Story of Cakravartin in the History of China*.
20. The concept of *cakravartin* was already mentioned as one of the supernatural powers that one can attain in the practice of *bodhisattvacaryā* associated with a woman's practice of transformation of the body. This Sarvāstivāda idea of transformation of the body was established before the rise of the Early Mahāyāna. See Cheng-mei Ku, the *Mahāyānic View of Women*, 102–106.

21. The *Mahāsatyanirgranthaputravyākaraṇa-sūtra*, translated by Bodhiruci in the Northern Wei Dynasty, *T*. 272 vol. 9, 330–337.
22. See the *Karuṇāpuṇḍarīka-sūtra*, translated by Dharmakṣema of the Northern Liang Dynasty, *T*. 157 vol. 3, pp. 174–181.
23. The *MHP*, p. 330.
24. The *Biography of King Aśoka*, translated by An Fa-qin of the Western Chin Dynasty, *T*. 2042 vol. 50, 99 ff.
25. The *Mahāparinirvāṇa-sūtra*, *T*. 374, 549a.
26. See the *Maitreyavyākaraṇa-sūtra*, *T*. 453.
27. The *Mahāvaipulya (vedalla)-mahāsannipāta-sūtra*, translated by Dharmakṣema of the Northern Liang Dynasty, *T*. 397 vol. 13, 214.
28. See D.B. Spooner, "Excavation of Sahribahlol," *Archaeological Survey of India*, Annual Report, 1909–10, pl. xix; see also Sir John Marshall, "Excavation at Taxila," *Archaeological Survey of India*, Annual Report, 1912–13.
29. *Ibid*.
30. See the *Biography of Ju-qu-mong-xun*, collected in the *History of the Northern Dynasties*, the Juan 81; see also Chang-ru Tang, *Collected Works on the History of the Wei Jin Northern and Southern Dynasties*, (Peking: San-lien, 1978), 404.
31. See the *Biography of Dharmakṣema*, collected in the *Biographies of Monks*, T. 2059, vol. 50, 336.
32. *Ibid*.
33. See the *Biography of Ju-qu-mong-xun*, collected in the *History of the Northern Dynasties*, the Juan 81.
34. See the *Biography of Dharmakṣema*, *T*. 2059, 336a.
35. *Ibid*.
36. See the *Biography of Xie-huai-yi* of the *Book of the Old Tang*, the Chuan 183.
37. See the *Biography of Yi-jing*, collected in the *Biographies of Monks Composed in the Sung Dynasty*, *T*. 2061 vol. 50, 710a.
38. See Michael Sullivan, *The Cave Temples of Maichisan*, (London: Faber and Faber, 1969), 21; see also Su Bai, "The Remains of Liang-zhou Stone Caves and the 'Liang-zhou Model,'" taken from the *Kao-gu-xue-bao*, 1986, no. 4, 435–443.
39. *Ibid*.
40. See the *Notes on the Translation of the Upāsakaśīla-sūtra*, taken from the *Chu-san-zang-ji-ji-*, *T*. 2145 vol. 55, 64c.
41. See the *Biography of Dharmakṣema*, *T*. 2059, 336a.
42. The *Bodhisattvaprātimokṣa*, translated by Dharmakṣema, *T*. 1500 vol. 24, 1107.
43. *Ibid*., 1107a.
44. See Cheng-mei Ku, *The Mahāyānic View of Women*, 157.
45. The *Upāsakaśīla-sūtra*, *T*. 1488 vol. 24, 1045.
46. *Ibid*., 1034.
47. *Ibid*., 1041a, 1047, etc.
48. *Ibid*., 1041a.

49. *Ibid.*, 1041c.
50. Upendra Thakur, *The History of Suicides in India*, (Delhi: Munshi Ram Manohar Lal, 1963), 106.
51. The *Sūtra Spoken by the Buddha on the Girl Nāgadatta*, *T*. 558, 910a.
52. *Ibid.*, 909–10.
53. The *Mahāparinirvāṇa-sūtra*, 383c–84.
54. *Ibid.*, 384a.
55. See the *Biography of Fa-jing*, taken from the *Biographies of Monks*, *T*. 2059, vol. 50, 404a–b.
56. For instance the stories are mentioned in the *Damamukanidāna-sūtra*, translated by Hui-jue of the Northern Liang Dynasty, *T*. 202 vol. 4, 352–53, 351c–52.
57. The *Upāsakaśīla-sūtra*, 1041c.
58. See the *Transmission of the Dharma*, *T*. 2058 vol. 50, 297a.
59. See the *Saddharmapuṇḍarīka*, *T*. 262 vol. 9, 53b.
60. *Ibid.*
61. See the *BM*, *T*. 2059, 404c–405.
62. *Ibid.*

13

CHINESE BUDDHIST CONFESSIONAL RITUALS

THEIR ORIGIN AND SPIRITUAL IMPLICATIONS

Hsiang-Chou Yo

The Main Functions of Religious Rituals

FROM THE STANDPOINT OF RELIGIOUS EVOLUTION, ritual is one of the common elements of religion. But from the standpoint of the Buddhist fundamental doctrine, ritual is not a necessity – because from primitive Buddhism to Māhāyana Buddhism, the highest objective of Buddhism is to realize "emptiness" (*śūnyatā*). In the context of the doctrine of "emptiness," ritual is not a necessary element which cannot be dispersed with. However, during the process of development and wide diffusion, Buddhism has gradually formed many rituals. Obviously, ritual has its own function, but it also has its own limitation. We can neither reject the value of rituals from the extreme super-mundane standpoint, nor consider rituals as the whole and absolute content of Buddhism from the standpoint of ritualism. In essence, we must recognize the value of some Buddhist traditional rituals from a middle standpoint of not-adopting-and-not-forsaking.

First, I would like to define the main functions of rituals in ordinary religions. These functions consist of at least the following:

1. *The concrete manifestation of religious concept*. Concept is originally abstract, but it can be concretely manifested through rituals. Because of this, ritual possesses the educational function of religious concept. Many believers learn the contents of their faith from rituals. This educational function of ritual, achieved by means of hint, force, or the effect of collective activities or reasonable persuasiveness, is quite strong, hence deserving our special attention in our analysis of religious activities.

2. *The stimulation, concentration, and enforcement of religious experience*. Religious experience itself is a very subjective experience and not easily introduced or transmitted to others by means of language alone. But through rituals, religious experience can be easily stimulated. Also, it can be concentrated and continuously enforced during the process of repeated rituals. Some mystic experience can be realized through rituals. This is the reason why rituals are widely utilized in the propagation of many religions.

3. *The objectification of religious ethics*. Every religion, following internal metaphysical presuppositions, has its own orientation and structure of ethical value. This orientation and structure can be fully objectified through the formation and execution of rituals. The religious authority which is established on the basis of religion and its opposite, religious taboos, can be clearly positioned through the design of rituals.

Basically, no matter what functions rituals manifest, these functions themselves are of neutral value only. It is worthy of our attention that sometimes rituals may develop into the ladder for upward elevation of human spirit through the rationalization of religion itself, but sometimes it may become the tool of anesthetizing the human mind through internal corruption and rational retreat of some religions. Judging from the forms of religion, it is very difficult to determine promptly which are good rituals and which are the bad ones. The spiritual implications manifested by the ritual and the religious experience to which it leads constitute the criteria for judgment. The former is the cause and the latter is the effect.

Based on this premise, I wish to take the confessional rituals of Chinese Buddhism as examples, by exploring the background of their formation and their spiritual implications, to explain what sort of attitude we should adopt in dealing with rituals.

The Formation of the Confessional Rituals of Chinese Buddhism

Confession is one of the important themes of religious practice. This is because religious behavior should inevitably involve the principles of "good" and "evil." Meanwhile, confession is the most important psychological factor in the process of forsaking evil and cultivating goodness. The Chinese Confucianists always insist that, "If you have an error, yet you don't correct it, this is called an error. If you have an error, but you correct it, nothing could be better than this." This is a clear admission that confession is the basic expression of the moral life. Judaism also deems confession as an important means of saving the human soul. In the process of the development of Chinese Buddhism, not only did confession receive great emphasis, but also since the 4th century A.D., Chinese Buddhism has taken confession as the springboard to create many complete rituals. Its formation and development are outlined as follows:

The Creation of Monastic Confessional Rituals

According to the literary records, Buddhism was introduced into China in the 1st century A.D. Buddhism spread rapidly in China due to the fact that its ideas were compatible with those of traditional Chinese culture in many ways, and the translation of Buddhist sūtras was undertaken with enthusiasm between the second and third century. In the fourth century A.D., the outstanding Buddhist leader in northern China, Master Tao An (312–385 A.D.), promulgated the rules for monks and nuns. He stressed that monasteries should have morning and evening practices. He also formally requested that confession for correcting one's error should be one of the major daily practices.[1] These rules were widely followed by the monasteries throughout China at that time and are in vogue even at present. Confession has thus become one of the major components of a Chinese Buddhist's daily schedule of practices. Around the 9th century A.D., a literature entitled "Great Confessional Text" was adopted as a guide to morning and evening practices. This served as an extensive yet compact document to be utilized in the formal system of practice since then.

In reality, Master Tao An inherited the tradition of South Asian Buddhism. Yet, before Buddhism was introduced into China, the emphasis on moral rules and rituals was an important part of original Chinese culture. This background can help us understand why confessional rituals could become very popular and persistent since Master Tao An promulgated them.

The Formation of Dharma Blossom Samādhi Confessional Rituals

The further expansion of the idea of confession through sūtras was made by Master Chi Yii (538–597 A.D.), the great founder of the Tentai sect. He established a set of systematic self-confessional rituals by adopting the form of confessions and worship based upon the Māhāyana sūtras translated from Sanskrit. The most representative work was "Dharma Blossom Samādhi Confessional Ritual."[2] It has at least three important effects on the development of Chinese confessional rituals of a later age:

1. *Definite procedure of confession provided the blueprint for future development.* The whole procedure consists of nine steps: (1) cleaning the temple premises, (2) cleaning one's body, (3) offering of the karma of body, speech, and thought, (4) taking refuge in the triple gem, (5) worshipping the Buddhas and Bodhisattvas of the ten directions, (6) expressing the intention to repent, (7) walking in a circle, (8) reciting the *Dharma Blossom Sūtra*, and (9) meditating. These nine steps have become the important preliminaries of most Chinese Buddhist confessional rituals.

2. *The use of* sūtra *chanting and meditation to facilitate the rationalization of rituals.* Confession is made by *sūtra* reciting and meditation. This reflects Master Chi Yii's attempt to balance "mindfulness" and "contemplation." Chanting *sūtras* can arouse one's wisdom by eradicating the feeling of guilt. In addition, meditation can appease the mind so as to reduce the tendency to commit evil and eliminate guilty feelings. "Mindfulness" is identical with "contemplation (*samādhi*)." *Samādhi* is thus achieved through confessional rituals. This is the most unique part of "Dharma Blossom Samādhi Confessional Rituals" which, accordingly, are intended not simply as means of generating religious feelings or as rules for morning and evening sūtra reciting, but as important ways of practicing *samādhi*. The Buddhists, therefore, can practice *samādhi* through confessional rituals. Thus, the rituals came to be highly rationalized.

3. *Worshipping the Buddhas and* bodhisattvas *of the ten directions*. This ritual is derived from the fundamental thought of Māhāyana which implies that all sentient beings can become Buddhas. Since all sentient beings can become Buddhas, the real purpose of worshipping the Buddhas and *bodhisattvas* of the ten directions is to form good relations with the Buddhas and *bodhisattvas* and to emulate them. Accordingly, people should encourage themselves to become a Buddha. In other words, worshipping in itself is not the ultimate purpose.

The Diffusion of Confessional Rituals on a Large Scale

Since Master Chi Yii invented the Dharma Blossom Samādhi Confessional Rituals in the 6th century A.D., a variety of confessional rituals based on the different sūtras or schools appeared.

In the 6th century, many confessional rituals were created according to such popular sūtras as *Medical Buddha Sūtra*, *Golden Light Sūtra*, and *Prajna Sūtra*. They were very similar to Dharma Blossom Samādhi Confessional Rituals despite the difference in procedure or the content of the sūtras.

The appearance of various confessional rituals accommodated more and more people who had different purposes in practicing confessional ritual. Some people practiced confessional rituals in order to attain happiness and to prevent calamities, some for the sake of saving the deceased, others for stabilizing spiritual life, and still others for the retribution of grace. The religious functions of confessional rituals were thus broadened. As a result, they became increasingly popular.

In the 7th and 8th centuries A.D., various Chinese schools such as Pure Land, Tantric, and Hua Yen founded their own confessional rituals. Founder of the Pure Land school, Master Shan Tao (613–618 A.D.), invented *The Ode to Western Pure Land*.[3] In it he used the method of chanting and explaining the *Amitābha Sūtra* paragraph by paragraph. Finally, it ended with taking vows and donating merit. His work not only established the fundamental structure of the Pure Land school's confessional rituals at a later age, but also strengthened greatly the activities of teaching and rationalizing of rituals, through the explaining of *sūtra*, as well as by chanting them. Later, Master Hua Chao (?–821 A.D.) invented *Ode to the Pure Land's Five Gatherings and Buddha-name Reciting*.[4] It used primarily the recitation of the name of the Buddha and increased the variance of chanting to produce the effect of rituals. Besides, Master Pu Kung (705–774 A.D.) of the Tantric school translated into Chinese *The Confessional Text of the Names of 35 Buddhas*.[5] It seems to be a response of the Tantric school toward the popularity of confessional rituals after it was introduced into China. Although the text is quite short, its structure still maintains the forms of Buddha-name reciting, confession, taking vows and donating merit. Master Chung Mi (780–841 A.D.) of the Hua Yen school also established a set of confessional rituals for the Hua Yen school in his work *The Ritual of Practice and Realization at the Sanctuary of Complete Enlightenment Sūtra*.[6] Later on, Master Tze Hsuan (809–881 A.D.) developed it into *Loving-Kindness and Compassion Water Confessional Ritual*.[7] It was practiced widely and continues to this day.

Although the Vinaya school has a few unique confessional rituals, it underscored their significance. Only the Three-Sastra school, the "Mind-only" school and the Ch'an school lay little emphasis on complex rituals. This is because the Three-Sastra school, following the thoughts of Nagarjuna, stresses the contemplation of emptiness and the destruction of attachment; the "Mind-only" school stresses the establishment of theory of "mind-only"; and the Ch'an school emphasizes "pointing to the original mind."

The Diffusion of the Emperor Liang's Confessional Ritual

Since the rise of confessional rituals in the 4th century until today, the Emperor Liang's Confessional Ritual is the most widely adopted in the context of Chinese Buddhism. Its original name is *Loving-kindness and Compassion Sanctuary Confessional Rituals*.[8] It is a very long text, with precise structure and beautiful phrases. Although in the preface it is claimed to be the collective work of many monks of the Northern Liang Dynasty of the 6th century, the compilation of the preface and the wide diffusion of the text took place during the 13th century.

We find it very difficult to ascertain, from literary records, the age of its establishment, yet there is still one hint worth our attention. That is, in the repeated chants of the names of the Buddhas of the ten directions, "Nan Mo Maitreya Buddha" is given first. The founder of Buddhism, Sakyamuni Buddha, is sometimes chanted in the second position and sometimes in the eighth. The name of Amitābha Buddha, who was widely recognized since the 4th century, is chanted only twice; once it is given as the Amitābha (Infinite Light) Buddha and the other time as the Amitāyur (Infinite Life) Buddha. A rationale for this very special phenomenon may be found in a historical fact. That is, in the 6th and 7th centuries, the Maitreya faith, which stresses the rebirth in the Tusita Heaven's Maitreya Inner Palace, was in conflict and confrontation with the Amitābha faith, which stresses the rebirth in Western Blissful Pure Land.[9] The background reflected in the Emperor Liang's Confessional Ritual should be the Maitreya faith. Accordingly, we can infer that the fundamental structure of the Emperor Liang's Confessional Ritual was laid down in the 6th and 7th centuries, but its completion awaited the 8th century.

Concerning the contents of the Emperor Liang's Confessional Ritual, there are two points worthy of our special attention.

1. *The precise Buddhist ethical system*. The rituals were upgraded, level by level, according to the stage of moral development represented by the conception of six realms. The cause and effect relationship of each level is explained in detail. Based on this precise ethical structure, these rituals can be widely adopted in the context of Chinese Buddhism.

2. *The ever-expanding thought of loving-kindness and compassion*. When participating in these rituals, the people in prayer should imagine themselves plunging into all states of life, perhaps of heavens, perhaps hells. At all times and at all places, they should utilize their infinite thoughts of loving-kindness and compassion for all sentient beings, and finally to return to the supreme enlightened state. This ever-expanding thought of loving-kindness and compassion is really the highest realization of the religious person. From it, we can see the religious spirit of Māhāyana Buddhism in caring about the masses while renouncing selfish thoughts.

The Popular Confessional Rituals in Recent Ages

In China, the confessional rituals reached their climax in the 10th century. Master Chuen Shih (963–1032 A.D.) made a great contribution to the appraisal of various confessional rituals.[10] The important confessional rituals of the Tendai and Pure Land sects were finalized by him. Since the 10th century, the Chinese emperors of various dynasties held nationwide confessional rituals frequently. Among ordinary people, the confessional rituals became the major Buddhist medium to harmonize their social life. Until today, confessional rituals are very popular in the context of Chinese Buddhism. From Taiwan, Hongkong, Singapore, Mālaysia to North America, most Chinese Buddhists still hold non-periodical confessional rituals. Among them, the Emperor Liang's Confessional Rituals, the Loving-kindness and Compassion Samādhi Water Confessional Rituals, the Medical Buddha Confessional Rituals, the Pure Land Confessional Rituals, and the Earth-storing Confessional Rituals are the more popular. Besides, the Great Compassion Confessional Rituals which worship the Avalokiteśvara Bodhisattva, the Ullumbana Meeting which confesses for both the dead and the living and expounds filial piety, the Water and Land Great Dharma Function which is the most extensive of all Chinese Buddhist rituals, are also widely practised.

These above-mentioned confessional rituals all stress the intonation of chanting, the arrangement of the sanctuary, the rules and the procedure of entering and leaving the sanctuary. After a period of more than 1,500 years, these rituals are still maintained completely and adeptly. This continuity can be attributed to the existence of so many distinguished representatives in the history of Chinese Buddhism. But what is more important, the confessional rituals really have their own rich contents and practical value so that they can continue to be living rituals satisfying the religious needs of Buddhists.

The Main Characteristics of the Chinese Buddhist Confessional Rituals

From the viewpoint of rituals, the Chinese Buddhist confessional rituals have at least the following six characteristics:

1. *Religion is a system of ethics*. All confessional rituals usually illustrate the cause and effect relationship between good/bad and happiness/unhappiness. In other words, the main contents of the whole system of religion is ethics. Since the moralism of original Chinese Confucianism was fully manifested in the Chinese Buddhist confessional rituals, Buddhism has become an indivisible part of Chinese culture.

2. *Union with the spirit of the principle of filial piety*. The principle of filial piety is an important characteristic of original Chinese culture. The Chinese Buddhist confessional rituals usually expressed the principle of filial piety by the oath "wish to donate this merit to my parents." Because offering sacrifice is an important aspect of filial piety, and because the confessional rituals resonate with the principle of filial piety, the confessional rituals harmonized with the Chinese traditional offering of sacrifice. This is a most important reason for the popularity of the confessional rituals among the Chinese people.

3. *Benefitting the sentient beings of the six realms and the three lives*. Most confessional rituals involve not only praying for oneself, but also for relatives and friends; not only for mankind, but also for the sentient beings of the six realms including the gods, the animals, the beings in hell, and even ghosts. In principle, the participation in the confessional rituals can be expanded indefinitely. And, the benefits can be extended to the past life, the present life, and the future life.

4. *The balance between reason and emotion, the integration of theory and practice*. The Chinese Buddhist confessional rituals emphasize not only rationalized contents such as sūtra-chanting, dharma-expounding and meditation, but also the revealing and sublimation of religious feelings. The participants can easily obtain a balance between emotion and reason. Furthermore, most confessional rituals illustrate the profound contents of contemplation, on the one hand, and point out the actual methods of practice on the other. In other words, participating in the confessional rituals implies not only the communication of religious concepts, but also the actualization of religious practice. The participants will neither stick to theory and forget the practice, nor stick to the practice and forget the theory.

5. *The nature of the ritual procedure and texts*. All confessional texts follow a common language and the procedures are stated very clearly. Therefore, in spite of the extent of the Chinese land mass and the

existence of many dialects, the rituals could be adapted and followed without much difficulty.

6. *The inclusion and integration of* sūtras *and* tantras. Since the 8th century, most confessional rituals, no matter what schools they belong to, attempted to integrate *sūtras* and *tantras*. This fact really points to one important direction for the future development of Buddhism.

The Spiritual Implications of the Chinese Buddhist Confessional Rituals

In summary, the spiritual implications of the Chinese Buddhist confessional rituals can be listed as follows:

The Concept of Karma-based Soul

The texts of most confessional rituals mention the phenomenon of reincarnation. Buddhism recognizes that the soul is the center of reincarnation, and the soul is everlasting. But Buddhism insists that soul is not static, with no change, and is not created by or flows from some supreme god. According to Buddhism, each one's soul is formed by karma. Karma means volitional behavior. Karma has inertia. Karma can direct, press, and induce results. Based on the principle of sowing and reaping, if you face bad luck or disaster, the only resolution is self-examination and adjusting your volition and volition-oriented behavior. The function of confession is revealed here. It can change your karma. Therefore, the so-called way of liberation (the saving of souls) in Buddhism lies in self-awakening. And confession is the first step toward self-awakening.

The Concept of Mind-only Causality

The concept of "mind-only" does not involve any cosmogonic theory of the soul as the substance or source of the universe, but stresses the idea of the soul's guiding function towards the spiritual cause and effect relationship. "Evil comes from the mind. You must confess your mind." This expression is frequently used at the end of the various Buddhist confessional rituals. Because of its emphasis on the "mind-only" cause and effect relationship, confession and correcting error become very important. Whether in elevating yourself or in degenerating yourself, the key lies in your thought. And, confession is the key in developing good thoughts.

The Concept of Tolerance Implied in Recognition of the Buddhas of Ten Directions and Manifold Gods

Although some confessional rituals are designed especially for particular objects of faith, such as the Avalokiteśvara Bodhisattva, Amitābha

Buddha, and the Earth-storing Bodhisattva, most confessional rituals chant the names of the Buddhas of ten directions. This means that according to Buddhism, on the one hand, the universe is an ever-expanding universe, and, on the other hand, the realization of "Buddhahood" is the realization of common moral personality. All sentient beings have equal opportunity. It is totally unnecessary to eliminate each other. Besides, the confessional rituals also recognize the existence of gods – beings of various levels of spiritual achievement in the ten directions. From the viewpoint of Buddhism, the superiority or inferiority of godhood depends not on magical power, but on the residue of the delusions. The five basic delusions include greed, hatred, ignorance, arrogance, and suspicion. The less residue of delusions one has, the higher wisdom one will obtain, and, accordingly, the higher godhood one will attain. Buddha is the one who has realized the highest perfection. According to this concept, the word "*Buddha*" is not the monopoly of Buddhism. The gods of all religions are also *Buddhas* if they can reach the state of no-delusions and obtain total wisdom. The exploration of this concept will surely promote communication and harmony among the major religions in the world.

The Concept of Loving-kindness and Compassion

Based on the concept of karma and "mind-only" causality, Buddhism does not hold that there are absolute criminals in this world. All sentient beings are equal from the very beginning. The reason why some people commit crimes is because of their ignorance. Everybody can be a Buddha right away if he can arouse the wisdom which everybody has from the very beginning. The Chinese Buddhist confessional rituals also emphasize this concept. The premise of equality, as well as the loving-kindness and compassion manifested by confessional rituals, do not represent charity on the part of a superior being nor simply a negative consolation, but a kind of respect and expectation of promise and blessing. The ultimate of loving-kindness and compassion is giving equal care towards all sentient beings no matter whether they are your enemies or benefactors, relatives or aliens.

The Concept of Dedication

The original meaning of dedication is redirecting. In most Chinese Buddhist confessional rituals, dedication is the last procedure. Why should one dedicate one's merit at the end of confessional rituals? The following are the reasons:

1. *Dedication of oneself toward others*. It is also called "the universal dedication." This is a state of being egoless or selfless. It is a wish to

redirect one's personal achievement for the sake of others.

2. *Dedication of smallness toward greatness*. This is not to be satisfied with small achievement. It is a wish to redirect the present small achievement such as Hināyāna towards a future great achievement such as Māhāyana.

3. *Dedication from below toward above*. It is also called "the supreme dedication." This is not to be self-satisfied. It is a wish to redirect the present low-level achievement towards the supreme *bodhi* (the most perfect self-awakening).

4. *Dedication from above toward below*. This is the willingness to redirect the supreme spiritual achievement toward the salvation of all sentient beings.

The concept of dedication can continuously reveal the higher objectives to the participants of the confessional rituals and make them surpass the attachment to the present achievement and spare no efforts in practice. It can also remind the participants to expand the universal care and prevent their reverting to another kind of selfishness because of one's temporary personal spiritual achievement.

The Concept of Śūnyatā

Śūnyatā is the central conception of Buddhism. It is very rich in implication. Some people are frightened by *śūnyatā* or they oppose it. As a matter of fact, why they are afraid of or oppose it is only because they misunderstand *śūnyatā*. The original meaning of *śūnyatā* is absence of self-nature. The absence of self-nature carries the same meaning as the proposition: "All things are created by causes and conditions." If we can understand the fact that "All things are created by causes and conditions," there is no reason for us to be afraid of the expression "no self-nature." When the Chinese Buddhist confessional rituals mention the concept of *śūnyatā*, they emphasize three points:

1. *The nature of crime is* śūnyatā. The commission of crime comes from bad karma. Why are there bad karmas? They are made up of ignorance and other relevant causes. The confession is not a synonym for regret. Regret is simply to recollect one's error and do nothing about it. Confession is intended to eliminate the cause of error from the entirety of the mind so that it will not, at least after facing the result of the error, recur in the future. If one cannot thoroughly observe the cause of the past error and just let the history of that error occupy one's mind, it will create a feeling of guilt and become an obstacle in the practice of *samādhi*. Therefore, one of the steps in the completion of confession is eliminating the feeling of guilt. Only if one can thoroughly identify the nature of guilt as *śūnyatā* and know that it is caused by the combination

of various factors, can one really eliminate one's guilt.[11]

2. Śūnyatā *is liberation*. All confessional rituals claim that only a thorough understanding of *śūnyatā* can bring liberation. Why is it said that *śūnyatā* can bring liberation? *Śūnyatā* implies that all things are made by the continuous combination of various causes and have no self-nature. Only if one can thoroughly understand this reality, one may eliminate meaningless attachment. Absence of attachment is absence of delusions, and this means liberation.

3. Śūnyatā *is no self-appearance*. No self-nature is no self-appearance. No self-appearance is without anything to depend on. Because there is nothing to depend on, there is nothing to be attached to. Following this principle, although confessional rituals have their own practical value, one still cannot be attached to them. Because if one is attached to the confessional rituals, one stands against the reality of no self-nature. Then, confessional rituals will lead to bondage rather than liberation.

The Middle Way and Harmony

In conclusion, the Chinese Buddhist confessional rituals are used as means to reveal and transmit the religious concepts of Buddhism as explained above. If we understand the various confessional rituals in terms of these concepts, we will find that no confessional ritual is absolutely necessary to express the religious concepts of Buddhism. In other words, a relationship between concept and confessional ritual is not absolute. Yet, if we don't use such confessional rituals, how difficult would the explanation and diffusion of the concepts be? This is a very practical problem. The best way to solve this problem is to look back to the most fundamental religious concept of Buddhism, i.e., the principle of the middle way.

The so-called principle of the middle way, in short, is that one should not adopt an extreme attitude in treating any difference or contradiction. One must follow the middle way. For example, in the *Complex Āgama Sūtra*, some people raised the question whether there is a world or not. Ānanda responded by quoting the Buddha's words: "If you truly observe the existence of the world, you will not create the opinion that there is no world. If you truly observe the extinction of the world, you will not create the opinion that there is the world. The Tathāgata keeps away from the two extremes and recommends the middle way."[12] Ānanda meant that the world is created, exists, changes, and extinguishes according to the various causes and conditions. Therefore, we cannot make an arbitrary judgment about the world from one single standpoint.

Looking at the confessional rituals from the standpoint of the middle way, we can elicit one simple principle: no-adopting and no-forsaking. The so-called no-adopting is non-attachment. The Buddha once said, "You must understand my dharma-expounding in terms of the parable of the raft. You must abandon even the dharma. Why not the non-dharma?"[13] It is meaningless for someone to bear the raft on his shoulders after crossing the river. Rituals have many functions, just like the raft used in crossing the river; but after it is used, we need not remain attached to it. This is the so-called no-forsaking is no-repelling. Nāgārjuna once said, "Just as when someone uses the finger to point to the moon the ignorant sees only the finger, not the moon."[14] The function of rituals is just like the finger used in pointing to the moon. Though the finger is not the moon, it has the function of directing, hence its usefulness. Yet, the ignorant ritual-performer takes ritual as the absolute truth. In short, we should follow the principle of the middle way. We should value rituals but not blindly believe in them; we should participate, but not attach ourselves to them; we should support, but not avoid them; we should surpass them, but not get confused by them.

If we cannot understand the middle way, if we cannot adopt the attitude of no-adopting and no-forsaking in the progression of confessional rituals, we will simply perform the rituals of chanting and worshipping and miss the true spirit of confessional rituals themselves. This is because the key to confession and worshipping lies in sincerity. If there is no sincerity, how can confession be productive? How can there be repentance? The meaning of sūtra-reciting and chanting lies in the contemplation of *śūnyatā*. Without such contemplation, sūtra-recitation becomes meaningless.

Following the middle way, we can also find that the Chinese confessional rituals exemplify the spirit of harmony:

1. *The harmony between emptiness and achievement*. This is the harmony on the level of concept. The confessional rituals themselves are oriented toward achievement, but their achievement is related to "emptiness." On the surface, these two may seem to be contradictory. But from the standpoint of spiritual practice, the rituals are an achievement; the "emptiness" provides for liberation. Therefore, in the actual experience of a spiritual pilgrim, "emptiness" and "achievement" are harmonious and not contradictory.

2. *The harmony between* sūtric *and* tantric *Buddhism*. This is the harmony of the different sources.

3. *The harmony between reason and emotion*. This is the harmony relating to theory and practice.

4. *The harmony between theory and practice*. This is the harmony in the procedure of rituals.

(Items 2–4 are already explained in the above.)

In addition to the above-mentioned four points, the spirit of harmony involved in the Chinese Buddhist confessional rituals can be also realized in the modes of the confessional rituals such as the harmony in chanting and rhythm, the harmony in the roles of monks and lay people in the sanctuary, the harmony relating the sages and the ordinary people. In other words, the middle way is harmony. The Buddha dharma and its confessional rituals which are established on the middle way fully exemplify the spirit of harmony.

According to the Chinese Buddhist historical records, the confessional rituals have produced many spiritual achievements. This means that confessional rituals are not merely forms of theoretical religious rituals but also have outstanding value in religious experience. From the study of the Chinese Buddhist confessional rituals, we may argue for their positive value. In the primitive religions, rituals may be only the tools in stimulating emotion and may have many anti-rational elements. But for a highly rationalized religion, rituals can become effective methods of practice. Concepts are thus fully united with practice.

Rationalism provides important direction for the future development of the world's religions. If religious people can follow the middle way of no-adopting and no-forsaking to develop and utilize the religious rituals with reasoned attitude, rituals will be valuable for the future development of human culture.

NOTES

1. Cf. T'ang Yung-T'ung, *Han Wei liang-Chinnan nan-Pei Ch'ao Buddhist History*, 2 vols., Shanghai, 1938, 213.
2. Collected in *Dainihon Kotei Daizōkyō* (abbreviated *DKD*), Kyoto, 1902–1905, vol. 46, 949–955.
3. Collected in *DKD*, vol. 47, 424–438.
4. Collected in *DKD*, vol. 47, 474–490.
5. Collected in *DKD*, vol. 12, 42–43.
6. Cf. Lin-Chu-Ching, *Buddhist Rituals* (in Chinese), Taipei: Buddhist Publications, 1986, 95–102.
7. Collected in *DKD*, vol. 45, 967–978.
8. Collected in *DKD*, vol. 45, 922–967.
9. Cf. Chiang Wei-Chua, *A History of Chinese Buddhism*, Taipei: Historical Research House, 1972, vol. 2, 7.
10. Cf. *DKD*, vols. 46–47.
11. Cf. Chi Yii, *Dharma Blossom Samādhi Confessional Rituals*, Collected in *DKD*, vol. 46, 954.
12. *Complex Āgama Sūtra*, Collected in *DKD*, vol. 2, 66.
13. *Dimond Sūtra*, Collected in *DKD*, vol. 8, 749.
14. Nāgārjuna, *Mahā Prajñā-pāramitā śāstra*, Collected in *DKD*, vol. 25, 125.

List of Contributors

Lily de Silva, Professor, Department of Pali and Buddhist Studies, University of Peradeniya, Peradeniya, Sri Lanka.

R.D. Guneratne, Associate Professor and Head, Department of Philosophy, University of Peradeniya, Peradeniya, Sri Lanka.

Masao Ichishima, Director of International Affairs, Taisho University, Tokyo, Japan.

David J. Kalupahana, Professor of Philosophy, Department of Philosophy, University of Hawaii at Manoa, Honolulu, Hawaii.

Y. Karunadasa, Professor and Head, Department of Pali, University of Kelaniya, Kelaniya, Sri Lanka.

Cheng-Mei Ku, Research Fellow, Institute of East Asian Philosophies, Singapore.

Sanath K. Nanayakkara, Editor, Encyclopedia of Buddhism, Colombo, Sri Lanka.

P. Don Premasiri, Associate Professor of Philosophy, Department of Philosophy, University of Peradeniya, Peradeniya, Sri Lanka.

Hammalawa Saddhatissa, Vice-President, Pali Text Society, Sanghanayaka Thera of Great Britain; President, Sangha Council, London, England. (Deceased)

Heng-ching Shih, Associate Professor, Department of Philosophy, National Taiwan University, Taipei, Taiwan, Republic of China.

Hsiang Chou Yo, Associate Professor, Chinese Culture University, Taipei, Taiwan, Republic of China.

Index

C

D

M

N

O